THE LIFE FRANCES OF ROME

By

Georgiana Fullerton

OF BLESSED LUCY OF NARNI

OF DOMINICA OF PARADISO

AND OF ANNE DE MONTMORENCY

WITH

An Introductory Essay
ON THE MIRACULOUS LIFE
OF THE SAINTS

BY J. M. CAPES, ESQ

Contents

Authorities

The authorities on which the History of St. Frances of Rome rests are as follows:

Her life by Mattiotti, her Confessor for ten years. Mattiotti enjoined her, as a matter of obedience, to relate to him from time to time her visions in the minutest detail. He was a timid and suspicious man, and for two or three years kept a daily record of all she told him; afterwards, as his confidence in her sanctity and sanity grew complete, he contented himself with a more general account of her ecstasies, and also put together a private history of her life. After her death, he wrote a regular biography, which is now to be found in the Bollandist collection (Venice, 1735, vol. ii.).

Early in the seventeenth century, Ursinus, a Jesuit, wrote a life, which was highly esteemed, but which was never printed, and, except in certain fragments, is now lost.

In 1641, Fuligato, a Jesuit, wrote the second life, in the Bollandist collection, which contains particulars of events that happened after Mattiotti's time.

Other well-written lives have since appeared: especially a recent one by the Vicomte de Bussière, in which will be found various details too long to be included in the sketch here presented to the English reader.

INTRODUCTORY ESSAY.

THE MIRACULOUS LIFE OF THE SAINTS.

In presenting to the general reader a newly-written Life of so extraordinary a person as St. Frances of Rome, together with the biographical sketches contained in the present volume, it may be useful to introduce them with a few brief remarks on that peculiar feature in the histories of many Saints, which is least in accordance with the popular ideas of modern times. A mere translation, or republication of a foreign or ancient book, does not necessarily imply any degree of assent to the principles involved in the original writer's statements. The new version or edition may be nothing more than a work of antiquarian or literary interest, by no means professing any thing more than a belief that persons will be found who will, from some motive or other, be glad to read it.

Not so, however, in the case of a biography which, though not pretending to present the results of fresh researches, does profess to give an account new in shape, and adapted to the wants of the day in which it asks its share of public attention. In this case no person can honourably write, and no editor can honourably sanction, any statements but such as are not only possible and probable, but, allowing for the degree of authenticity in each case claimed, on the whole historically true. No honest man, who absolutely disbelieves in all documents in which the original chronicler has mingled accounts of supernatural events with the record of his own personal knowledge, could possibly either write or edit such Lives as those included in the following pages; still less could they be made public by one who disbelieves in the reality of modern miracles altogether.

In presenting, then, the present and other similar volumes to the ordinary reader, I anticipate some such questions as these: "Do you really put these stories into our hands as history? Are these marvellous tales to be regarded as poetry, romance, superstitious dreaming, or as historical realities? If you profess to believe in their truth, how do you reconcile their character with the universal aspect of human life, as it appears *to us and to our friends?* And finally, if you claim for them the assent to which proved facts have a right from every candid mind, to what extent of detail do you profess to believe in their authenticity?" To these and similar questions I reply by the following observations:

The last of these questions may be answered briefly. The lives of Saints and other remarkable personages, which are here and elsewhere laid in a popular form before the English public, are not all *equally* to be relied on as undoubtedly true in their various minute particulars. They stand precisely on the same footing as the ordinary events of purely secular history; and precisely the same degree of assent is claimed for them that the common reason of humanity accords to the general chronicles of our race. No man, who writes or edits a history of distant events, professes to have precisely the same amount of certainty as to all the many details which he records. Of some his certainty is all but absolute; of others he can say that he considers them highly probable; of a third class he only alleges that they are vouched for by respectable though not numerous authorities., Still, he groups them together in one complete and continuous story, and gives them to the world as *history;* nor does the world impute to him either dishonesty, ignorance, credulity, or shallowness, because in every single event he does not specify the exact amount of evidence on which his statement rests.

Just such is the measure of belief to be conceded to the Life of St. Frances, and other biographies or sketches of a similar kind. Some portions, and those the most really important and prominent, are well ascertained, incontrovertible, and substantially true. Others again, in all likelihood, took place very much, though not literally, in the way in which they are recorded. Of others, they were possibly, or even probably, the mere colouring of the writer, or were originally adopted on uninvestigated rumour. They are all, however, consistent with known facts, and the laws on which humanity is governed by Divine Providence; and therefore, as they may be true, they take their place in that vast multitude of histories which all candid and well-informed persons agree in accepting as worthy of credit, though in various degrees.

Supposing, then, that miraculous events may and do occur in the present state of the world's history, it is obvious that these various degrees of assent are commanded alike by the supernatural and the natural events which are here so freely mingled together. Some are undoubtedly true, others are probably either fictitious or incorrectly recorded. The substance rests on the genuine documents, originally written by eye-witnesses and perfectly competent judges; and as such, the whole stands simply as a result of the gathering together of historical testimony.

Here, however, the ordinary English reader meets us with the assertion, that the supernatural portions of such lives are simply *impossible*. He assumes—for I am not exaggerating when I say that he never tries *to prove*—that these marvellous interruptions of the laws of nature never take place. Consequently, in his judgment, it is purely ridiculous to put forth such stories as history; and writers who issue them are guilty either of folly, ignorance, superstition, or an unprincipled tampering with the credulity of unenlightened minds. Of those who thus meet the question of historical evidence by an assumption of a universal abstract impossibility, I earnestly beg an unprejudiced attention to the following considerations:

If it be once admitted that there is a God, and that the soul is not a mere portion of the body, the existence of miracles becomes at once probable. Apart from the records of experience, we should in fact have expected that events which are now termed miraculous would have been perhaps as common as those which are regulated by what we call the laws of nature. Let it be only granted that the visible universe is not the *whole* universe, and that in reality we are ever in a state of most intimate *real* communion with Him who is its Creator; then, I say, we should have expected to have been as habitually conscious of our intercourse with that great Being, as of our intercourse with one another. The true marvel is, that we are not thus habitually conscious of the Divine Presence, and that God is really out of our sight. If there is a God, who is ever around us and within us, *why* does He not communicate with us through the medium of our senses, as He enables us to communicate with one another? Our souls hold mutual communion through the intervention of this corporal frame, with such a distinct and undeniable reality, that we are as *conscious* of our intercourse as of the contact of a material substance with our material bodies. Why, then,—since it is so infinitely more important to us to hold ceaseless

3

communication with our Maker,—why is it that our intercourse with Him is of a totally different nature? Why is it that the material creation is not the ordinary instrument by which our souls converse with Him? Let any man seriously ponder upon this awful question, and he must hasten to the conclusion, that though experience has shown us that the world of matter is not the *ordinary* channel of converse between God and man, there yet remains an overwhelming probability that some such intercourse takes place *occasionally* between, the soul and that God through whose power alone she continues to exist.

In other words, the existence of miracles is probable rather than otherwise. A miracle is an event in which the laws of nature are interrupted by the intervention of Divine agency, usually for the purpose of bringing the soul of man into a conscious contact with the inhabitants of the invisible world. With more or less exactness of similitude, a miracle establishes between God and man, or between other spiritual beings and man, that same kind of intercourse which exists between different living individuals of the human race. Such a conscious intercourse is indeed asserted by infidels as well as by atheists, to be, if not impossible, at least so utterly improbable, that it is scarcely within the power of proof to make it credible to the unbiased reason. Yet surely the balance of probability inclines to the very opposite side. If there *is* a God, and our souls *are* in communication (of some kind) with Him, surely, prior to experience, we should have expected to be habitually conscious of this communion. And now that we see that we are not at any rate habitually so, still the burden of proof rests with those who allege that such conscious intercourse *never* takes place. Apart from all proof of the reality of any one professed miracle, the infidel is bound to show *why* all miracles are improbable or impossible; in other words, why man should never be conscious of the presence and will of his ever-present God.

Protestants, however, and even weak Catholics, regard the record of one of those mysterious lives, in which the soul of a man or woman has been repeatedly brought into this species of communion with invisible beings, as a tale which, though it is just possible that it may be true, is yet, on the face of it, so flagrant a violation of the laws of nature, as to be undeserving of positive hearty belief. They confound the laws of physical nature with the laws of universal nature. They speak of the nature of this material earth, as if it was identical with the *nature of things*. And this confusion of thought it is to which I would especially call attention. Miracles are contrary to the ordinary laws of physical nature, and therefore are so far improbable, but they are in the

4

strictest conformity with the nature of things, and therefore *in themselves* are probable. If the laws of nature rule God as they control man, a miracle is almost an impossibility; but if God rules the laws of nature, then it is wonderful that something miraculous does not befall us every day of our lives.

Again, it is in a high degree probable that miraculous events will generally, so to say, take their colour from the special character of that relation which may exist between God and man at the time when they come to pass. If, in the inscrutable counsels of the Almighty, man is placed, during different eras in his history, in different circumstances towards his Creator and Preserver, it would seem only natural that the variations in those circumstances should be impressed upon the extraordinary intercourse between God and His people. Or, to use the common Christian term, each *dispensation* will have its peculiar supernatural aspect, as well as its peculiar spiritual and invisible relationship. If man was originally in a higher and more perfect state of being than he is now, it is probable that his communion with God was singularly, if not totally, unlike what it has been since he fell from primeval blessedness. If after his fall, two temporary states have been appointed to him by his God, then the miracles of each epoch will bear their own special corresponding characteristics. And lastly, if by a new exercise of regenerating and restoring power it has pleased the Invisible One to rescue His creatures from the consequences of their ancient ruin, then again we may expect to recognise the history of that redemption in the whole course of the miraculous intercourse between the Redeemer and the redeemed until the end of time. The supernatural elements in the Paradisiacal, the Patriarchal, the Mosaic, and the Christian states, may be expected to be in many respects distinct, each embodying with awful and glorious power the invisible relations which the God of nature and of grace has thought fit to assume towards His creatures.

And such, in fact, has been the case. Not only is the ceaseless existence of a miraculous intercourse between God and man one of the most completely proved of all historical events, but the miracles of each dispensation are found in a wonderful degree to correspond with the relationship of God to man in each of the separate epochs. The same superhuman consistency is found to pervade all the works of God, both where nature and grace are separate from one another, and where the common laws of nature are burst through, and the material universe is made as it were the bondslave of the unseen. The impiously meant assertions of unbelief are fulfilled in a sense which unbelievers little look for; and they who cry out in their hatred of miracles, that all things are governed by unchanging *law*, may learn that in truth unchanging laws do rule over all, although those laws have a range and a unity in the essence and will of God, of which mortal intelligence never dreamed. The natural and the supernatural, the visible and the invisible, the ordinary and the miraculous, the rules of the physical creation and the interruptions of those rules,—all are controlled by one law, shaped according to one plan, directed by one aim, and bound to one another by indissoluble ties, even where to human eyes all seem lost in confusion and thwarted by mutual struggle.

Of what we should now call the miraculous, or supernatural, communion between God and man in Paradise, we know historically but little. The records of revelation being for the most part confined to the state of man as he is, and his actual and future prospects, present but a glimpse of the conscious communion which was permitted to the first of our race in their original bliss. It is, however, believed by theologians, that in Paradise what we should now term miracles did not exist; for this reason, that what is now extraordinary was then ordinary. God conversed with man, and man held communion with angels, directly and habitually; so that in a certain sense man saw God and the world now unseen[1]. For it is not the mere possession of a body which binds the soul with the chains of sense; it is the corruption and sinfulness of our present frames which has converted them into a barrier between the spirit within and the invisible universe. As Adam came forth all pure and perfect from the hands of his Creator, a soul dwelling in a body, his whole being ministered fitly to the purposes of his creation, and with body and soul together he conversed with his God. It was not till the physical sense became his instrument of rebellion, that it was dishonoured and made his prison-house, and laid under a curse which should never be fully removed until the last great day of the resurrection.

Upon the fall of Adam, a new state was introduced, which lasted about two thousand five hundred years. During its continuance, the supernatural intercourse between Almighty God and His degraded creatures took an entirely different character. What had originally been continual, and as it were natural, became comparatively rare and miraculous. Henceforth there *seemed* to be no God among men, save when at times the usual laws of the earth and the heavens were sus-

---

[1] : See St. Thomas, Summa, pars prima, quæst. 94. art. 1,2.

pended and God spoke in accents which none might refuse to hear. Of these supernatural manifestations the general aspect was essentially typical of the future redemption of the lost race by a Saviour. That promise of deliverance from the consequences of sin, which Almighty God had vouchsafed to the first sinners, was repeated in a vast variety of miraculous interventions. Though there may have been many exceptions to the ordinary character of the Patriarchal miracles, still, on the whole, they wear a typical aspect of the most striking prominence.

The first miracle recorded after the fall is the token granted to Abel that his *sacrifice* was accepted. A deluge destroys all but one family, who are saved in an ark, the type of the Church of God, and a rainbow is set in the sky as a type of the covenant between God and man. A child is miraculously born to Abraham in his old age, who is afterwards offered to God as a type of the Redeemer, and saved from death by a fresh supernatural manifestation of the Divine will. The chosen race become captive in Egypt, as a figure of man's bondage to sin; a series of awful miracles, wrought by the instrumentality of Moses himself, a type of Jesus Christ, delivers them from their slavery, terminating with the institution of the Passover, when the paschal lamb is eaten, and they are saved by its blood, as mankind is saved by the blood of the Lamb of God. The ransomed people miraculously pass through the Red Sea, foreshadowing the Christian's regeneration by baptism; as they wander afterwards in the desert, manna descends from heaven to feed them, and water gushes from the rock to quench their thirst, and to prefigure that sacred food and those streams of grace which are to be the salvation of all men. Almost every interruption of the laws of nature bespeaks the advent of the Redeemer, and does homage to Him as the Lord of earth and heaven.

At length a code of laws is given to the chosen race, to separate them completely from the rest of men, and a promise of perpetual temporal prosperity is granted to them by God as the reward of their obedience, and as a figure of the eternal blessedness of the just. From that time with, as before, occasional exceptions, the supernatural events which befall them wear a new aspect. Their peculiarly typical import is exchanged for one more precisely in conformity with the leading principle of the new dispensation. The rites and ceremonies of the new Law prefigure the Sacrifice and Redemption of the Messias; but the miracles of the next fifteen hundred years are for the most part directed to uphold that rule of present reward and punishment, which was the characteristic feature of the Jewish theocracy. The earth opens to punish the disobedience of Core and his companions. Fiery serpents smite the murmuring crowd with instant death; while the promised Saviour is prefigured, not by a miracle, but by the erection of a brazen serpent by the hands of Moses. The walls of Jericho fall prostrate before the trumpets of the victorious Israelites; one man, Achan, unlawfully conceals some of the spoil, and an immediate supernatural panic, struck into his countrymen, betrays the committal of the sin. Miraculous water fills the fleece of Gideon, to encourage him to fight for his country's deliverance. An angel foretells the birth of Samson to set his people free, when they are again in bondage. Samson himself is endowed with supernatural strength; exhausted with the slaughter of his foes, he prays for water to quench his thirst, and a stream bursts forth from the ass's jawbone with which he had just slain the Philistines. Bound in chains, blinded, and made a jest by the idolaters, his prayer for a return of his strength is heard by God, and he destroys a multitude in his last moments.

And thus, through all the history of the Kings and the Prophets, the power of God is repeatedly put forth to alter the laws of nature for the purpose of enforcing the great rule of the Mosaic law. The disobedience of the Jews might, if God had so pleased, have been invariably punished by the instrumentality of the ordinary course of events, shaped by the secret hand of Divine Providence so as to execute His will, just as now we find that certain sins inevitably bring on their own temporal punishment by the operation of the laws of nature. And so, in the vast majority of instances in which the Jews were rewarded and punished, we find that the Divine promises and threats were fulfilled by the occurrence of events in the natural order of things. But yet frequently miracles confirmed and aided the work of chastisement and blessing; and of the numerous wonders which were wrought from the giving of the law to the coming of Christ, we find that nearly all bore this peculiar character. For many centuries also a constant miraculous guidance was granted to the people in the "Urim and Thummim," by which they were enabled, when they chose to remain faithful, to escape all national calamities and enjoy the fullest blessings of the promised land.

Under the Christian dispensation, again, a new character is imprinted upon the supernatural history of the Church, which is, in fact, the impression of the Cross of Christ. While the characteristics of the Patriarchal and Jewish miracles are not wholly obliterated, an element, which if not entirely new, is new in the intensity of its operation, is introduced into the miraculous life of the children of Christ, which life is really the prolongation of the supernatural life of Jesus Christ Himself. It is accompanied also with a partial restoration of that peculiar power which was possessed by man before he fell, when his body became a veil to hide the world of spirits from his soul. While prophecies of future events have not wholly ceased in the Christian Church, and miracles are frequently wrought for the conferring of some temporal blessings, yet these other wonderful features distinguish the supernatural records of Christianity from those of both Patriarchal and Jewish times. The undying power of the Cross is manifested in the peculiar sufferings of the Saints, in their mystic communion with the invisible world, and in that especial sanctity to which alone miraculous gifts are for the most part accorded under the Gospel. Not that all these three peculiarities are to be observed in the life of every Saint under the Gospel. Far from it, indeed. The supernatural life of the Saints varies with different individuals, according to the pleasure of that Almighty Spirit, who communicates Himself to His elect in ten thousand mysterious ways, and manifests Himself according to His own will alone. Still, at times, they are found united, in conjunction with those miraculous powers which were possessed under the old dispensations in one individual. In such cases we behold the Life and Passion of the King of Saints visibly renewed before our eyes; the law of *suffering*,—that mysterious power, as life-giving as it is unfathomable,—is set before us in an intensity of operation, which at once calls forth the scoffs of the unbeliever, and quickens the faith of the humble Christian; the privileges of eternity are anticipated, and the blessings of a lost Paradise are in part restored. Jesus Christ lives, and is in agony before us; the dread scene of Calvary is renewed, united with those ineffable communications between the suffering soul and its God, which accompanied the life and last hours of the Redeemer of mankind. Our adorable Lord is, as it were, still incarnate amongst us, displaying to our reverent faith the glories of His Passion in the persons of those who are, in the highest sense that is possible, His members, a portion of His humanity, in whom He dwells, who dwell in Him, and whose life, in a degree incomprehensible even to themselves, is hid with Christ in God. Such a Saint was St. Frances of Rome, one of those glorious creations of Divine grace by means of which, at the time when the Holy City was filled with bloodshed and ravaged with pestilence, and when the heaviest disasters afflicted the Church, Almighty God set forth before men the undying life of the Cross, and the reality of that religion which seemed to be powerless to check the outrages of its professed followers.

In Paradise, then, as has been said, the whole nature of man ministered to the fulfilment of the end for which he was created, namely, the
knowledge and love of God. He came forth from his Maker's hands
endowed not only with a natural soul and body untainted with sin, but
with such supernatural gifts, arising from the Divine Presence within
him, that nothing was wanting but perseverance to his final perfection.
The various elements in his nature were not, as now, at war with one
another. His body did not blind the eye of his soul, and agitate it with
the storms of concupiscence; nor did the soul employ the body as its
instrument of rebellion against God. Though not yet admitted to that
glorious vision of the Eternal which was to be the reward of his obedience, yet he lived in direct commerce with the world of spirits. He
knew and conversed with God and His angels in a way which is now
wholly incomprehensible to the vast majority of his descendants.

When Adam fell, he became, in one word, what we all are now by
nature. Not only was he placed under a curse, but his God was hidden
from his eyes; and that corporeal habitation, which he had abused to
his soul's destruction, became the prison of his soul's captivity. Though
created in the image of God, and retaining, even when fallen, certain
traces of his celestial origin, he became a mere helpless denizen of
earth, and a veil descended and hid his God and all spiritual beings
from his mind. From that time forwards *suffering* became not merely
the law of his daily life, but the only means by which he could be first
restored to the Divine favour, and finally be taken to a happy eternity.
And inasmuch as he was to be redeemed by the sufferings of One who
was at once man and not man, He was in a certain sense to share those
sufferings, in order to partake in the blessings they purchased for him.
A mystic union was to take place between the Saviour and the fallen
race, of which a community in suffering, as the instrument of restoration, was to be for ever and in every case established. This anguish,
further, was to be twofold, including all the faculties both of the body
and the soul. Man had sinned in his whole being; in his whole being,
therefore, he was to suffer, both in the person of his Redeemer, who
was to suffer for him, and in himself, who was to suffer with his Saviour. A "holocaust" was to be offered to the offended Majesty of God;
an offering, not only of his *entire* nature, but a *burnt* offering; a sacrifice which should torture him in the flames of Divine vengeance, and
kill him with its annihilating fierceness.

As, however, it pleased the Divine Wisdom to postpone for forty
centuries the advent and atonement of the Redeemer, so, for the same
period, the race redeemed participated, in a comparatively slight de-

gree, in those restorative sufferings which derived all their virtue from the sacrifice upon the Cross. Pangs of body and bitterness of soul were, in truth, the lot of man from the moment that Adam sinned; but they were the pangs and bitterness of a criminal under punishment, far more than the sacrificial pains of the members of Christ crucified. Asceticism formed but a small portion of the religious worship of the people of God, until the great atonement was completed upon Calvary. Not that any degree, even the lowest, of acceptable obedience could ever be attained without some measure of the crucifixion of the natural man. Patriarchs and Israelites alike felt the power of the Cross as the instrument of their sanctification. But still earthly prosperity, including bodily pleasures, was, as a rule, the reward with which God recompensed His faithful servants. That which became the rule under the Gospel, was the exception from Adam till Moses, and from Moses until Christ. Here and there some great example of Christian asceticism enforced upon a sensual people the nature of perfect sanctity. Elias fasted on Mount Carmel, and beheld the skirts of the glory of the Most High. The Baptist fasted and tamed his natural flesh in the wilderness, and beheld not only the Incarnate Son of God, but the descent of the Eternal Spirit upon Him. Yet, for the most part, the favoured servants of God lived the lives of ordinary men; they possessed houses, riches, and honours; and married wives, even more than one.

At length the Cross was set up in all its awful power; suffering received its perfect consecration, and took its ruling place in the economy of man's redemption. Jesus, in descending from the Cross, bestowed that Cross upon His children, to be their treasure until the end of the world. Crucifixion with Him, and through Him, as their Head, became their portion and their glory. Every soul that was so buried in His wounds as to receive the full blessings of His sacrifice, was thereby nailed, in Christ, to the Cross, not to descend from its hallowed wood until, like Christ, it was dead thereon. Henceforth the sanctity of God's chosen servants assumes its new character. It is no longer written, "I will bring you into a land flowing with the milk and honey of this earth;" but, "Blessed are the poor, and they that suffer persecution." The lot of Abraham and of David is exchanged for that of St. Peter and St. Paul. In place of triumph in war with the idolaters, the Christian is *promised* persecution; in place of many herds and flocks, and treasures of gold, God *gives* him poverty and sickness; the fast, the vigil, the scourge, take place of the palaces of cedar and the luxuriant couch; marriage gives way to celibacy; and long life is a privilege in order that in many years we may suffer much, and not that we may enjoy much. Such is the ordinary course of the Divine dealings with the soul since the Cross received its full mysterious saving power.

And to the full as mysterious is the new character imprinted upon the miraculous life of Christian sanctity. The phenomena of that new existence, in which certain souls are brought into mystic communion with the unseen world, bear the print of the wounds of the Eternal Son in a manner which fills the ordinary Christian mind with amazement and trembling. It is by a painful crucifixion of the natural man, both soul and body, carried to a far more than ordinary perfection, that the soul is introduced into this miraculous condition. Imprisoned in her fleshly tabernacle, which, though regenerated, is through sin foul, earthly, and blinding as ever, the mind can only be admitted to share in the communion which Jesus Christ unceasingly held with His Father and with the world invisible, by attaining some portion of that self-mastery which Adam lost by his fall. The physical nature must be subdued by the vigorous repetition of those many painful processes by which the animal portion of our being is rendered the slave of the spiritual, and the will and the affections are rent away from all creatures, to be fixed on God alone. Fasting and abstinence are the first elements in this ascetic course. The natural taste is neglected, thwarted, and tormented, till, wearied of soliciting its own gratification, it ceases to interfere with the independent action of the soul. The appetite is further denied its wonted satisfaction as to quantity of food. By fasts gradually increasing in severity, new modes of physical existence are introduced; that which was originally an impossibility becomes a second law of nature; and the emaciated frame, forgetting its former lusts, obeys almost spontaneously the dictates of the victorious spirit within. The hours of sleep are curtailed under judicious control, until that mysterious sentence which compels us to pass a third of our existence in unconscious helplessness is in part repealed. The soul, habituated to incessant and self-collected action, wakes and lives, while ordinary Christians slumber, and as it were are dead. The infliction of other severe bodily pains co-operates in the purifying process, and enables the mind to disregard the dictates of nature to an extent which to many Catholics seems almost incredible, and to the unbeliever an utter impossibility. Physical life is supported under conditions which would crush a constitution not supported by the miraculous aid of almighty power; and feeble men and women accomplish works of charity and heroic self-sacrifice from which the most robust and energetic of the human race, in their highest state of *natural* perfection, would shrink back in dismay as hopeless impossibilities. The senses are literally tyrannised over, scorned, derided, insultingly trampled on. The sight, the smell, the hearing, the touch, and the taste, are taught to exercise themselves upon objects revolting to their original inclinations. They learn to minister to the will without displaying one rebellious symptom. Matter yields to spirit; the soul is the master of the body; while the perceptions of the intelligence attain an exquisite sensibility, and the mind is gifted with faculties absolutely new, the flesh submits, almost insensible to its condition of servitude, and scarcely murmurs at the daily death it is compelled to endure.

The process is the same in all that regards the affections and passions of the mind itself. The heart is denied every thing that it desires, which is not God. However innocent, however praiseworthy, may be the indulgence in certain feelings, and the gratification of certain pursuits in ordinary Christians, in the case of these favoured souls nature is crushed in *all* her parts. Her faculties remain, but they are directed to spiritual things alone. Possessions of all kinds, lands, houses, books, pictures, gardens, husband, wife, children, friends, —all share the same tremendous sentence. God establishes Himself in the soul, not only supreme, but as the *only inhabitant.* Whatsoever remains to be done in this world is done as a duty, often as a most obnoxious duty. Love for the souls that Christ has redeemed is the only human feeling that is left unsubjugated; and wheresoever the emotions of natural affection and friendship mingle with this Christian love, they are watched, and restrained with unsparing severity, that the heart may come at last to love nothing, except *in* Christ Himself.

All this, indeed, repeatedly takes place in the case of persons in whom the purely miraculous life of the Christian Saint is never even commenced. It is that which all monks and nuns are bound to struggle for, according to the different rules to which they have respectively received their vocation. And, by the mercy of God, this perfect detachment from earth, and this marvellous crucifixion of the flesh, is accomplished in many a devout religious, to whom the *extraordinary* gifts of the Holy Ghost are as unknown as His extraordinary graces are familiar. Still, in those exceptional instances where miraculous powers of any species are bestowed, this bitter death, this personal renewal (as far as man can renew it) of the agonies of Calvary, is ordinarily the necessary preparation for admission to the revelations of the Divine glory, and to the other mysteries of the miraculous life.

The physical nature, then, being thus subdued, and taught to be the obedient servant of the sanctified will, the history of the Catholic

Church records a long series of instances in which the soul has been brought into direct communion with God, with angels, and with devils, more or less through the *sensible* instrumentality of the bodily senses, thus spiritualised and exalted to a new office. The ineffable glories of the *life* of Christ are renewed in those who have thus endured the *cross* of Christ. The death of the body is the life of the soul; and the Son of God is, as it were, again visibly incarnate in the world which He has redeemed.

The phenomena of this miraculous state are as various as they are wonderful. There is scarcely a natural law of our being which is not found to be frequently suspended. Such is the *odour of sanctity*, a celestial perfume that exhales from the person of the Saint, in conditions where any such delicious fragrance could not possibly spring from natural causes, and where even, as in the case of a dead body, nature would send forth scents of the most repulsive kind. In such instances, sometimes in life, sometimes in death, sometimes in health, sometimes in loathsome diseases, there issues from the physical frame an odour of unearthly sweetness, perhaps communicating itself to objects which touch the saintly form.

Or a strange supernatural warmth pervades the entire body, wholly independent of the condition of the atmosphere, and in circumstances when by the laws of nature the limbs would be cold; sometimes, while sickness has reduced the system to such a degree of exhaustion, and brought on so morbid an action of the functions, that the stomach rejects, with a sort of abhorrence, every species of food, the most holy Eucharist is received without difficulty, and seems not only to be thus received, but to furnish sufficient sustenance for the attenuated frame. Not unfrequently corruption has no power over a sacred corpse; and without the employment of any of the common processes for embalming, centuries pass away, and the body of the Saint remains untouched by decay, bearing the impress of life in death, and not crumbling to dust, as in cases of natural preservation, when exposed to the action of the atmosphere. Add to these, the supernatural flexibility and lightness with which at times the living body is endowed by Divine power; the physical accompaniment of ecstasy; the elevation of the entire body from the ground, and its suspension in the air for a considerable space of time; and we have sufficient examples of the mysterious ways in which the bodies of Saints bespeak the purity which dwells within them, and in a degree anticipate the corporeal perfections of those glorified habitations in which the souls of the just will dwell after the resurrection.

By another class of miraculous powers possessed by Christian Saints, they are enabled to recognise the true nature or presence of purely spiritual objects by the instrumentality of their natural organs of sense. Thus, a mere touch at times reveals to them the moral condition of the person on whom they lay their hands. A singular distaste for natural food is accompanied by a perception of a celestial sweetness in the holy Eucharist. Gross sinners appear to the sight in the form of hideous monsters, demoniacal in their aspect, or as wearing the look of the most repulsive of the brute creation. The sense of smell, in like manner, detects the state of the soul, while the ear is opened to heavenly sounds and voices, and Almighty God speaks to the inner consciousness in a manner which, inexplicable as it is when defined in the language of human science, is shown by incontestable proofs to be a real communication from heaven to the enlightened intelligence.

In certain cases the animal creation are taught to do homage to the presence of a Saint. As God opened the eyes of Balaam's ass, and it beheld the messenger of Divine wrath standing with a sword in his hand, so birds, fishes, insects, sheep, and the wildest beasts of the forests, have at times saluted the Saints with joy and sweetness, laying aside their natural timidity or their natural ferocity, and recalling the hour when Adam dwelt in sinless peace in Eden, surrounded by the creatures which the hand of God had made. All nature is bid thus to arise to welcome the elect of the Lord of nature. Flowers spring up beneath their feet; fruits suddenly ripen, and invite them to gather and eat; storms cease, and gentle winds refresh the sky. Every where the presence of Him who lulled the tempest with a word is recognised in the souls in whom He dwells, and in whom He thus, in a mystic sense, fulfils His own promise, that the meek shall possess the land.

Thus, again, time and space are in their degree comparatively annihilated for the sake of some of these favoured servants of the Eternal and Omnipresent. St. Pius V., while bodily in Rome, was a witness of the naval victory of the Christians over the Turks; St. Joseph of Cupertino read letters addressed to him while their authors were writing them far away; St. Dominic foresaw the war of the Albigenses, and the death of Peter of Arragon; and St. Ignatius beheld his successor in the Duke of Gandia. A similar mysterious faculty enables its possessor to discern the presence of relics and other sacred objects, more especially of the adorable Eucharistic species; or even to behold Jesus Christ Himself in His glorified human form, in place of the usual appearance of bread and wine; while in some instances the Host has darted, unborne by mortal hand, into the mouth of a Saint about to communicate at the foot of the altar.

On those species of miracles which are in no way peculiar to the Christian dispensation I need not linger. Such is the gift of healing, whether by the Saint's will and touch while alive, or by his relics and intercession when dead. Such is the gift of prophecy, which abounded, as we might have expected, far more in the Saints before the advent of the Redeemer than since His coming, and which, indeed, was not rigidly confined to men of religious character. Such are those supernatural powers by which our present temporal blessings, in addition to the cure of diseases, are conferred upon individuals or communities by the instrumentality of holy men and women. I confine myself to those more peculiarly Christian privileges, which, though they were not wholly unknown to the Patriarchal and Mosaic Saints, are yet eminently characteristic of those times in which the glorification of the humanity of Jesus appears to have shed a measure of glories upon the bodies of those who most intensely share the sufferings of His cross.

Some of these tokens of the perpetual death of the Son of God in His Saints were, indeed, for several centuries either unknown, or extraordinarily rare in the Christian Church herself. Such is that most awful of the displays of the undying power of the Cross, in which the actual wounds and tortures of the crucified Jesus are visibly renewed, by a miraculous agency, in the persons of His chosen ones. This most terrible of the gifts of the great God is generally preceded by some supernatural occurrence foreshadowing the visible representation of the scene on Calvary about to be set up before the eyes of men. At one time it is a species of bloody sweat, like that of Jesus Christ in the garden of Gethsemani; at another, a visible print of the cross is impressed upon the shoulders; or angels present a mystic cup of suffering to the hands of the self-sacrificing Saint. Then follows what is termed *stigmatisation*, or the renewal of the actual wounds of the Crucified, accompanied with the bloody marks of the crown of thorns upon the sufferer's head; for the most part one by one, until the whole awful commemoration is complete, the skin and flesh are rent on the forehead and round the head, in the hands, in the feet, and in the side; a stream of gore pours forth, at times trickling down in slow drops, at times (as on Fridays) in a fuller tide, accompanied with agonising pangs of body, and except in the fiercest moments of spiritual conflict, with interior consolations of ravishing sweetness. The wounds pierce deep down into the flesh, running even through the hands and the feet.

The state of *ecstasy* is another of the most wonderful of the elements of the miraculous life of the Saints. Under the Divine influence the physical frame undergoes a change in many respects similar to that which is supposed (whether truly or falsely) to result from the operation of magnetism or somnambulism. Many features, at the same time, distinguish the Christian ecstatic condition from that which is produced by purely physical or (it may be) diabolical causes, on which we cannot at present enter in detail. It is sufficient to say, that the results of the true ecstasy are in the strictest conformity with the doctrines of the Christian revelation, and in perfect harmony with the perfections and rules of the *moral* world.

The soul in this state becomes, as it were, independent of the power of the body, or she uses her physical senses in an absolute subordination to her own illumined will. Visions, such as are recorded in the Old Testament in the case of the prophets, are presented to her faculties. She is introduced into the courts of heaven, and beholds and converses with Saints in glory, with the Mother of God, with Jesus Christ Himself. Or the whole mystery of the Passion is re-enacted before her spiritualised sight, the evangelical history being filled up with all those actual but minuter details which are omitted in the written records of the Gospels. In certain cases, the body itself is lifted up from the ground, and so remains for a while in the presence of a crowd of bystanders. In others, the soul, while in ecstasy, is the medium of communication between Almighty God and other persons then present, and the Saint's voice repeats the revelations to those for whom they are designed. Or, again, an unearthly flame shining around the head or whole person of the ecstatic, like the cloven tongues upon the Apostles at Pentecost, attests the presence of the Invisible, and symbolises the message sent forth from His throne to men.

A more purely intellectual vision or revelation is another of the works of the Holy Ghost in His Saints. By such revelations, for the most part, the truths of holy Scripture were communicated to its writers. God, who created the human soul with all its faculties, and who is able to make known His will in any way that He pleases to the intelligence, has His own mysterious but not less accurate tests, by which He enables the favoured spirit to discern a revelation from a mere product of the human imagination, and to distinguish between the voice of God and the suggestions of Satan. Nor was this mode of intercourse between the soul and her God confined exclusively to the elder dispensations or to apostolic ages. Many a Christian Saint has been privileged to contemplate God Himself, in a certain sense, in His essence; beholding the depths of such mysteries as those of the Holy Trinity, the Incarnation, the Eucharistic Presence, or the true nature of sin, with a directness of vision, and comprehending them to an extent, which passes the powers of human language to define.

Lastly, all that we read in the Bible respecting the visible and tangible intercourse between man and the angelic and diabolic host is continued in the times of Christianity. The reality of the ministration of angels and of the assaults of demons, in the case of all Christians, is believed by every Catholic; but in very many cases the Saints have become as conscious of the presence and actions of their unseen friends and foes as of the presence and actions of mortal men. To some Saints, our blessed Lord Himself has appeared in human form, perhaps in that of the most despised and miserable of the poor and sick; to others, their guardian-angels or other pure spirits have presented themselves, sometimes in the guise of ordinary men, and sometimes in a manifestly supernatural shape. Often, too, the enlightened soul has beheld Satan and his accursed spirits, either working it some bodily injury, or assaulting it with some subtle temptation, or seeking to scare it by assuming some hideous loathsome shape, or assuming the garb of an angel of light for the purpose of accomplishing his hellish ends. Of all these supernatural phenomena, however, illustrations will readily occur to those who are familiar with the lives of Saints, or, indeed, to those who have studied the Bible only, and who read the inspired writings as really *true*, remembering that the miraculous events there recorded did not cease the moment that the canon of Scripture was closed, but that such as was the relation between God and man and angels and devils for more than four thousand years, such it has been until this very hour.

Such, then, are the doctrines and opinions which are implied in what may be termed the miraculous life of Catholic Saints, and of which the history of Frances of Rome presents one of the most remarkable examples. They are here but briefly sketched: but I trust that enough has been said to indicate the general character of the principles involved in these wonderful histories; and I now pass on to offer a few remarks on the self-contradictions into which those persons fall who refuse to investigate this species of subject on the ordinary rules of historical evidence.

I need hardly remind the reader that an immense number of persons, both infidels and Protestants, especially in sober-minded England and Scotland, treat every professed Catholic miracle as a portion of the vast gigantic system of deliberate fraud and villany which they conceive to be the very life of Catholicism. From the Pope to the humblest priest who says Mass and hears confessions in an ugly little chapel in the shabbiest street of a country town, all are regarded as leagued in one wide-spreading imposture. Pius IX., for instance, it is imagined, *knows* the liquefaction of St. Januarius's blood to be a trick of the Neapolitan clergy; but he keeps up the falsehood for the sake of gain and power. In like manner, he has an extensive Roman laboratory ever at work for the manufacture of all the instruments of delusion which his emissaries propagate throughout Christendom. There he makes false relics, from portions of the true cross downwards; there he sells pardons and indulgences; and there he has a *corps* of writers employed in the invention of fictitious miraculous tales, saints' lives, and the like. All over the world he has "agents" for the sale of these goods, the Catholic Bishops in England being his "English Correspondents," who doubtless receive a handsome percentage on the profits realised. The staff of underlings is also complete, energetic, and well paid. Thus, the Oratorian Fathers are busily employed in scattering "Saints' Lives" throughout this country, greatly to their own profit. Thus, too, I am myself engaged in a similar work, either laughing in my sleeve at the credulity on which I practise, or submitting from sheer intellectual incompetence to be the tool of some wily Jesuit who enjoins the unhallowed task. Such, when drawn out into details, and stripped of the pompous declamation of the platform, is, in serious truth, the idea which innumerable persons imagine to be the Catholic system of propagandism and deceit; and every Catholic miracle is thus accounted for by the supposed wickedness of all Catholics, except a few blinded ignorant devotees.

Any argument, therefore, addressed to prejudgments of this class must merge in the general argument, which shows that, whether the Catholic religion be true or false, it is beyond the limits of credibility that its ruling principle can be one of intentional deception. I insist, then, that it would not merely be a miracle,—if is an *impossibility* that such an imposture should remain undetected to this day, and that men and women of all ranks, ages, and countries, the ablest and the most simple, including uncounted fathers and mothers of families, should persist in submitting to and upholding the authority of a few thousand priests, who are really no better than incarnate devils. Whether the Catholic system be an error or not, it must have fallen to pieces a hundred times over, if its chief ruler and his subordinates were mere tricksters, playing upon the credulity of a fanatical and besotted world. By this same test, then, its miraculous histories must be judged, like the general characters of its supporters. They who propagate these stories believe them to be true. They do not, of course, assert that *every* supernatural story is what it professes to be. They may even admit that many are the mere creations of well-meaning but ill-informed report. Nor is every Catholic priest, monk, or layman to be accounted a sincere and honest man. There are betrayers of their Lord, from Judas Iscariot to the last wretched apostates, who remain for years in the Church, deceiving others without deceiving themselves. But on the whole, and viewed as a body, the Catholic Church is as honest and truthful, when she asserts that many wonderful miracles are incessantly taking place within her, as the most scrupulous of moralists can desire.

"But she is herself deceived," exclaims the more candid separatist or sceptic, taking up the argument declined by his scoffing brother. Catholics, it is supposed, are under the dominion of so abject a superstition, that the moment the subject of their religion is introduced, they cease to exert their ordinary common sense and powers of criticism, and believe any thing and every thing that seems to be marvellous. Granting them to be sincere, the charitable Protestant is of opinion that they are intellectually incapable of testing the pretensions of these wonders to be real and true miracles. If, in plain words, Catholics are not knaves, they *must be* fools. Now, let me ask any candid person who thus accounts for our belief in modern miracles, to furnish me with an intelligible answer on two points. First, let him explain how it comes to pass that an innumerable multitude of persons, many of them distinguished for the highest intellectual powers, and proving by their lives and their deaths that they are ready to make every sacrifice for the sake of religion, should suffer themselves to be imposed upon in so momentous a subject, should willingly accept as true a series of absurd fabrications, whose falsehood they might detect by the exercise of any ordinary acuteness, and should risk their reputation with the world by professing to believe these fictions. If we *are* sincere in our faith, it is impossible to suppose us so willing to be imposed upon. The hollowness of these supernatural pretensions must have betrayed itself to *some* amongst us. The bubble must have burst *somewhere*. If not at Rome, where Protestants imagine Catholic intellect to be at its lowest ebb, at least in England, or France, or Belgium, or Germany, *some* of our great Catholic philosophers, historians, politicians, and men of science, must have unveiled the truth[1].

And, secondly, I desire to be told *who* are the deceivers. If our numerous miracles are all errors, there must be gross deception in a host of instances *somewhere*. *Where* is it, then? I ask; which are the dupes, and which the rogues? Do the clergy cheat the laity? Or do the laity (who have quite as much to do with these miracles) cheat the clergy? Do the Jesuits entrap the Pope? Or does the Pope mystify the Jesuits? When missionaries shed their blood in hundreds in heathen lands, are we to believe that *they* are the fabricators of the wonderful tales which they have been in the habit of sending home to Christendom? Or did they leave Europe with the intention of becoming martyrs, without troubling themselves to ascertain whether they were not the dupes of delusions already surrounding them in a Christian land? Again I say, if Catholic miracles are all false, there must be boundless trickery *somewhere*, and I demand to know *where* it is. In an English court of justice a charge of conspiracy cannot be entertained unless the accuser can point out certain parties on whom to fasten his charge. Judge and jury would laugh at a plaintiff who came into court crying out that he was victimised by some invisible, indescribable, and unknown, but yet very numerous band of foes. So it is with this popular theory about Catholic miracles. We are told that we are deceived. We are all cheated together. The bishops are victims; the priests are victims; monks and nuns are victims; the laity are victims; the old Catholics in England are victims; the converts are victims; the best of us all are victims; the most learned, the most pious, the most able, the most self-denying,—all *these* are dupes. If there are deceivers, they are the few, the ignorant, the cunning, and the vile. The Roman Church, as a Church, is supposed to be under the dominion of a band of conspira-

---

[1] : It is a remarkable fact, that the most celebrated work on the supernatural gifts accorded by God to Christians, is the production of one of the greatest intellects, and by far the most influential political writer, that modern Europe has seen. Görres, the author of the *Christliche Mystik*, was the Wellington of literature during the last European war. The influence which he exercised over the whole German mind by his *Rhenish Mercury* is altogether without parallel in the history of journalism. It was, indeed, regarded as so formidable by Napoleon himself, that he styled Görres a *fourth continental power*. Yet this first of publicists devoted his whole life to the investigation of the wonders of Catholic mysticism, and believed with undoubting conviction in their reality.

tors, who have blinded her eyes without her having found it out, and who are now using her for their own godless purposes. Does not such a supposition confute itself? Is it worth admitting, even as an hypothesis? Would such a statement be endured for a moment by a judge and twelve men in a jury-box? I say, therefore, before moving a step to overthrow the Protestant accusation, "Make a distinct and intelligible charge of certain definite crimes against certain definite individuals. When that is done, the proof still remains with you. Show us both who are the deceivers, and how they deceive us; or admit that there is no credulity so open-mouthed as that of Protestants when they attack Catholics; no superstition so base as that which worships this visible order of nature as an eternal rule which not even God Himself can ever interrupt."

The fact is, however, that no Protestant ever attempts any thing like a profound investigation of the Catholic miracles. A calm, critical, and judicial inquiry into the worth of the Roman process of canonisation has never been risked. Here is an enormous catalogue of incidents, whose supernatural character is vouched for by the decrees of a long series of Popes, professedly based upon the most prolonged and anxious legal examination. For centuries a tribunal has been declaring that one series of miracles after another has come before it; that it has weighed them all with the utmost care; that it has heard every thing that could be urged against them; that it has rejected, as not proved, a very large number; and that, after the most searching inquiry, it *has* found such and such supernatural incidents to be established by every law of human evidence[1]. No man can look at the processes of the canonisation of Catholic Saints without admitting that very few of those secular events which we unhesitatingly believe are supported by so overwhelming a weight of proof. Men's fortunes and lives are incessantly taken away by law at our very doors on lower degrees of evidence, and no one exclaims. And yet the decisions of this Catholic tribunal are set aside without hesitation. People think them not even worthy of listening to. The whole affair they count a childish trifling; and with a shrug or a sneer they pass it by.

And it is the same with those miracles which have not been brought before any such high tribunal, but which rest on undeniable private evidence. Those who are not Catholics put them aside simply as in-

---

[1] For the steps followed in the processes of canonisation, see Faber's *Essay on Beatification, Canonisation, and the Processes of the Congregation of Rites.*

credible. They assume that they cannot be true, and therefore that they are not true. Press them in argument, and they will shirk your most stringent proofs. You can make no impression upon their *wills*. They will believe any thing but that God has interrupted the course of nature in favour of any one but themselves. In short, if we wish to see human reason in its most irrational mood, we have but to enter into conversation with a Protestant who asserts and thinks that he believes the Bible miracles to be true, and urge upon him the proofs of such modern miracles as are recorded of St. Frances of Rome. You will perceive first, that though he has made up his mind on the subject with unhesitating dogmatism, he has never investigated its bearings or facts, even in outline. Nevertheless, to your surprise, you will find him perfectly ready to start some random theory, at a moment's notice, unconscious of the momentous, the awful nature of the matter he is handling. You see, perhaps, that his mind is powerfully influenced by the singular character of many Catholic miracles. He thinks them strange, unnecessary, unaccountable, absurd, disgusting, degrading. His nervous sensibilities are shocked by an account of the fearful pangs accompanying the *stigmata*. In the phenomena of ecstasy he can see nothing more than the ravings of delirium, or (if he believes in mesmerism) than the tales of a clairvoyante, and the rigidity of catalepsy. His physical frame, accustomed to its routine of breakfast, luncheon, and dinner, its sofas and easy-chairs, and its luxurious bed, shudders at the thought of the self-inflicted penances of the Saints, and at the idea of God's bestowing a miraculous power of enduring such horrors. He would be as much surprised to be told that Smithfield was literally the abode of incarnate demons, as to hear that demons have often assumed the shapes of beasts and monsters in their conflicts with the elect. The notion that an angel might visibly appear to a pious traveller on the Great Western or Birmingham railroad, and protect him from death in a frightful collision of trains, makes him open his eyes and contemplate you as scarcely sane to hint at such a thing. That "the Virgin," as he calls her, should come down from heaven and enter a church or a room, and hold a conversation with living men, women, or children in the nineteenth century, and give them a trumpery medal, or tell them to wear a piece of cloth round their neck, or cure them of some disease, he regards about as likely and rational as that the stories in the *Arabian Nights* and the *Fairy Tales* should turn out to be true histories. Be as serious as you please, he simply laughs in his sleeve, thinking to himself, "Well, who would have believed that the intellect of an educated Englishman should submit itself to such drivelling as this?"

Perceiving that this is the state of his mind, you open the Bible, which lies, handsomely bound, upon his table, and running rapidly through the four Gospels and the Acts of the Apostles, point out to him a long series of supernatural events there recorded; and show him that in their nature they are precisely the same as those modern miracles which provoke his disgust or contempt. You remind him, first of all, that our Lord Jesus Christ is the Head of the Church, and that all His people are made *like Him*, in His life and His sufferings, as well as in His glory; and then proceed to your summary. He accounts the penances of Saints needless and impossible; you remind him of our blessed Lord's fast of forty days and forty nights. He is horror-struck at the details of the sufferings of those in whom the Passion of Christ has been visibly renewed; you beg him to attempt to realise the bloody sweat in the Garden of Olives. He speaks of mesmerism and clairvoyance, and derides the thought of a Saint's being illuminated with radiant light, or exhaling a fragrant odour; you ask him how he explains away the transfiguration of Jesus. He says that it is physically impossible that a man's body can be (as he expresses it) in two places at once; you desire him to say by what law of nature our Lord entered the room where the disciples were when the doors were shut; how St. Peter was delivered from chains and imprisonment by the angel; how St. Paul was rapt into the third heaven, *whether in the body or out of the body, he could not tell*. He says that when a Saint has thought himself attacked by devils in hideous shapes, his brain has been diseased; you entreat him to beware of throwing a doubt on the temptation of Jesus Christ by Satan in the wilderness. He pities you for believing that the Mother of God has appeared for such needless purposes to excited devotees; you ask him why the Son of God appeared long after His death and ascension to St. Paul, and told him what he might have learnt in a natural way from the other Apostles. He calls your miraculous relics childish trumpery; you ask whether the handkerchiefs and aprons which cured the sick, after having touched St. Paul's body, were trumpery also; and whether St. Luke is countenancing superstition when he relates how the people crowded near St. Peter to be healed by his very shadow passing over them. Then, as he feels the overwhelming force of your rebukes, he insinuates that there is something divine, something evidently touching, pure, and strict in morality in the Bible narratives, which is wanting in these lives of Catholic Saints; and you refer him to such biographies as that of St. Frances of Rome, and compelling him to read the narratives of her revelations, ask him if all that she says when in a state of ecstasy does not wear, even in his judgment, the impress of a Divine origin, and seem to be dictated by the God of all purity, humility, and love.

At length your opponent, after brief pondering, changes his ground, and asserts that you are yourself deceived; that the real defect in Catholic miraculous stories is the want of evidence. He tells you that he would believe, if he could; but that you have not proved your point. You next call his attention to the distinct promise made by our blessed Lord to the Church, that miracles should always continue with her; and ask him how, on his theory, he accounts for the non-fulfilment of this promise. You desire him to lay his finger on the epoch when its fulfilment ceased; and not only to assert that it then ceased, but to prove his assertion. He says nothing, for he has nothing to say which he can even attempt to prove; and you proceed to furnish a few examples of miracles, from patristic, mediæval, or modern times, or perhaps of the present day, which are supported by at least as cogent an amount of evidence as the historical proof of the Scripture miracles. You insist upon his *disproving* these. He cannot. He resorts to some new hypothesis. He says that there is deception *somewhere*, though he cannot tell where; and probably by this time is showing symptoms of a wish to end the discussion. You urge him again, and press him to give an intelligible reason for supposing that there *must* be deception any where. He thinks a while; and when at length you are looking for a rational conclusion, he starts backwards to his old assumption that the Catholic miracles *cannot* be true. He begs the whole question, and says that they are in favour of Catholicism, and that Catholicism is false. You too recur to your old reference to the Bible, and so on. And thus you run again the same round; and you may run it a thousand times over, till you perceive that there is but one reason why your opponent is not convinced; which is, that he *will not* be convinced. And thus it was in the days when those very miracles were wrought which Protestants profess to believe. The Jews *would not* believe our Lord's words and doctrines. He then bade them believe Him because of His miracles; and they instantly imputed them to the power of the devil. He showed them that this theory was impossible; but, so far from being convinced and converted, they went their ways, and plotted His death. Now, our controversialists cannot, or do not wish, to take away our lives; but when not a word is left them in the way of argument, they go their ways, and protest to their fellows, that we are obstinate, unfair, superstitious, and insolent; and too often encourage one another in the bitterest persecution of those who are convinced by our reasonings, and submit to the Church.

I now turn to the objections which are at times felt by Catholics themselves to the publication of Saints' Lives, abounding in supernatural incidents. Such persons are, indeed, not numerous; and their number is rapidly diminishing. Still it can scarcely be doubted that conscientious Catholics *are* to be found who take the view I am speaking of, from ideas which, though erroneous (as I believe), are yet so truly founded in sincerity, as to demand respect and explanation from those who differ from them.

The objections they raise are twofold. First, they allege that such books scandalise Protestants and drive them from the Church; and secondly, they do not see *how* incidents, wholly unlike our ordinary daily experience, *can* practically serve us in our private Christian lives.

To the idea that non-Catholics are thus needlessly prejudiced against the faith, I reply, that this assertion is wholly unproved. That they do, as a matter of fact, laugh and attack such biographies, I fully admit; but they laugh at them on grounds which we cannot admit without giving up the Christian revelation itself. They scoff at them, not because they think them not supported by credible testimony, but because they are not what they call dignified, refined, and just such as they should have supposed all things to be that come from God. That such a temper of mind is indicative of pure Deism, it needs no words to prove. A man who derides a miraculous event merely as *trifling*, thereby asserts that he himself is the judge of what is great and what is little in the sight of God. He lays down laws for the guidance of the Almighty. He is adopting the identical reasoning of professed infidels, who on this very ground reject Christianity itself. And it is obvious that nothing can be more perilous than the encouragement of so fatal a principle of judgment. Once let the acute and logical Protestant perceive that you move one step backwards in deference to this objection, and he will press you with fresh consequences of the very same admission until he lands you in undisguised scepticism, if not in the blackest Atheism.

Can any single instance, in fact, be named in which a mind that was apparently determined to seek salvation at all costs, has been actually deterred from entering the Catholic Church by meeting with these extraordinary histories? Are they not a butt for determined and obstinate Protestants, and for such Protestants only? Ask any convert whether, on looking back, he can say that the knowledge of these peculiarities in Catholic hagiology ever practically held him back for four-and-twenty hours in his journey towards the Church. That the world is angry, and that the world vents its spleen and its contempt in bitter jests, is true enough; but *pious souls are not made to sin, or kept away from their Saviour*, by any thing of the kind. And that the rage and mocking of man afford not the slightest reason for inducing the Church to turn out of her natural path, I shall not dishonour my readers by attempting to prove to them.

That it *is* her natural course to make these histories public, for the practical edification of her children, is clear from one fact alone,— they are precisely parallel to the life of our blessed Lord, as narrated in the four Gospels. The whole question resolves itself into this: If such lives as that of St. Frances, and many others, recently published in England, are not edifying to the ordinary Christian, then the life of Jesus Christ is not edifying. The Gospels, as well as the Acts of the Apostles and the Epistles, must be rigorously expurgated and cut down to the type of the common domestic life of the present day. Nothing can be further removed from the circumstances of most men than the records of our Lord's miracles and supernatural acts in general. What has the temptation, the transfiguration, the driving the devils into the swine, the turning the water into wine at what we should now call a "wedding-breakfast," and, in fact, almost every *act* in our blessed Lord's life, in common with our amusement, our business, our society, our whole experience? Yet, to say that a devout soul can meditate on these transcendently mysterious events, and not derive from them practical instruction to enable her to fulfil her little trivial earthly duties with Christian perfection, is nothing short of blasphemy. The Son of God incarnate, all glorious, all awful, all unfathomable as He was even in the days of His sojourning on earth, was yet our example, our model, our embodied series of precepts. The eye of the simplest regenerate child cannot be turned for an instant upon His Divine glories and ineffable sufferings without drawing light therefrom to guide it even in its play with its fellows, or in the most trivial of the duties towards its parents and teachers.

And such, I am convinced, is the experience of Catholics of all ranks, of every age and every degree of intellectual cultivation, who study religiously the miraculous lives of the Saints, believing them to be, on the whole, correct histories. It is not needful that they should regard them to be literally true in all their details, as the Bible is true. We have but to regard them as we regard other authentic human narratives, with the addition of that veneration and confidence which is due to such portions of them as have been formally sanctioned by the Church, to derive from them unceasing spiritual comfort and instruction. Doubtless, if we are so ignorant as to fancy that all Saints' histories are to be alike in details, and that therefore we ought to wish that the circumstances of our lives were the same as theirs, we shall be doing ourselves great mischief. But let us study them with a true knowledge of the mere elements of the Christian faith, and they will be to us what St. Paul desires his disciples to seek for in *his* life, namely, a continuation, as it were, of the life of Jesus Christ, carried on through all the successive ages of His Church on earth. They will impress upon our minds with an intensity peculiarly their own, the reality of the invisible world and the ensnaring tendencies of every thing that we possess. Weak and ignorant as is the imaginative and sensitive portion of our nature, it needs every possible help that it can find to counteract the paralysing effects of the worldliness of the world, of the lukewarmness of Christians, and of the enthralling nature of the universe of sight and sense. Our courage is wonderfully strengthened, and our love for things invisible is inflamed, by every thing that forces us, as it were, to *see* that this visible creation *is not* the only thing that is real, mighty, and present. The general precepts and the dogmatic statements of religion acquire a singular and living force when we perceive them carried out and realised in the actual affairs of life in a degree to which our personal experience is a stranger. Influenced as human nature is by example, these unpretending narratives, whose whole strength lies in the facts which they record, and not in the art of the biographer, undeniably *strike* the mind with an almost supernatural force. They enchain the attention; they compel us to say, Are these things true? Are these things possible? Is religion, after all, so terribly near to us? Are this life and this world so literally vain and worthless, so absolutely nothing worth? Are suffering and awful bodily anguish blessings to be *really* coveted? Are the maxims which I daily hear around me so hopelessly bad and accursed? Are angels and devils so near, so very near, to us all? Is purgatory so terrible and so inevitable to all but the perfect, that these fearful visions of its pains are in substance what I myself shall endure? And if I fall from grace and die in sin before one of the innumerable temptations that hourly beset me, is it true that nothing less than an eternity of such torments, the very reading of which even thus represented makes me shudder with horror, will be my *inevitable* lot? And is the bliss of the Saints and the joy of loving God so inexpressibly sweet to any souls here on earth? Is it possible that any one should escape from a state of coldness, deadness, worldliness, and unwilling performance of his religious duties, and positively come to lose all taste for bodily and mere intellectual pleasures through the absorbing of his whole being into the love of Jesus and of

Mary, and through a burning thirst for the beatific vision of the Eternal Trinity?

And who will venture to say that it is not good *for us all* to have such thoughts frequently pressed upon our attention? If there is any meaning in the command that we are to aim at being perfect, whatever be the state of life *in which* we are called to seek perfection, surely it is no ordinary advantage thus to have the essentially supernatural character of our religious life forced again and again upon our attention. For, be it never forgotten, this very *supernaturalness* is one of its essential features. There are innumerable varieties in our vocations. The earthly circumstances in which we are to serve God are almost innumerable in their variety; but the supernatural element appertains to them all alike. Our actual relationship to the awful and glorious realities of the unseen world is precisely the same in kind as that of the most miraculously endowed Saints. The only difference is this, that in their case that relationship was perceived and visibly manifested in a peculiar mode, to which we are strangers. Heaven, purgatory, and hell are as near to us as if we beheld the visions of St. Frances. The cross is as literally our portion, in its essential nature, as if the five sacred wounds were renewed physically in our agonising frame. Our angel-guardian is as incessantly by our side, as if our eyes were opened to behold his effulgent radiance. Satan strikes the same blows at our souls, whether he shows himself to our sight or not. The relics of Saints, which we carefully look at or criticise, *may be* at any moment the vehicles of the same miraculous powers as the handkerchiefs from the body of St. Paul. Who would say to a blind man, "Forget the tangible realities of this life, because you cannot see them"? Who would not rather say, "Bear constantly in mind what is the experience of those who *can* see, that you may practically remember their ceaseless nearness to you"? And just such is the experience of the Saints, in whose histories faith has partly merged into sight, and the veil which blinds our eyes has been partially and at certain seasons withdrawn. It tells us, as few things else can tell, of the *reality* of the objects of our faith.

I add a word or two on the question, how far the actual conduct of the extraordinary persons whose lives are here related is to serve as a model for practical imitation by ordinary Christians. To the well-instructed Catholic, it would be an impertinence in me to suggest that they are not in every detail thus to be followed. It is the duty of a Christian to follow the rules for daily life which it has pleased Almighty God to lay down in the Gospel, and not to imagine that those exceptional cases of conduct to which He has supernaturally prompted certain individuals are to be imitated by those who have only the ordinary graces of the Holy Spirit.

The general reader, however, may be reminded that Catholics believe, that as the Creator of the universe occasionally interrupts the order of the laws of nature, so He at times interrupts the relative order of the laws of duty; not, of course, the essential laws of morality, but those positive laws which are obligatory simply because they are enacted by competent authority. No person, indeed, can be justified in acting on such an idea in his own case, unless guided by supernatural light, beyond the usual spiritual illumination given to all Christians. This supernatural light is rarely vouchsafed, and it is accordingly in the highest degree presumptuous in any person to overstep the ordinary routine of distinctly ordered duty, under the idea that he is called by God to break the rules given for the guidance of mankind in general. In all such supposed cases, the Catholic Church has the proper tests to apply, by which the soul can learn whether she is led by a Divine afflatus, or betrayed by her own disordered imagination, or the deceits of an invisible tempter.

J.M.C.

THE LIFE OF ST. FRANCES OF ROME

CHAPTER I.

GENERAL CHARACTER OF THE SAINT'S LIFE—HER CHILDHOOD AND EARLY PIETY.

There have been saints whose histories strike us as particularly beautiful, not only as possessing the beauty which always belongs to sanctity, whether exhibited in an aged servant of God, who for three-score years and more has borne the heat and burden of the day, or in the youth who has offered up the morning of his life to His Maker, and yielded it into His hands before twenty summers have passed over his head; whether in a warrior king like St. Louis, or a beggar like Benedict Labré, or a royal lady like St. Elizabeth of Hungary; but also as uniting—in the circumstances of their lives, in the places they inhabited, and the epochs when they appeared in the world, much that is in itself poetical and interesting, and calculated to attract the attention of the historian and the man of letters, as well as of the theologian and the devout. In this class of saints may well be included Francesca Romana, the foundress of the religious order of the Oblates of Tor di Specchi. She was the model of young girls, the example of a devout matron, and finally a widow, according to the very pattern drawn by St. Paul; she was beautiful, courageous, and full of wisdom, nobly born, and delicately brought up: Rome was the place of her birth, and the scene of her labours; her home was in the centre of the great city, in the heart of the Trastevere; her life was full of trials and hair-breadth escapes, and strange reverses; her hidden life was marvellous in the extreme: visions of terror and of beauty followed her all her days; favours such as were never granted to any other saint were vouchsafed to her; the world of spirits was continually thrown open to her sight; and yet, in her daily conduct, her character and her ways, minute details of which have reached us, there is a simplicity as well as a deep humility, awful in one so highly gifted, touching in one so highly favoured.

Troubled and wild were the times she lived in; perhaps if one had to point out a period in which a Catholic Christian would rather not have had his lot cast,—one in which there was most to try his faith and wound his feelings, he would name the end of the fourteenth century, and the beginning of the fifteenth. War was raging all over Europe; Italy was torn by inward dissensions, by the rival factions of the Guelphs and the Ghibellines. So savage was the spirit with which their conflicts were carried on, that barbarism seemed once more about to overspread that fair land, and the Church itself was afflicted not only by the outward persecutions which strengthen its vitality, though for a while they may appear to cripple its action, but by trials of a far deeper and more painful nature. Heresy had torn from her arms a great number of her children, and repeated schisms were dividing those who, in appearance and even in intention, remained faithful to the Holy See. The successors of St. Peter had removed the seat of their residence to Avignon, and the Eternal City presented the aspect of one vast battle-field, on which daily and hourly conflicts were occurring. The Colonnas, the Orsinis, the Savellis, were every instant engaged in struggles which deluged the streets with blood, and cut off many of her citizens in the flower of their age; strangers were also continually invading the heritage of the Church, and desecrated Rome with massacres and outrages scarcely less deplorable than those of the Huns and the Vandals. In the capital of the Christian world, ruins of recent date lay side by side with the relics of past ages; the churches were sacked, burned, and destroyed; the solitary and indestructible basilicas stood almost alone, mournfully erect amidst these scenes of carnage and gloom; and the eyes of the people of Rome were wistfully directed towards that tutelary power, which has ever been to them a pledge of prosperity and peace, and whose removal the signal of war and of misery.

It was at that time, during the Pontificate of Urban VI., in the year 1384, that Francesca was born at Rome; that "she rose as a star in a dark night," according to the expression of the most ancient of her biographers. Her father's name was Paul Bussa; her mother's Jacobella de' Roffredeschi; they were both of noble and even illustrious descent, and closely allied to the Orsinis, the Savellis, and the Mellinis. On the day of her birth she was carried to the church of Santa Agnese, in the Piazza Navona, and there baptised. Little could the worshippers who may have been praying there that day for a blessing on their bereaved and distracted city, have guessed in what form that blessing was bestowed, and that that little babe, a few hours old, was to prove a most powerful instrument in the hands of God for the extinction of schism, the revival of piety, and the return of peace.

From her infancy, Francesca was not like other children. Her mother, when she held her in her arms or hushed her to sleep on her knee, had always an involuntary feeling of reverence for her little daughter; it was as if an angel of God, not an earthly child, had been lent her; a heavenly expression shone in her eyes, and the calm serenity of her infant features struck all who approached her with admiration. Francesca learned to read at the same time that she began to speak; the first words she was taught to utter were the sacred names of Jesus and Mary; at her mother's knee she lisped the Little Office of the Blessed Virgin, and during the whole course of her life she never omitted that practice.

At two or three years old she had the sense and intelligence of a grown-up person; an extraordinary piety revealed itself in all her words and actions. She never played like other children; but when left to herself would often retire into silent corners of her father's palace, and kneeling down, join her little hands in prayer; and lifting up her infant heart to God, would read a devout book, or repeat hymns to the Blessed Virgin, her own dear mother as she used to call her. Silence appeared to be the delight of this young child—the deepest reserve and modesty an instinct with her. At the age of six years the practices of the saints were already familiar to her. She had left off eating meat, eggs, or sweets of any description, and lived on plainly boiled vegetables and bread. The necessity of eating at all seemed irksome to her, and she never drank any thing but pure water. Then also had begun her unwearied study of the lives of holy women, and especially of the virgin martyrs who have shed their blood for the love of Jesus Christ. The Sacrament of Confirmation, which she received at that time in the church of Santa Agnese, the same in which she had been baptised, filled her with ardour to show her love for her Lord by every imaginable means, even those the most painful to the flesh.

Her mother was a very devout person, and in the habit of visiting every day some of the churches, especially those where indulgences were to be gained, and she also frequented the stations with affectionate assiduity. For in that troubled epoch, as in the earliest times of the Church, as now, as always, on certain days, in certain places, the relics of apostles, of martyrs, and of confessors were exhibited to the faithful, often on the very spot where they had finished their course with joy, having kept their faith and won their crown. The devotion of "the stations," as it is performed in Rome, is one of the most touching links with the past that it is possible to conceive. To pass along the street, so often trod by holy feet in former and in latter days, and seek the church appointed for that day's station; to approach some time-worn basilica, or ancient sanctuary, without the city walls may be, and pausing on the threshold, give one look at the glorious works of Almighty God in the natural world,—at the wide Campagna, that land-sea, so beautiful in its broad expanse and its desolate grandeur, at the purple hills with their golden lights and their deep-blue shadows, and the arched sky telling so vividly the glory of its Maker; and then slowly lifting the heavy curtain that stands between that vision of earthly beauty, and the shrine where countless generations have come to worship,—to tread under feet the green boughs, the sweet-smelling leaves, the scattered flowers, that morning strewn upon the uneven, time-trod, time-honoured pavement; bowing in adoration before the Lord in His tabernacle, to thank Him for the wonders that He has worked in His saints,—for the beauty of the world of grace, of which that of the visible world is but the type and the shadow; and then move from one shrine to the other, wherever the lights upon the altars point the way, and invoke the assistance, the prayers of the saints whose relics are there displayed;—all this is one of those rare enjoyments which at once feed the soul and awake the imagination, and which the devout Christian can find in no place but Rome.

It was these "stations" that Francesca's mother frequented, and took her little daughter with her. Sometimes she went to some church in the heart of the city; sometimes to some lonely shrine without the walls. Then, as now, the beggars (so we find it mentioned later in the life of the Saint) congregated at the doors, and clamoured for alms. Then, as now, the lights burned upon the altars, and the sweet smell of fragrant and crushed leaves perfumed the air. During sermons the little girl's attention never wandered; and on her return home she was wont to repeat what she had heard with unction and delight.

Her mother's favourite church was that of Santa Maria Nuova; in our day more frequently called that of San Francesca Romana. It stands in the Toro Romano, close to the ruins of the ancient Temple of Peace. It was served at that time by the Benedictine monks of Mount Olivet; and to one of them, Don Antonio di Monte Savello, Jacobella de' Roffredeschi intrusted the spiritual direction of her daughter. He was a man of great learning and piety, and continued her director for five and thirty years. Every Wednesday the little maiden came to him for confession. She consulted him about her occupations, her religious exercises, and her studies, and exactly obeyed his most minute directions, even in indifferent things. Often she tried for his permission to practise greater austerities; and such was her fervour, and the plain indications of God's designs upon her, that he occasionally allowed her to perform penances which might have been considered in ordinary cases too severe for her tender age. At other times he forbade them altogether; and she submitted cheerfully to his commands, without a word of remonstrance or complaint, and resumed them again at his desire, with the equanimity of one who well knew that the spirit of perfect obedience is more acceptable to God than any works of devotion.

"A celestial brightness, a more eternal beauty,   Shone on her face, and encircled her form, when after confession   Homeward serenely she walked, with God's benediction upon her.   When she had passed, it seemed like the ceasing of exquisite music."[1] Francesca's daily life was as perfect as a child's could be. No untrue words sullied her pure lips; no gross thought dwelt in her mind. She seldom laughed, though a sweet smile was often on her lips. Up to the age of eleven, her life was one long continual prayer. Every little action was performed with a view to the glory of God. Her trifling failings she deplored with anguish; every stain on the pure mirror of her conscience was instantly washed away by tears. It was not long before it pleased God to vouchsafe to her extraordinary graces. Her early and almost intuitive acquaintance with the mysteries of religion was wonderful. Every day she meditated on the Incarnation and the Passion of Jesus Christ; and her devotion to the Blessed Virgin increased in proportion to her love for our Lord. Her face flushed with delight, and a seraphic expression beamed in her eyes, when she spoke of the sufferings of Jesus, and the glories of Mary. From the little oratory where she held secret communion with heaven, she went out into the world with the most ardent desire to serve the poor, to console the afflicted, to do good to all. The affection of her young heart found vent in numerous works of charity; and Francesca's name, and Francesca's sweet voice, and Francesca's fair face, were even then to many of the sufferers of that dark epoch a sign of hope,—a pledge that God was still amongst them as of yore, and His Spirit at work in the hearts of men.

---

[1] Longfellow: *Evangeline.*

CHAPTER II.

FRANCESCA'S EARLY INCLINATION FOR THE CLOISTER—BY HER FATHER'S DESIRE SHE MARRIES LORENZO PONZIANO—HER MARRIED LIFE—HER ILLNESS AND MIRACULOUS CURE.

From the time that Francesca had understood the meaning of the words, her greatest desire had been to enter a convent; but with that spirit of humility and reserve which so particularly belonged to her, she had kept her desire concealed in her heart, and had manifested it to none but God and her director. Don Antonio encouraged her to persevere in this silence, and to prove her own resolution by secretly adhering to the rules, and practising the austerities of one of the strictest religious orders. She gladly assented to this, and persevered in it for a considerable time. Stronger and deeper every day grew her inclination to forsake the world, and to hold communion with God alone in the solitude of the cloister; with that God whose love had already driven from her heart all care for comfort, for pleasure, and for self. But not so smooth was to be her path through life; not much longer was she to sit in silence at the feet of her Lord, with no other thought than to live on the words, which fell from His lips.

Though she concealed as much as possible the peculiarities of her mode of life, they could not altogether escape the notice of her parents; and they soon questioned her on the subject. When she informed them of her wish to embrace the religious life, her father chose to consider her vocation as a childish fancy, and informed her in return that he had already promised her in marriage to Lorenzo Ponziano, a young nobleman of illustrious birth, and not less eminent for his virtues and for his talents than from his fortune and position. He reckoned amongst his ancestors St. Paulianus, pope and martyr; his mother was a Mellini; and his eldest brother Paluzzo had married Vannuzza, a daughter of the noble house of Santo Croce. Francesca's heart sank within her at this announcement, and falling on her knees she implored her father to alter his determination, and allow her to follow what she believed to be the will of God in her regard. She went even so far as to protest that nothing should induce her to consent to this marriage; torrents of tears fell from her eyes as she poured forth her supplications and urged her request. But it was all in vain that she wept and prayed. Paul Bussa turned a deaf ear to her pleadings; declared that his word was pledged, that nothing should ever persuade him to retract it; and he insisted that, as a dutiful daughter, she should submit herself to his will. Seeing him thus immovable, Francesca rose from her knees, withdrew in silence from his presence, and retiring into her little oratory, prostrated herself before the crucifix, and asked counsel of Him at whose feet she wished to live and to die; and implored Him, if such was His good pleasure, to exert His Almighty Power, and raise obstacles to the projected marriage. Then, strengthened by prayer, she was inspired to seek direction from him who was the organ of the divine will to her, and hurrying to Santa Maria Nuova, she requested to see Don Antonio Savello.

Kindly and gently the good priest spoke to his afflicted penitent. He promised to consult the Lord for her in prayer, and suggested some devotions to be used by herself for that purpose. Then, seeing her countenance assume a calmer expression, he endeavoured to prepare her mind for what he doubtless already knew was the will of God, and the true, though in one so minded, the singular vocation of Francesca. "If your parents persist in their resolution (he said), take it, my child, as a sign that God expects of you this sacrifice. Offer up to Him in that case your earnest desire for the religious life. He will accept the will for the deed; and you will obtain at once the reward of that wish, and the peculiar graces attached to the sacrament of marriage. God's ways are not as our ways, Francesca. When St. Mary Magdalene had sent for the Lord Jesus Christ to come and heal her brother, it was no doubt a severe trial to her that He came not; that the long hours of the day and of the night succeeded each other, and that He tarried on the way, and sent no message or token of His love. But when her brother rose from the dead, when the shroud fell from his limbs, and he stood before her full of life and strength, she understood the mystery, and adored the divine wisdom of that delay. God indeed asks of you your heart, Francesca; but He also claims your whole self as an oblation, and therefore your will that He may mould it into entire conformity with His own. For works may be many and good, my daughter, and piety may be fervent, and virtues eminent, and yet the smallest leaven of self-love or self-will may ruin the whole. Why do you weep, Francesca? That God's will is not accomplished, or that your own is thwarted? Nothing but sin can mar the first, and in this your trial there is not the least shade of sin. As to your own will, bend, break, annihilate it, my child, and take courage. Have but one thought—the good pleasure, the sweet will of God; submit yourself to His Providence. Lay down your wishes as an oblation on His altar; give up that highest place which you had justly coveted; take the lower one which He now appoints you; and if you cannot be His spouse, be His loving and faithful servant."

Francesca went home, and awaited in silence her father's further commands. She was very pale, for the struggle was a painful one. She prayed night and day, watched and fasted. When Paul Bussa renewed his injunctions, she gently gave her assent, begged him to forgive her past resistance, and henceforward gave no outward signs of the suffering within, all the greater that it came in the form of rejoicing, and that others deemed that to be happiness which cost her so many secret tears. The family of Ponziano were overjoyed at the marriage,—the bride was so rich, so beautiful, and so virtuous; there was not a young man in Rome who did not look with envy on Lorenzo, and wish himself in his stead. There was no end to the banquets, the festivities, the merry-makings, which took place on the occasion; and in the midst of these rejoicings Francesca left her father's palace for that of the Ponziani. It stood in the heart of the Trastevere, close to the Yellow River, though not quite upon it, in the vicinity of the Ponte Rotto, in a street that runs parallel with the Tiber. It is a well-known spot; and on the 9th of March, the Festival of St. Francesca, the people of Rome and of the neighbourhood flock to it in crowds. The modern building that has been raised on the foundation of the old palace is the Casa dei Esercizii Pii, for the young men of the city. There the repentant sinner who longs to break the chain of sin, the youth beset by some strong temptation, one who has heard the inward voice summoning him to higher paths of virtue, another who is in doubt as to the particular line of life to which he is called, may come, and leave behind them for three, or five, or ten days, as it may be, the busy world, with all its distractions and its agitations, and, free for the time being from temporal cares, the wants of the body provided for, and the mind at rest, may commune with God and their own souls. Here they listen daily, nay hourly, to the instructions of devout priests, who, in the manner prescribed by St. Ignatius, place before them in turn the most awful truths and the most consoling mysteries of the Kingdom of God. Resolutions are thus taken, conversions often effected, good purposes strengthened in a way which often seems little short of miraculous. The means are marvellously adapted to the end; and though many a wave may sweep over the soul, when it again returns to the world, a mark has been stamped upon it not easily effaced.

Over the Casa dei Esercizii Pii the sweet spirit of Francesca seems still to preside. On the day of her festival its rooms are thrown open, every memorial of the gentle saint is exhibited, lights burn on numerous altars, flowers deck the passages, leaves are strewn in the chapel, on the stairs, in the entrance-court; gay carpets, figured tapestry and crimson silks hang over the door, and crowds of people go in and out, and kneel before the relics or the pictures of the dear saint of Rome, and greet on each altar, and linger in these chambers, like kinsfolk met on a birthday to rejoice together. The well-dressed and the ragged, the rich and the poor, without distinction, pay their homage to her sweet memory whose living presence once adorned the spot which they visit. It is a joyous and touching festival, one which awakens tender thoughts, and brings the world of memory into close connection with that of hope. The mind is forcibly carried back to the day when the young bride of Lorenzo Ponziano entered these walls for the first time, in all the sacred beauty of holiness and youth—

"Pure as the virgin snow that dwells
Upon the mountain's crest,
Cold as the sheet of ice that lies
Upon the lake's deep breast."

Pure from the least taint of worldly vanity, cold to all that belongs to human passion; but with a heart burning with love to God, and overflowing with charity to every creature of His.

She was received tenderly and joyfully by Lorenzo himself, by his father Andrew, his mother Cecilia, and Vannozza, the wife of his elder brother. Francesca smiled sweetly as she returned their caresses; but the noise, and the gaiety, and the visiting, that attended a wedding in those days weighed heavily on her spirits; and though she never complained, Vannozza perceived that her little heart was oppressed with some secret sorrow, and tenderly inquired into its cause. Francesca could not resist the gentle appeal, and disclosed her grief to her kind sister. She told her that the world had never given her pleasure, that her affections were elsewhere set, that she longed to live for God alone, and felt sad, in spite of all her efforts, at the tumult and dissipation, which was now her portion. "If such are your feelings, my beloved little sister," exclaimed Vannozza, "my sympathy may serve to console you; for neither do I find any delight in the vanities of the world, but only in prayer and meditation. Let us be friends, Francesca; I will help you to lead the life you desire, and together we shall arrive at the end we have in view."

These kind words filled Francesca's heart with joy; and from that day forward there sprung up a friendship between these two young women, which lasted for eight-and-thirty years, and was a source of the greatest consolation to them through all the trials they had to encounter, at the same time that it edified all those who beheld that tender affection.

In her new home Francesca followed the same mode of life which she had pursued in her father's house; but her zeal was tempered with so much wisdom and prudence, that she offended no one, and contrived to win the affection of all her relations. Her good sense, her sweetness of temper, her earnest piety, charmed them all; and they were astonished that so young a girl could at once assume the part and fulfil the duties of a devoted wife and a noble matron. Anxious in every way to conform herself to Lorenzo's wishes, she received the visits of the high-born ladies her equals and companions, and returned them with punctuality. She submitted to appear in public with all the state which belonged to her position, and accepted and wore the costly dresses and the splendid jewels which her husband lavished upon her; but under those gorgeous silks and rich brocades a hair-shirt was concealed. Always ready to comply with any observance which duty or propriety required, she at the same time steadily abstained even from the innocent amusements in which others indulged; and never danced or played at cards, or sat up late at night. Her manner was so gentle and kind, that it inspired affection in all who approached her; but there was also a profound and awful purity in her aspect and in her demeanour, which effectually checked the utterance of a free or licentious word in her presence. Faithful to her early habits of piety, she continued every Wednesday her visits to Santa Maria Nuova; and after confessing to Don Antonio, she went to communion with such fervent devotion, that those who saw her at the altar absorbed in adoration, foresaw that God would ere long bestow extraordinary graces on her soul. Rising betimes in the morning, Francesca devoutly said her prayers, made her meditation, and read attentively out of a spiritual book.

In the course of the day, whenever she had a moment's leisure un-claimed by any of the duties of her state, she withdrew into a church or into her own room, and gave herself up to prayer. Every Saturday she had a conference with Fra Michele, a Dominican monk, the prior of San Clemente, and an intimate friend of her father-in-law. He was a learned theologian, as well as a man of great piety and virtue, and in-structed her with care in all the doctrines of religion.

At the same tune, so austere and devout a life in a young person of twelve years old could not fail to attract the attention and draw down the censures of the worldly. Many such began to laugh at Francesca, and to turn her piety into ridicule. They intruded their advice on Lo-renzo Ponziano, and urged him to put a stop to what they termed his wife's eccentricities. But happily for Francesca, he was not one of those men who are easily influenced by the opinion of others. He formed his own judgment, and pursued his own line of conduct undis-turbed by the comments and animadversions of his would-be advisers. His young wife was much too precious to him, much too perfect in his sight, her whole life bore too visibly the stamp of God's dealings with her, for him to dream of interfering with the course she had taken. On the contrary, he looked upon her with that affectionate veneration which the presence of true sanctity always awakens in a noble and re-ligious mind. His father and mother were of the same way of thinking, and all but idolised the holy child who had come amongst them as an angel of peace. They regarded her as the blessing of their house, and the comfort of their old age. Paluzzo, Lorenzo's brother, delighted in encouraging the intimacy that had arisen between his young sister-in-law and his own wife Vannozza. There was not a single member, friend, or servant, of that noble family, that did not look with delight upon Francesca. She was the joy of every heart, the sweet consoler of every sorrow, the link that bound them all by the sacred cord of love. Day by day her influence—her tender, noiseless, gentle influence—was felt, subduing, winning, drawing them all to God.

The happiness which the family of Ponziano had enjoyed since Lo-renzo's marriage was interrupted by the sudden and dangerous illness of his wife, which baffled all medical skill, and soon brought her to the verge of the grave. The affliction of her husband and of his whole fam-ily was extreme. Their pearl of great price seemed about to be taken from them. No remedies afforded the slightest relief to her sufferings; she was unable to rest, or to retain any nourishment; and every day her strength declined. The consternation of her friends knew no bounds; her father was inconsolable. He secretly reproached himself with the constraint he had placed on her inclinations, and considered her illness as a Divine chastisement. Francesca alone remained unmoved amidst the general affliction. She placed her life in the hands of God, and waited the event with perfect submission. Unable to speak, or even to move, the sweet expression of her earnest eyes alone spoke her gratitude to those who nursed her and wept over her sufferings. At other times they were fixed on the Crucifix with an unutterable look of trust and love. Once only she was disturbed, and indignation gave her strength to protest against the guilty suggestions of some friends of the family, who, according to the notions of that time, persisted in believing that a spell had been cast upon her, and proposed to have recourse to some persons in Rome who dealt, or pretended to deal, in magic arts. Francesca declared herself ready to die, rather than countenance so impious a proceeding. After all medical resources had been exhausted, when despair had succeeded to hope, Almighty God restored her health for a while; and the news of her recovery was hailed with rapture within and without the palace.

Her sufferings, however, returned with double violence; she endured the most excruciating pains; and was again considered to be at the point of death. During a whole year she remained as it were on the brink of eternity: her soul prepared to take its wing; continually sustained by the Sacraments of the Church, her only remaining thought was to soothe the anguish of her husband and parents. Once again, those persons who had previously proposed to resort to magic arts for her cure, managed to thrust into her room, on some pretence or other, a woman celebrated in that line. Francesca, enlightened by a divine inspiration, instantly detected the fraud; and raising herself in her bed, with a voice, the strength of which astonished the bystanders, exclaimed, "Begone, thou servant of Satan, nor ever venture to enter these walls again!" Exhausted by the effort, she fell back faint and colourless; and for a moment they feared that her spirit had passed away. But that very day God was preparing a miracle in her behalf; and as she had refused to hold any communication with the Evil One, He was about to send His young servant a heavenly messenger, with health and healing on his wings. It was the eve of the Festival of St. Alexis,—that noble Roman penitent, who passed so many years at the threshold of his own palace, unpitied, unrecognised by his own relations, who went in and out at the gate, and stopped not to question the silent, lonely, patient beggar, who lay there with his face hid in a poor cloak, finding peace in the midst of bitterness.

The Ponziani had all withdrawn to rest for a few hours; the women who attended on the dying Francesca had fallen asleep. She was lying motionless on her couch of pain. Her sufferings had been sharp; they were sharper than ever that night. She endured them in the strength of the Cross, from which neither her eyes nor her thoughts wandered. The whole house, and apparently the city also, was wrapt in slumber; for not a sound marred the stillness of the hour,—that stillness so trying to those who watch and suffer. Suddenly on the darkness of the silent chamber a light broke, bright as the day. In the midst stood a radiant figure, majestic in form and gracious in countenance. He wore a pilgrim's robe; but it shone like burnished gold. Drawing near to Francesca's bed, he said: "I am Alexis, and am sent from God to inquire of thee if thou choosest to be healed?" Twice he repeated the words, and then the dying one faintly murmured, "I have no choice but the good pleasure of God. Be it done unto me according to His will. For my own part, I would prefer to die, and for my soul to fly to Him at once; but I accept all at His hands, be it life or be it death." "Life, then, it is to be," replied St. Alexis; "for He chooses that thou shouldest remain in the world to glorify His name." With these words he spread his mantle over Francesca and disappeared, leaving her perfectly recovered.

Confounded at this extraordinary favour, more alive to the sense of God's wonderful mercy than to her own sudden freedom from pain, Francesca rose in haste, and prostrate on the floor, made a silent and fervent thanksgiving; then slipping out of her room without awaking her nurses, she hurried to the bedside of her friend and sister. Putting her arm round her neck and her cheek next to her's, she exclaimed, "Vannozza cara! Vannozza mia!" (My dear Vannozza, my own Vannozza.) And the bewildered Vannozza suddenly awoke out of her sleep, and distrusting the evidence of her senses, kept repeating, "Who calls me? Who are you? Am I dreaming? It sounds like the voice of my Cecolella."[1] "Yes, it is your Cecolella; it is your little sister who is speaking to you." "My Francesca, whom I left an hour ago at the point of death?" "Yes, the very same Francesca who now holds you to her breast; you, you, my beloved companion, who day and night have comforted and consoled me during my long illness, and who must now help me to thank God for His wonderful mercy." Then sitting upon her bed, with her hands clasped in her's, she related to her her vision, and

---

[1] The Italian diminutive for Francesca.

the instantaneous recovery that had followed it; and then, as the light was beginning to break into the chamber, she added with eagerness, "Now, now the day is come. Let us not delay a moment longer, but hasten with me to Santa Maria Nuova, and then to the church of St. Alexis. I must venerate his relics, and return him my thanks, before others learn what God has done for me."

This pious purpose fulfilled, they returned home, where Francesca was looked upon as one risen from the dead. The affection she inspired was mingled with awe; every one considered her as the special object of the Divine mercy, and venerated her accordingly. Not so joyfully had Lorenzo received her on their bridal-day, as when she came to him now, restored to his arms by the miraculous interposition of a merciful God.

CHAPTER III.

FRANCESCA PROCEEDS IN HER MORTIFICATIONS AND WORKS OF CHARITY—HER SUPERNATURAL TEMPTATIONS AND CONSOLATIONS.

Not in vain had Francesca been brought so near to death, and so wonderfully restored to perfect health. A favour such as she had received could not fail of producing signal results in one who so well corresponded with every degree of grace vouchsafed to her. This last manifestation of God's mercy disposed her to meditate deeply and earnestly on the designs of Providence in her regard. She seemed now to discern, in a clear and overpowering manner, the nature of the particular judgment which she had been about to undergo, the amount of responsibility incurred by every grace conferred on her soul, the severe account which would be demanded of every talent committed to her charge; and at the sight she shuddered, as a man draws back affrighted at the distinct appearance of a precipice which he has skirted in the night, or at the waves dashing wildly on a beach on which he has been landed in safety. Her meditations at that time assumed a very solemn character; every moment that she could spare was spent in the neighbouring church of St. Cecilia or in her own oratory, and employed in a minute review of her past life, and in forming heroic resolutions for the future.

The government of the tongue is one of the most difficult and important points in the spiritual life. From this time forward Francesca avoided all unnecessary conversations, and became habitually silent. There was no moroseness in her silence; it never interfered with the kindnesses or the courtesies of life; but as in childhood she had been remarkable for it, so in womanhood it distinguished her, and especially since her illness and miraculous recovery. Vannozza inquired of her one day what it was that made her so habitually silent, and she answered, "God expects more of us than heretofore;" and then she proposed to her a still stricter mode of life than they had yet adopted. Vannozza willingly assented, and they agreed to give up all useless amusements, fashionable drives, and diversions, and to devote to prayer and to good works the hours thus withdrawn from the service of the world. They resolved to observe with the most exact punctuality every law of God, and every precept of the Church; to obey their husbands with the most attentive and Christian-like submission; to be invariably docile to their ghostly father, and submit to him their actions, their words, and even their thoughts; and thus to secure themselves against the deceits of the evil one. They then proceeded to arrange for themselves a place of retreat, where they could withdraw to pray at any hour of the day or of the night. It was not easy to accomplish this in a palace inhabited by a numerous family and a large number of servants; but in a sort of cave at one end of the garden, and in a little room that happened to be unoccupied under the roof of the house, they established two oratories, which they furnished with crucifixes, images of our Blessed Lady, and pictures of saints, as well as with various other objects of devotion and with instruments of penance. These two little cells became their comfort and delight; whenever their domestic duties or their religious observances out of doors left them at liberty, they were in the habit of retiring into the garden oratory, and at night they frequently spent whole hours in prayer in the upper chamber. The first dawn of day often found them at their orisons. The hours that were not devoted to prayer or to the duties of their state, they employed in works of charity. Almost every day they went to the hospital of San Spirito, and nursed the sick with the kindest attention; consoling them by their gentle words and tender care, bestowing alms upon the most needy, and above all, tending affectionately the most disgusting cases of disease and infirmity. Throughout their whole lives they never omitted this practice. To serve Christ in His afflicted brethren was a privilege they never consented to forego.

Francesca was at this time very anxious to lay aside the insignia of wealth and rank, and to dress as simply as the poor she so much loved; but, always obedient, she would not attempt to do so without the permission of her spiritual guide. Don Antonio Savello would not give her leave to relinquish the splendid robes then worn by persons of her rank; he feared it might annoy her husband, and that there might be danger of ostentation in any thing that attracted public attention; but he allowed both the sisters to wear a coarse woollen garment under their magnificent dresses, and to practise in secret several other austerities. Their fasts and abstinences became more rigid than ever; but were carried on with so much simplicity, and such a total absence of display, that the very persons who habitually took their meals in company with them, scarcely remarked their mortifications, or else attributed them to a peculiarity of taste or the observance of a regimen. Disciplines and other bodily penances of a very severe nature were by this time habitual to Francesca, and she persevered in them to the end of her life. With whatever care they concealed all these things, it was not possible that the city of Rome should remain ignorant of their piety and their generosity to the poor. The common people looked upon Francesca and Vannozza as two saints; and their example began to tell beneficially upon the women of their own class. Several noble ladies were inspired with the desire to walk in their steps, and to imitate their virtues. But it was not likely that Satan should behold unmoved the work of grace thus advancing in the hearts of these two young servants of God, and through them on many others. He chafed at the sight; and now began that long series of attacks, of struggles, and of artifices, by which he endeavoured to mar the glorious progress of these heroic souls. Almighty God seems to have granted to the prince of darkness, in San Francesca's case, a permission in some respects similar to that which He gave him with regard to His servant Job. He was allowed to throw temptations in her way, to cause her strange sufferings, to persecute her by fearful manifestations of his visible presence, to haunt her under various shapes, some seductive in their appearance, others repulsive and terrific in their nature; but he was not permitted (as, thanks be to God, he never is permitted,) to deceive or to injure His faithful servant, who for every trial of the sort obtained some divine favour in compensation; who for every vision of diabolical horror, was allowed a glimpse into the world of glory; and to whom at a later period was appointed a heavenly guardian to defend her against the violence of her infernal foe.

The first time that Satan presented himself in a visible form to Francesca's sight, God gave her an earnest of His protection in the strife about to be waged between her and the old serpent by miraculously revealing to her the character of her visitor. It was under the aspect of a venerable hermit, emaciated with fasts and watchings, that he entered the Ponziano palace: his intention was, by some artful words, to inspire Francesca with aversion and disgust for the solitary life, and at the same time for that hidden life which she so zealously practised in the midst of the world. He was shown into a large room, where the assembled family were sitting and conversing together. No sooner had Francesca set her eyes upon him, than she was supernaturally enlightened as to his true character; she knew at once the dreadful enemy, thus for the first time made manifest to her sight; and, suddenly changing colour, she rose and left the room. Vannozza followed (alarmed at her hasty departure), and found her in the oratory kneeling before the Crucifix, and as pale as death. She inquired into the cause of her emotion; but Frances simply desired her to return to the sitting-room, and request Lorenzo to dismiss the hermit. As soon as he was departed, she re-appeared amongst them as serene and calm as usual; and to no one but to her confessor did she mention the circumstance. Yet it was a most awful moment, that first initiation into the supernatural world, that first contact with the powers of darkness, that opening of the visible war between her and the great enemy. No wonder that she was habitually silent; her soul must have lived in very close communion with the invisible world, and the presence of God must have been realised in an extraordinary decree by one whose spiritual discernment was so miraculously keen.

A more ordinary snare was the tempter's next resource, and he chose as his instrument a person of piety and virtue, but whose human fears and affections were too strong for her faith. He suggested to Cecilia, the mother-in-law of the two saints, who was most fondly attached to them, and maternally solicitous about their healths, that the ascetic life which they led must necessarily impair it; that amusements were essential to young persons; and that the singularity of their conduct reflected discredit on the family. Under this impression, she strove by every means in her power to counteract their designs, to thwart them in their devotional and charitable practices, and to induce them to give up more of their time and of their attention to the world. She thus gave them occasion to practise a very peculiar kind of patience, and to gain the more merit in the eyes of God, in that they had daily to encounter a sort of opposition particularly trying to young and ardent spirits. It is related, that one day, when they had gently but steadily refused to pay some visits which, far from being absolute duties, were only pretexts for gossip and the most frivolous conversations, Francesca and Vannozza had retired into the garden oratory; and after spending some time in prayer, began conversing together on the life which the early Fathers were wont to lead in the deserts, and of the happiness it must be to live entirely devoted to the service of God, and to commune with Him above, far from the distracting thoughts and cares of the world. They went on picturing to themselves the manner in which they would have divided their time and arranged their occupations under similar circumstances, and together they made out a complete rule of life.

Absorbed in the subject, Vannozza exclaimed, with childlike simplicity, "But what should we have to eat, sister?" and Francesca replied, "We should search for fruits in the desert, dearest; and God would surely not let us seek in vain." As she said these words they rose to return home, and from a tree which grew out of a ruined wall on one side of the garden there fell at her feet a quince of the largest size and most shining colour, and another similar to it was lying in Vannozza's path. The sisters looked at each other in silent astonishment; for the time of the year was April, and nothing but a miracle could have brought these apples to maturity at this unwonted season. The taste of the fruit was as excellent as its colour was beautiful. They were divided amongst the members of the family, who wondered at the marvels which seemed continually to attend the steps of Francesca. She was profoundly grateful for such favours, but probably marvelled less than others at their occurrence. Her youth; the simplicity of her faith; her total abstraction from worldly thoughts; her continual study and meditation of the Holy Scriptures and of the lives of the Saints,— must have necessarily familiarised her mind with such ideas. It could not seem incredible to her, that the God who in less favoured times, and under a severer dispensation, had so often suspended the laws of nature, in order to support, to guide, and to instruct His people; that the Saviour who had turned water into wine by a single word, and withered the unprofitable fig-tree by a look,—should at all times display the same power in favour of His children, in ways not a whit more marvellous or mysterious.

Cecilia made one more effort to check what she considered exaggeration in the mode of life of her daughters-in-law. She urged their husbands to interfere, and by their authority to oblige them to mix more with the world. But Paluzzo and Lorenzo had too deep an esteem for their wives, and too great a sense of the advantages they derived from their singular virtues, to be persuaded into putting a restraint on their actions. Since they had come into the family, and united their pious efforts for their own and others' spiritual improvement, disputes and quarrels had given way to the most edifying concord. The servants, moved by their example, performed their duties with exemplary zeal, frequented the churches and the sacraments, and abstained from profane or idle words. They accordingly entreated their mother to give up her fruitless attempts, and allow the two young women liberty to follow the rule of life they had adopted; and thus put an end to the kindly meant but trying persecution they had gone through.

About this time the devil, thwarted in his designs, but always on the watch, was permitted to vent his anger against Francesca and her sister-in-law in a way to which he often had recourse, and which, while it seemed to display a momentary power over their bodies, only proved in the end that a stronger one than he was always at hand to defeat his malice, and snatch from him his prize. Francesca and Vannozza had gone to St. Peter's on an intensely hot day in July, in the year 1399. Absorbed in prayer, they had hardly noticed the lapse of time, and twelve o'clock had struck when they set out on their way home. In order to avoid observation, and the marks of veneration which the people lavished upon them as soon as they set eyes on the two saints (as they always called them), they chose the most unfrequented streets they could find. The heat grew intolerable. The sultry air seemed on fire, and not a breath stirred it. Exhausted with fatigue, their mouths parched with thirst, they reached the church of St. Leonardo; and holding each other's hands, approached the brink of the river, in order to cool their burning lips and throbbing heads with a little water. As they bent over the stream for that purpose, a violent blow from an invisible arm was aimed at Francesca, and hurled her into the Tiber. Vannozza fell with her; and, clasped in each other's arms, they were rapidly carried away by the current, and saw no means of escape. "They were lovely in their lives, and in their deaths they were not divided," might well have been said of them, had the watery grave, which seemed inevitable, swallowed up on that day the two brides of the Ponziani. But it was not the will of God that they should perish. Human aid was not at hand; the stream was rapid, the current deep, and the eddies curled around them; but they called upon God with one voice, and in an instant the waters, as if instinct with life, and obedient to a heavenly command, bore them gently to the shore, and deposited them unhurt on the green margin of the river.

About this time also a supernatural favour of the most extraordinary nature was vouchsafed to Francesca. Her guardian angel, who was one day to accompany her, not by an invisible presence only, as in the case of all Christians, but, by a rare privilege of grace, in a visible form, ever manifest to her spiritual sight, now began to reveal himself to her by the most watchful observance of her conduct. At all times and in all places, by day and by night, her slightest faults were noticed and punished by this still invisible, but now evidently present monitor. At the least imperfection in her conduct, before she had time to accuse and to condemn herself, she felt the blow of a mysterious hand, the warning of an ever-attentive guardian; and the sound of that mystical chastisement was audible to others also. Great was the astonishment of those who could thus discern something of God's dealings with this chosen soul. Once, when she had abstained through human respect from interrupting the course of a very frivolous and useless conversation, the warning was inflicted with such severity that she bore the mark of the blow for several succeeding days.

Such a rapid advance in holiness, such new and ever-increasing virtues, were the results of this supernatural tuition, that Satan now attempted to seduce her by the wiliest of his artifices, the master-piece of his art, his favourite sin,—"the pride that apes humility." So many miracles wrought in her favour, such strange revelations of God's peculiar love for her soul, awakened in Francesca's mind, or rather the devil suggested to her the thought, that it might be better to conceal them from her director, or at least to acquaint him with only a portion of the wonders that were wrought in her behalf; and accordingly, the next time she went to confession she refrained from mentioning the signal grace which had been vouchsafed to her. At the very instant she was thrown prostrate on the ground, and recognised the hand of her heavenly monitor in the blow which thus warned her of the grievous error into which she was falling. In that short moment she had time to perceive and acknowledge it; and with intense contrition she confessed to her director the false humility which had beguiled her into a dangerous reserve, with perfect openness revealed to him the whole of God's past and present dealings with her soul, and explained to him the meaning of what had just taken place. Don Antonio listened with astonishment and gratitude, and thus addressed her: "You have just escaped from a great danger, my daughter; for those who aim at perfection cannot conceal any thing from their spiritual guide without running the risk of delusion. By your mistaken silence you were complying with the suggestions of Satan, who, under the semblance of humility, was seeking to awaken in you a secret and baneful pride. You would have been led by degrees to over-estimate these supernatural favours, to deem them not merely means of grace, but rewards due to your merits; to despise those to whom God does not grant them; and to give yourself up to extravagant and unauthorised austerities in order to secure their continuance, and to distinguish yourself in your own and others' sight. I should have forbidden you to practise them; you would have been tempted to renounce my guidance, to take one confessor after another, until you had found one weak or blind enough to approve your self-will; and then the arch-enemy of mankind, under the garb of an angel of light, would have made you the prey of his delusions, till at last you might have fallen from one error into another, and made shipwreck of your faith. Such has been the downward course of many a soul, that has begun by yielding to a false humility—the offspring of pride—and has ended in sin and perdition."

From that time forward, Francesca was on her guard against every species of pride and self-reliance, however disguised and refined. She related her faults and temptations, the graces she received and the favours she obtained, with the same childlike openness and simplicity. It was at the age of sixteen that she was thus advanced in the science of the saints; and every day her virtues and her piety increased.

CHAPTER IV.

THE BIRTH OF FRANCESCA'S FIRST CHILD—HER CARE IN HIS EDUCATION—SHE UNDERTAKES THE MANAGEMENT OF HER FATHER-IN-LAW'S HOUSEHOLD—A FAMINE AND PESTILENCE IN ROME—FRANCESCA'S LABOURS FOB THE SICK AND POOR—THE MIRACLES WROUGHT IN HER BEHALF.

The year 1400 was opening under melancholy auspices. Boniface IX. was at that moment in possession of the pontifical throne, and celebrating the jubilee, the periodical recurrence of which at the end of every fifty years had been decreed by Clement VI. in 1350; but Rome was even then in a lamentable state, and presages were not wanting of still more disastrous times. The wars for the succession of the kingdom of Naples, between Louis of Anjou and Ladislas Durazzo, were agitating the whole of Italy; and the capital of the Christian world was exposed to all the fury of the contending parties. The powerful faction of the Colonnas, in arms against the Pope, invaded the Capitol at the head of a numerous body of insurgents on horseback and on foot; and the air resounded with the cries of "Long live the people! Death to the tyrant Boniface IX.!" On that day the signal was given for a division of parties, which led shortly afterwards to the appalling tragedy which decimated the nobility of the Eternal City and deluged her streets with blood.

Lorenzo Ponziano, from his rank and his great possessions, as well as from his fidelity to the Church and the Sovereign Pontiff, was especially marked out as an enemy by the adverse faction. But while on every side the storm was brewing, and the aspect of public affairs each day more gloomy, a blessing was granted to him which for the last five years he had ardently desired. The expectation of an heir to the family of Ponziano filled him and his parents with inexpressible delight. Francesca, in the meantime, was incessantly occupied in recommending to God the child she was about to bear; and offered up her every little act of devotion in its behalf, with the hope of drawing down the Divine blessing on its future existence. In the same year she was happily delivered of a son, who was immediately baptised in the church of Santa Cecilia in Trastevere, and received the name of Giovanni Baptista. It was not at that time the custom for ladies of rank to nurse their children; but Francesca set aside all such considerations, and never consented to forego a mother's sacred privilege. She did not intrust her child for a moment to the care of others, afraid that, in her absence, the utterance of unworthy sentiments, bad manners and habits, which even in infancy may cause impressions not easily eradicated, should taint with the least evil the heart and mind of her son. It is remarkable how careful the holy mothers which we read of in the lives of the Saints appear to have been of the circumstances attending the infancy of their children,—that period during which we are apt to suppose that no impressions can be given or received. Are we not perhaps in error on that point?—As much that we read and apparently forget leaves notwithstanding a certain deposit in our minds, which comes into play when called forth by association, so, may not certain sights, sounds, and words, not understood at the time, impart a certain colour, stamp certain images on the mind of an infant, which, however dim and confused, deepen and grow with it as it expands? There have been curious psychological instances of names, of languages, of dormant recollections, reawakening as it were under a peculiar condition of the nervous system, and which could only be traced to impressions received in the earliest stages of existence.

Francesca, in obedience to her director, as well as guided by her own sense of duty, modified for the time being her usual mode of life, and occupied herself with the care of her child in preference to all other observances of charity or of devotion. She did not complain or regret that she had to give up her habitual religious exercises, in order to tend and to nurse the little creature whom she looked upon as the gift of God, and whose careful training the best offering she could make in return. The joy which she had felt in her infant's birth was marred by the death of her father, who, when his grandson was placed in his arms, exclaimed in the words of St. Simeon, "Lord, now lettest

Thou thy servant depart in peace;" and the words seem to have been prophetic, for he died almost immediately afterwards, and was buried in the vaults of Santa Agnese, in the Piazza Nuova. At a later period, when that church was reconstructed, his remains were transported to the cloisters of Tor Di Specchi, where the simple inscription, "Here lies Paul Bussa," remains to this day. Francesca, in pursuance of her desire, not only to exclude evil, but to infuse good dispositions at the earliest possible period into her baby's soul, lost no opportunity of imparting to him the first notions of religion. Before he could speak, she used to repeat to him every day the Lord's Prayer and the Hail Mary, clasp his little hands together, and direct his eyes to heaven, and to the images of Jesus and Mary, whose names were of course the first words he learned to utter. She checked in him by grave looks, and slight punishments fitted to his age, every ebullition of self-will, obstinacy, and anger; and later, of deceit, envy, and immodesty. Though she had the most tender mother's heart, she seldom indulged in passionate caresses, and never left unchastised any of his faults, or gave way in any instance to his tears and impatience. When others objected that it was absurd to expect self-command from a creature whose reason was not developed, she maintained that habits of self-control are to be acquired at the earliest age, and that the benefit thus obtained extends to the whole of life. The child thus trained lived to prove the wisdom of her views, and became in difficult times the support of his family and an honour to their name.

About a year after the birth of Giovanni Baptista, Cecilia, Lorenzo's mother, died. Andreazzo Ponziano, and both his sons, fully conscious of the prudence and virtue of Francesca, resolved to place her at the head of the house, and to commit to her alone the superintendence of their domestic affairs and the whole management of the household. Distressed at the proposal, she pleaded her youth and inexperience, and urged that Vannozza, as the wife of the eldest brother, was as a matter of course entitled to that position. Vannozza, however, pleaded with such eagerness that it was her most anxious desire not to occupy it, and that all she wished was to be Francesca's disciple and companion, that, overcome by the general importunity, she found herself obliged to comply. Now it was that her merit shone conspicuously. Placed at the head of the most opulent house in Rome, no symptom of pride, of haughtiness, or of self-complacency, ever revealed itself in her looks or in her actions. She was never heard to speak a harsh or impatient word. Firm in requiring from every person in her house the proper fulfilment of their duties, she did it in the gentlest manner. Al-

ways courteous to her servants, she urged them to serve God with diligence, and watched over their souls redeemed by His precious blood.
Her address was so winning and persuasive, that it seldom failed of its
effect. She contrived to arrange the hours of their labour with so much
order and skill, that each had sufficient leisure to hear Mass, to attend
the parochial instructions on Sundays and holidays, to frequent the
Sacraments, and join every day in family prayer,—fulfilling the whole
of a Christian's duty. If by any chance (and it was a rare one in a house
thus governed) a quarrel arose between any of the servants, she was
always ready to come forward, appease angry passions, and reconcile
differences. If, in so doing, she had occasion to speak with what she
considered undue severity to one of the parties, she would immediately
apologise with tears, and in the humblest manner entreat forgiveness.
This extreme sweetness of disposition, however, did not degenerate
into weakness; and she could testify the utmost displeasure, and reproved with energy when offences were committed against God. It
was intolerable to her that His Divine Majesty should be insulted in
her abode; and she, the gentlest and most unassuming of women, could
display on such occasions the greatest firmness.

One day, it is recorded, several gentlemen had been dining with
Lorenzo; and one of them after dinner drew from his pocket a book
which contained a treatise on magic. Lorenzo took it up, and was examining it with some curiosity, when his wife stole noiselessly behind
him, took it out of his hands, and threw it into the fire. Nettled by this
proceeding, her husband reproached her in rather bitter terms for her
incivility to their guest; but she, who was habitually submissive to his
least word, only replied that she could not regret the destruction of
what might have proved to many an occasion of sin. She inexorably
consigned to the flames in the same manner every bad book that came
in her way.

Her tender charity was evinced when any of the inmates of the palace were ill. She was then the affectionate nurse of the sufferers, and
spent whole nights by their bedside. Nothing ever discouraged or wearied her; the lowest servant in the house was attended to, as if she had
been her own mother or sister. More anxious still for their soul's health
than their body's, she was known to go out herself alone at night in
search of a priest when a sudden case of danger had occurred beneath
her roof. Her charity was in one instance miraculously rewarded by a
direct interposition of Providence, in a matter apparently trifling, but
on which, humanly speaking, her dear sister Vannozza's existence
seemed to turn. She was dangerously ill, and had been for days unable

to swallow any food; the very sight of it caused her intolerable nausea; and from sheer exhaustion her life was reduced to so low an ebb, that the worst was apprehended. On Francesca's inquiring if she could think of any thing which she could imagine it possible to eat, she named a certain fish, which was not in season at that time. The markets were scoured by the servants, but naturally in vain, and they returned empty-handed to the dejected Francesca, who, kneeling by the bedside of her friend, betook herself, with arduous faith and childlike simplicity, to prayer. When she raised her head, the much-wished-for article of food was lying before her; and the first morsel of it that Vannozza eat restored her to health.

She had been about a year at the head of her father-in-law's house, when Rome fell under the double scourge of famine and pestilence. The Ponziani were immensely rich, and their palace furnished with every kind of provisions. Francesca forbade her servants to send away a single poor person without relieving their wants; and not content with this, she sought them out herself, invited them to come to her, and made them continual presents of corn, wine, oil, and clothing. She exhorted them to bear their sufferings with patience, to return to God and to their religious duties, and to strive by fervent prayer to appease the Divine wrath, provoked by the crimes of mankind. Vannozza and herself were indefatigable in their visits to the hospitals and the out-of-the-way corners of the city.

Andreazzo Ponziano, a good man, but not a saint, was alarmed at the excessive liberality of his daughter-in-law, and feared that it would end in producing a famine in his own house. He began by prudently withdrawing from their hands the key of the granary; and then, for greater security, afraid perhaps of yielding to their entreaties, which he was not accustomed to resist, he took to selling whatever corn he possessed beyond what was required for the daily consumption of the family. Nothing, therefore, remained in the corn-loft but a huge heap of straw. The provident old man followed the same plan with his cellar, and sold all the wine it contained, with the exception of one cask, which was reserved for his own and his children's use.

Meanwhile the scarcity went on increasing every day, and the number of starving wretches in proportion. Franceses, unable to meet their demands, and still more incapable of leaving them to perish, braved at last all false shame and repugnance, and resolved with Vannozza to go into the streets and beg for the poor. Then were seen those two noble and lovely women standing at the doors of the churches, knocking at the gates of the palace, following the rich in the public places, pleading with tears the cause of the sufferers, gladly receiving the abundant alms that were sometimes bestowed upon them, and not less gladly the sneers, the repulses, the insulting words that often fell to their share in these pilgrimages of mercy. At last the famine reached its height. At every side,—on the pavement, in the corners of the streets,—were lying crowds of persons, barely clothed with a few tattered rags, haggard with hunger, wasted with fever, and calling upon death to end their sufferings. It was a grievous, a horrible sight,—one that well-nigh broke the heart of our saint. The moanings of the dying were in her ears; the expression of their ghastly faces haunted her day and night. She would have gladly shed her blood for them, and fed them with her life. A sudden inspiration came over her one day: "Come to the corn-loft," she exclaimed, turning to Vannozza, and to Clara, a favourite and pious servant of theirs; "Come with me to the corn-loft; let us see if amongst the straw we may not succeed in finding a few grains of corn for the poor." And on their knees for several hours those patient, loving women sifted the straw, and by dint of labour collected about a measure of corn, which they were bearing away in triumph, when the God who caused the widow's oil not to fail, and made her barrel of meal last through a scarcely more grievous famine, was preparing their reward. Lorenzo had entered the granary just as they were carrying off their hard-earned treasure, and, looking about him, beheld in place of the straw which was lying there a moment before, 40 measures of bright yellow corn, so shining and so full, says Francesca's earliest biographer, that it seemed as though it had been raised in Paradise, and reaped there by angels. In silent astonishment he pointed out to them the miraculous supply, and must have felt in that hour what such virtue as his wife's and his sister's could even in this world win of mercy at God's hands. But corn was not enough; the sick wanted wine. They came, poor pallid ghosts, just risen from their beds of suffering, to beg it of Francesca; aged men and delicate children, mothers with infants at their breasts, poor worn-out priests sinking with exhaustion, and yet willing to assist others, they had recourse to her for a little wine to strengthen them in their works of mercy, and she had no wine to give, save out of the single cask in the cellar. She gave it, nevertheless; and day after day drew from it, till not a drop was left. Andreazzo, provoked, waxed very wroth; he had never before been angry with Francesca, but now he stormed and raved at her; he had been to the cellar to see the wine drawn for that day's use, and not a drop was in the cask. "Charity indeed!" he exclaimed, "charity begins at home; a pretty sort of virtue this, which, under the pretext of assisting strangers, introduces penury and privation into the midst of a person's own family." He vented his anger in bitter reproaches; Lorenzo and Paluzzo were also inclined to take his part, and joined in severely blaming Francesca. She the while, with a gentle voice and quiet manner, breathing most probably a secret prayer to her who at the marriage-feast of Cana turned to her Son and said, "They have no wine," doubtless with an inward assurance that God would befriend her in an extraordinary, but not to her an unprecedented manner, thus addressed them: "Do not be angry; let us go to the cellar; may be, through God's mercy, that the cask may be full by this time." They followed her with an involuntary submission; and on reaching the spot, saw her turn the cock of the barrel, out of which there instantly flowed the most exquisite wine, which Andreazzo acknowledged to be superior to any he had ever tasted. The venerable old man turned to his daughter-in-law, and, with tears in his eyes, exclaimed,

"Oh, my dear child, dispose henceforward of every thing I possess, and multiply without end those alms that have gained you such favour in God's sight."

The report of this miracle spread far and wide; and, in spite of her humility, Francesca did not object to its being divulged, as it testified to the Divine virtue of almsgiving, and encouraged the rich to increase their liberality, and minister more abundantly to the suffering members of Christ.

A kind of religious awe seems to have taken possession of Lorenzo's mind, at the sight of so many wonders wrought in his house. The great esteem in which he had always held his wife, now took the form of a profound veneration. He recommended her to follow in every respect the divine inspirations she received, and left her entirely free to order her life and dispose of her time in any way she thought fit. Francesca, after consulting with her director, took advantage of this permission to execute what had been her long-cherished desire. Selling all her rich dresses, her jewels, and her ornaments, she distributed the money amongst a number of poor families, and from that time forward never wore herself any other gown than one of coarse dark-green cloth. Her mortifications became so continual and severe, her fasts so rigid, that it is difficult to conceive how her health could have sustained them without miraculous support, or how she can have found time for all her duties, and the incredible number of good works which she daily performed. When we consider that she was unremitting in her attention to her children, that she was never known to neglect the diligent superintendence of household affairs, that she repeatedly visited the hospitals and the poor sick in their houses, that morning and evening she went to the churches where indulgences were to be gained, recited numerous vocal prayers, often spent hours in contemplation, and in the garden oratory, where with Vannozza, Clara, and Rita Celli, a devout young person who was admitted into their intimacy, she read spiritual books or conversed on religious subjects,—our admiration is quickened; for that zeal and strong will could work wonders all but incomprehensible to those who have not put their shoulder to the wheel in good earnest, or learnt to appreciate the priceless value of every minute of this short life.

CHAPTER V.

THE BIRTH OF FRANCESCA'S SECOND SON—HIS SUPERNATURAL GIFTS—THE BIRTH OF HER DAUGHTER—SATANIC ATTACKS UPON FRANCESCA—-TROUBLES OF ROME—FRANCESCA'S HUSBAND IS SEVERELY WOUNDED—HER ELDEST SON, WHEN GIVEN UP AS A HOSTAGE TO THE NEAPOLITANS, IS MIRACULOUSLY RESTORED TO HER.

FRANCESCA had just attained the age of twenty when her second son was born. He was baptised on the day of his birth, and received the name of Giovanni Evan—gelista. The contemporary biographer, some of whose sayings have been already quoted, mentions of this child that he was endowed with wonderful gifts of grace, and that the love of God was manifested in him even before he could speak. In his quaint language he thus describes him: "Evangelista was old in sense, small in body, great in soul, resplendent in beauty, angel-like in all his ways." He might well have been termed, in familiar language, his mother's own child; for in his veriest infancy his only pleasure was to be carried into churches, or to give alms to the needy, especially to the poor religious, for whom he had a special predilection. Francesca's delight in this lovely little infant was indescribable. He was to her as one of God's own angels, and tears of joy filled her eyes as she mused on the extraordinary signs of grace which he daily evinced. Supernatural had been the mother's virtues, supernatural were the qualities of the child; at the age of three years old he was endowed with the gift of prophecy, and the faculty of reading the un-uttered thoughts of men's hearts.

Singular instances of this power are on record. He was in his mother's arms one day, when two mendicant friars approached the Ponziano Palace. Instantly stretching out his little hands, Evangelista took from Francesca the alms she was wont to bestow on such visitors, and held it out to them; but at the same time looking steadfastly at one of the monks, he said to him, "Why will you put off this holy habit? you will wear a finer one; but woe to you who forget your vow of poverty."

The friar coloured and turned away; but it was soon evident that the words were prophetic, for within a short time, and after obtaining a bishopric through a simoniacal act, the unhappy man died a violent death. That same year, Evangelista was in his parent's room one day; and his father taking him up on his knees, was playing with him, and devouring him with kisses. In the midst of his sport, the child turned suddenly pale, and laying hold of a dagger which had been left on the table, he placed the point of it against Lorenzo's side, and said to him as he looked up into his face with a strange melancholy smile, "Thus will they do to you, my father." And it so happened that at the time of the invasion of Rome by the troops of Ladislas Durazzo, the lord of Ponziano was dangerously wounded in the exact place and manner which his little son had pointed out.

Evangelista was not quite three years old when his little sister Agnese was born, who in beauty, heavenly sweetness of temper, and precocious piety, proved the exact counterpart of her brother. Soon after her confinement, Francesca had a vision which impressed her with the belief that God would one day claim this child as His own. She saw a dove of dazzling whiteness, bearing in its beak a tiny lighted taper, enter the room; and after making two or three circles in the air, it stooped over Agnese's cradle, touched her brow and limbs with the taper, gently fluttered its wings, and flew away. Looking upon this as a sign that the little maiden would be called to the monastic life, she brought her up as a precious deposit only lent her for a time, and to be delivered up at no distant period. With even stricter care than she had used with her brother, if that were possible, she watched over the little girl; never leaving her for a single moment, and performing towards her the offices of a servant as well as of a mother. She kept her in complete retirement, never taking her out of doors except to church; teaching her to love Jesus supremely—better even than her parents— and entertaining her with descriptions of that dear Saviour's adorable perfections. She encouraged her to observe silence, to work with her hands at stated times, and taught her to read in the lives of the saints of holy virgins and martyrs. Agnese's character and turn of mind answered precisely to her mother's wishes; and the perfection of her conduct was such, that she was generally designated by all who knew her as the little saint or the little angel.

The years of Evangelista's and Agnese's infancy had been most disastrous ones to the unhappy inhabitants of Rome. The factions which had arisen in consequence of the schism, and of the intrigues of Ladislas of Naples, had banished all security, and converted the town into a field of battle, where bloody conflicts were daily taking place. The principles of union seemed banished from the world. The nations and sovereigns of Europe, given up to the most selfish policy, ceased to acknowledge the chief pastor of the Church; and the Eternal City, beyond any other place, had become an arena for ferocious struggles and sanguinary conspiracies. The year 1406 brought with it a momentary semblance of peace, and Francesca and Vannozza availed themselves of that breathing-time to revisit some of the distant churches, and attend the Italians as before. They used to walk to them on foot at the earliest break of day, accompanied by Rita Celli, the young person already mentioned, and Lucia degli Aspalli, a devout married woman nearly related to the Ponziano family. They repeated psalms and litanies on their way, or spent the time in pious meditation, and remained some hours in prayer before the altars which they visited in turn,—taking care to be at home again by the time that their presence was required. In that troubled epoch the voice of the preacher was seldom heard; sermons, however, were occasionally delivered by the Franciscans and the Dominicans in the churches of Ara Coeli and Santa Maria sopra Minerva; and at these our saints never failed to assist. Their spiritual guide had given them leave to go to communion several times a week. This was a privilege seldom granted and seldom sought for in those distracted times. The blessed practice of daily communion, which universally prevailed amongst the early Christians,—that practice which turns earth into heaven, and converts the land of exile into a paradise of peace and joy,—was all but entirely neglected, or only kept up in some few cloisters. The two sisters habitually communicated in the church of Santa Cecilia, the nearest to their house. One of the priests of that parish was scandalised at the frequency of their communions, and persuaded himself that it was incredible that young women of their age, and in such a position of life, could possibly be in possession of the requisite dispositions. This unhappy man ventured one day to give Franeesca an unconsecrated wafer; God instantly revealed to the saint the sin of the priest, and she informed her director of the fact. Don Antonio disclosed to the astonished offender the secret which had been confined to his own breast. He confessed his fault with the deepest contrition, implored God's pardon, asked forgiveness of the saint, and received the humiliation as a warning against rash judgments.

The warfare which Satan was permitted to carry on against Francesca became more and more violent at this period of her life. In actual outrages, in terrific visions, in mystical but real sufferings, which afflicted every sense and tortured every nerve, the animosity of the evil spirit evinced itself; and Almighty God permitted it, for she was of those chosen through much tribulation to ascend the steep path which is paved with thorns and compassed with darkness, but on which the ray of an unearthly sunshine breaks at times. She was to partake of the miraculous gifts of the saints; to win men's souls through prayer, to read the secrets of their hearts, to see angels walking by her side, to heal diseases by the touch of her hands, and hold the devils at bay, when they thought to injure the bodies of others or wage war with her own spirit. But such heights of glory are not gained without proportionate suffering; the cup of which Jesus drank to the dregs in His agony she was to drink of, the baptism of horror with which He was baptised was to be her's also in a measure; and that mysterious weakness, that divine helplessness of His, which allowed Satan to carry Him, the Lord of all, to the pinnacle of the temple or the brow of the mountain, was not unshared by His servant. Strange and bewildering were the assaults she endured, but still more wonderful the defeats of the evil one. Of her triumph, as of those of her Lord, it may be said, "that when the devil left her, then angels came and ministered unto her." Strange, that those who believe the history of Jesus should turn incredulously away from that of His saints; for did He not expressly say, that what He suffered, they should suffer; that where He had overcome, they would triumph; and that the works that He performed, aye and greater works still, they should accomplish?

On one occasion, when on the point of setting out for the Basilica of St. Peter's, Vannozza was violently precipitated down the stairs of the palace by the power of the evil spirit, and fell at her sister's feet, who at that instant heard a voice whispering in her ear, "I would kill thy sister, and drive thee to despair;" but at the same moment an inward revelation bade Francesca raise up the prostrate form of her friend, and apply to her bruised limbs an ointment which instantly relieved the pains of her fall. Another time our saint was lifted up by the hair of her head, and suspended over a precipice for the space of some minutes; with perfect calmness she called upon Jesus, and in a moment found herself in safety within her room. Her first act was to cut off her beautiful hair, and, offer it up as a thank-offering to Him who had saved her from the hands of the infernal enemy. These are only specimens of the trials of this nature to which Francesca was more or less subjected all her life, but to which it will not be necessary again to make more than casual allusion.

In the year 1409, when she was about twenty-seven years old, her temporal calamities began. After Ladislas of Naples, befriended by the enemies of the Pope, and in 1408 gained possession of Rome by fraudulent means he left behind him as governor of the city the Count Pietro Traja, a rough and brutal soldier, well fitted to serve the fierce passions of his master. He was continually looking out for occasions to persecute those Roman nobles who remained faithful to the cause of the Church. He was abetted in this by the faction of the Colonnas, and some other powerful families, who supported the pretensions of the anti-Popes Gregory XII. and Benedict XIII. against the legitimate pontiff Alexander V., recently elected by the Council of Pisa. The troops of Lewis of Anjou, the rival of Ladislas in the kingdom of Naples, had in the mean time entered that portion of Rome which went by the name of the Leonine City, and gained possession of the Vatican and the castle of St. Angelo. Several skirmishes took place between the forces of the usurper and the troops of the Pope and of Lewis of Anjou. Lorenzo Ponziano, who from his birth and his talents was the most eminent man of his party, and an ardent supporter of the legitimate cause, commanded the pontifical army on one of these occasions, and was personally engaged in a conflict with the Count of Traja's soldiers. In the midst of the fray he was recognised by the opposite party, and became the special mark of their attacks. Fighting with heroic courage, he had nearly succeeded in dispersing his assailants, when, as Evangelista had foretold the year before, a dagger was treacherously thrust into his side, and inflicted so deep a wound that he fell to the ground, and was taken up for dead. The terrible news was carried to the Ponziano palace, and announced to Francesca. The anguish that her countenance revealed filled the bystanders with compassion; but it was only for an instant that she stood as if transfixed and overwhelmed with grief.

Repressing by a strong effort her bursting sobs and the cries that were breaking from her heart, she soon raised her eyes to heaven with a steadfast gaze, forgave the assassin, offered up Lorenzo's life and her own, and murmured the words of Job, "The Lord had given him, the Lord has taken him away; blessed be the name of the Lord." Then, calm, composed, braced for endurance, she courageously advanced to meet the slow approach of those who were bringing back to his home the body of her murdered husband. As they laid him in the hall of the palace, she knelt by his side, and putting her face close to his, she discerned in the apparently lifeless form the faint symptoms of lingering vitality. The sudden revulsion of hope did not overcome her presence of mind. She instantly desired those about her to send for a priest and for a doctor; and then, bending over Lorenzo, she suggested to him, in words which found their way to the understanding of the dying man, whatever the most affectionate tenderness and the most ardent piety could devise at such a moment,—to prepare the soul for its last flight, pardon for his foes, and especially for his assassin, a firm trust in God, and the union of his sufferings with those of his Lord.

The palace presented a scene of wild confusion. Armed men were moving to and fro; the clash of arms was mingled with the groans of the servants: the weeping and waitings of the women and of the children, vows of vengeance, curses deep and loud, frantic regrets, were heard on every side. Francesca alone was as an angel of peace, in the midst of the uproar of passion and the outpouring of grief. Her's was the keenest sorrow of all; but it was kept under by the strength of a long-practised faith, and thus it interfered with no duty and staggered at no trial. Day and night she watched by Lorenzo's couch. Her experience in nursing the sick, and in dressing wounds, enabled her to render him the most minute and efficacious assistance. Her watchful love, her tender assiduity, received its reward; God gave her that life, far dearer to her than her own. Contrary to all expectation, Lorenzo slowly recovered; but for a long time remained in a precarious condition.

Meanwhile the Count of Traja, pressed on every side, began to foresee the necessity of leaving Rome; but, in his exasperation, resolved previously to wreak his vengeance on the families most devoted to the Pope, and especially on that of the Ponziani, which was especially obnoxious to him. He accordingly arrested Paluzzo, Vannozza's husband, and kept him in close confinement; and understanding that Lorenzo had a son of eight or nine years old, he commanded that he should be given up into his hands as a hostage, and swore that in case of a refusal he would put Paluzzo to death. Now, indeed, is Francesca tried almost beyond the power of endurance: now is her cup of anguish filled to the brim. She can ask counsel of none: Lorenzo she dares not consult: it might kill him to hear the fearful truth. Others would say, "Give up the child;" and she looks at his fair face, at his innocent eyes, at the purity of his spotless brow; and she cannot, she will not, she must not give him up. Oh, that she had the wings of a dove to fly away and carry him hence! She takes him by the hand, and, like a second Hagar, goes forth, whither she knows not. It is an instinct, an impulse, an inspiration. It is the mother's heart within her that bids her fly from the horrible dilemma, and save her child from the tyrant who seeks more than his life,—who would ruin his soul. Through out-of-the-way streets, into the deserted corners of the city she goes, clasping the boy's hand with an agonising grasp, with but one thought—to hide him from every eye. Suddenly she stops short; before her stands Don Antonio, her long-trusted director, who has led her through the green pastures in which her spirit has found rest. He questions her, and hears the incoherent account of her fears, her anguish, and her flight. By a supernatural light he sees the drift of this trial, and puts her faith to the test. "Francesca," he said, "you fly to save the child; God bids me tell you that it is to the Capitol you must carry him—there lies his safety; and do you go to the Church of Ara Cceli." A fierce struggle rose in Francesca's heart—the greatest storm that had ever convulsed it. "To the Capitol!" she is about to cry. "It is at the Capitol that the tyrant awaits him!" But ere the words are uttered, they die away on her lips. Grace has gained the mastery; the faith of the saint has asserted its power. The wild expression passes away from her eyes; she bows her head in silence, and with a firm step retraces her steps, in obedience to him who has spoken in God's name. In the mean time the report of the event had spread through Rome, and in the more crowded streets which she had to pass through a cry of pity and of terror arose. Crowds press about her, and bid her turn back; they tell her she is mad to surrender the child, they try to take him from her, and to carry him back by force to his father's palace; but in vain. She waves them off, and pursues her way till she has reached the Capitol. She walked straight up to the place where the Neapolitan tyrant was standing, and surrendered up the boy to him; and then, without once looking back, she hurried into the Church of Ara Coeli, fell prostrate at the feet of the Mother of Mercy, and before that sacred image, dear to this day to every Catholic parent, she made the sacrifice of her child, of her life, of her soul, of all that in that hour she had felt to give up. Then, for the first time, a torrent of tears relieved her tight-bound heart; and gazing on the picture, she saw the dove-like eyes of the Blessed Virgin assume the tenderest and most encouraging expression, and in her ears were whispered words welcome as the dew to the thirsty ground; sweet as the notes of the bird when the storm has subsided: "Be not afraid; I am here to befriend you."

She was at peace; she felt sure that her son was safe; and on her knees, in speechless prayer, she waited the event. Nor did she wait long. When she had left the Count of Traja's presence, he had ordered one of his officers to take the little Baptista on his horse, and carry him away to a place he appointed; but, from the instant that the child was placed on the saddle, no efforts could induce the animal to stir from the spot. In vain his rider urged him with spurs and whip: neither the severest blows, nor the accustomed voice of his master, succeeded in moving him an inch from the place, where he stood as motionless as a statue. Four of the knights of Naples renewed the attempt. Four successive steeds were tried for the purpose, and always with the same result. There is a strength greater than man's will; there is a power that defeats human malice. Struck with a secret terror and dismay by the evident prodigy, the Count of Traja gave up the unequal contest, and ordered the child to be restored to his mother. Before the altar of the Ara Coeli, at the foot of that image, where in her anguish she had fallen and found hope when hope seemed at end, Francesca received back into her arms the son of her love, and blessed the God who had given her strength to go through this the severest of her trials.

CHAPTER VI.

SUFFERINGS OF ROME FROM THE TROOPS OF LADISLAS—DEATH OF FRANCESCA'S SON EVANGELISTA—THE FAMINE AND PLAGUE IN ROME—FRANCESCA'S LABOURS FOR THE STARVING AND SICK—HER MIRACLES.

POPE ALEXANDER V. died at Bologna in 1410. Sixteen cardinals assembled in that city, and chose for his successor Balthazar Cossa, who took the name of John XXIII. While they were proceeding with the election, Ladislas seized the opportunity of the interregnum once more to advance upon Rome; and from Veletri he threatened it with a second invasion. The new Pope renewing the alliance with Lewis of Anjou, they combined their forces against Ladislas, and endeavoured to drive him back from the position he had taken. Their arms proved successful in a first battle; but Lewis having withdrawn his troops immediately after the victory, Ladislas deceived the Holy Father by a pretended peace, gained possession of Rome, and gave it up to pillage. The horrors of this invasion, and of the sack that followed it, surpassed in atrocity almost all those which had previously afflicted the capital of the Christian world. A number of palaces and houses were destroyed, the basilicas were despoiled of their treasures and desecrated by the most abominable orgies, the churches turned into stables, and many of the faithful adherents of the Church subjected to the torture or barbarously put to death.

The Ponziani were amongst the principal of the Pope's supporters; and Lorenzo, scarcely recovered from his long illness, was persuaded by his friends to withdraw himself by flight from the fury of the conqueror, and conceal himself in a distant province. It had been impossible to remove his wife and children; and Francesca remained exposed to a succession of the most trying disasters. The wealth of the family chiefly consisted in their country possessions, and the immense number of cattle which were bred on those broad lands; and day after day intelligence was brought to her that one farm-house or another was burnt or pillaged, the flocks dispersed or destroyed, and the shepherds murdered by a ruthless soldiery. Terrified peasants made their escape into the city, and scared the inhabitants of the palace with dreadful accounts of the death of their companions, and of the destruction of property which was continually going on. A cry of despair rang from Mount Soracte to the Alban Hill, extended to the shores of the Mediterranean, and resounded in the palaces of Rome, carrying dismay to the hearts of its ruined and broken-spirited nobles.

Francesca received the tidings with an aching heart indeed; for her compassion for the sufferings of others did not permit her to remain unmoved amidst such dire misfortunes. Still she never lost her habitual composure; her only occupation was to console the mourners: her first impulse on these occasions to bless God, and accept at His hands all that His providence ordained. It was well that she was resigned, and had learned the lesson of courage at the foot of the Cross; for, like a flood at spring-tide, her afflictions were increasing every day, threatening to overwhelm all landmarks but those of an indomitable faith. One fatal morning, a troop of savage ruffians, drunk with rage, and vociferating blasphemies, broke into the palace, clamouring after Lorenzo, and threatening to torture the servants if they did not instantly reveal his place of concealment; and ended by carrying away Baptista, who clung in vain to his mother's neck, and was only parted from her by force. When they had succeeded in tearing him away from her arms, they proceeded to pillage, and all but to destroy, the time-honoured residence of the Ponziani. In the space of a few hours that gorgeous abode was turned into a heap of ruins. Bereft of her husband, of her son, and of all the conveniences of life, Francesca, with her two younger children, remained alone and unprotected; for her brother-in-law, Paluzzo, who might have been a support to her in that dreadful moment, was still a prisoner in the tyrant's hands, and her innocent boy shared the same fate. It is not exactly known how long his captivity lasted; but it may be supposed that means were found of effecting his release, and sending him to Lorenzo; for it is mentioned that, at the period when the troubles were at an end, and peace restored to the city of Rome, the father and the son returned together.

In the mean time, Francesca took shelter in a corner of her ruined habitation; and there, with Evangelista and Agnese, she managed to live in the most complete seclusion. These two children were now their mother's only comfort, as their education was her principal occupation. Evangelista, as he advanced in age, in no way belied the promise of his infancy. He lived in spirit with the angels and saints, and seemed more fitted for their society than for any earthly companionship. "To be with God" was his only dream of bliss. Though scarcely nine years old, he already helped his mother in all the pains she took with Agnese's education

The hour for another sacrifice was, however, at hand. It was not long delayed. The second invasion of Rome had been succeeded by a dreadful famine, which was followed in its turn by a severe pestilence. Already one or two cases of the prevailing epidemic had appeared in the Ponziano Palace, and then Evangelista sickened with it; and one morning Francesca was told that the son of her love was dying. No sooner had he felt the first symptoms of the plague, than he asked for a confessor. He never doubted that his last hour was come; and she believed it too. Don Antonio hurried to the bed-side of the boy, who, after he had made his confession, sent for his mother, and taking her hand in his, addressed her in some such words as follow:

"Mother mine, I have often told you that God would not leave me with you long; that He will have me dwell with His angels. Jesus is my treasure, my hope, and my joy. I have ever lived with Him in thought, in desire, in unutterable longings. Every day I have said 'Thy kingdom come;' and now He calls me to it. There is a crown prepared for me, my beloved mother. The Lord is about to give it me, and we must part for awhile. But bless His name, oh my mother. Praise Him with me; for He delivers me from all that your love dreaded for me upon earth. There is no sin, no sorrow, no sickness where I am going. Nothing but peace and joy and the sight of God in that better land where the blessed are expecting me. I must not see you weep. I will not have you grieve. Rejoice with your child; for I see them even now, my holy advocates, St. Anthony and St. Vauplerius. They are coming to fetch me away. Dearest mother, I will pray for you. Evangelista will love you in heaven as he has loved you on earth, and you will come to him there."

The dying boy then remained silent for a few moments. Then a sudden light illumined his face; his features seemed transformed. Raising his eyes with a look of rapture, he exclaimed, "Here are the angels come to take me away. Give me your blessing, my mother. Do not be afraid. I shall never forget you. God bless you and my dear father, and all who belong to this house. Blessed be the name of the Lord." Then crossing his little arms on his chest, he bowed down his head, a last smile passed over his face—"she had her meed, that smile in death," and his young spirit passed to the regions of endless bliss.

A touching prodigy, well adapted to cheer the heart of our saint, took place that very day in a house adjoining her own. A little girl, who had been dangerously ill for a long time, and had completely lost the power of speech, at the very moment that Francesca's son had expired suddenly raised herself in her bed, and exclaimed several times in a loud voice, and in a state of evident rapture, "See, see! how beautiful! Evangelista Ponziano is going up into heaven, and two angels with him!" The mortal remains of the young boy were deposited in the family vault in the church of Santa Cecilia, in Trastevere. A monument was erected there with the simple inscription, "Here lies Evangelista Ponziano;" and a figure in stone, clothed in a long robe, was carved upon it.

Francesca wept over the loss of her dearly-beloved child, but did not grieve for him. How could she have done so? He was in bliss; and had only preceded her to that heaven for which she was day by day preparing. Nor was it a time for the idle indulgence of sorrow. Want and sickness were turning Rome into a charnel-house. Wild voices were screaming for bread on every side. The streets were encumbered by the victims of contagious disease; their frantic cries and piteous moanings re-echoed in each piazza and under every portico. Old men were dying surrounded by the corpses of their children; mothers pressed to their milkless bosoms their starving infants. Others crept about bereft of all their family, and haunting like pale ghosts the scenes of their past happiness. No carriages shook the public ways. The grass grew in the deserted streets; one mournful equipage alone slowly pursued its course through the doomed city, gathering as it passed the dead at every door; and when the dreadful cargo was completed, bearing it away to the crowded cemetery. The ruin of private property, the general penury occasioned by the cruelties of Ladislas, and the sacking of Rome by his soldiers, had cut off almost all the resources of private charity. Anxiety for self, and the fear of contagion, had worked so deeply on the mind of the multitude, that many persons abandoned even their near relatives and friends when they were attacked by the plague. Nothing but the charity which is of divine not of natural origin could meet such an emergency, or cope in any degree with the awful misery of those days. Francesca, bereaved of every thing but her one little girl, and lodged with Vannozza and Rita in a corner of their dismantled house, had no longer at her command the resources she had formerly possessed for the relief of the poor. A little food from their ruined estates was now and then supplied to these lonely women; and they scarcely partook of it themselves, in order to bestow the greatest part on the sick and poor. There was a large hall in the lower part of the palace which had been less injured than any other portion of the building. It was at least a place of shelter against the inclemencies of the weather. The sisters converted it into a temporary hospital; but of the shattered furniture that lay scattered about the house, they contrived to make up beds and covering, and to prepare some clothing for the wretched creatures they were about to receive. When all was ready, they went in search of the sufferers. If they found any too weak to walk, they carried them into the new asylum; there they washed and dressed their putrefying sores, and by means which saints have often employed, and which we could hardly bear even to think of, they conquered in themselves all repugnance to sights and employments against which the senses and the flesh rise in rebellion. They prepared both medicine and food; watched the sick by day and by night; laboured incessantly for their bodies, and still more for their souls. Many were those who recovered health through Francesca's care, and many more who were healed of the worst disease of the soul,—a hardened impenitence under the just judgment of God. She had the art of awakening their fears, without driving them to despair; to make them look upon their sufferings as a means of expiation (that great secret of Catholic consolation), and bring them by degrees to repentance, to confession, to the practice of long-forgotten duties, and of those Christian virtues which her own example recommended to their hearts.

The example which the ruined and bereaved wives of the Ponziani had given kindled a similar spirit among the hitherto apathetic inhabitants of Rome. The magistrates of the city, struck at the sight of such unparalleled exertions where the means were so slender, were roused from their inaction, and in several parts of the city, especially in the parishes of St. Cecilia and of Santa Maria in Trastevere, hospitals and asylums were opened for the perishing multitudes. Often and often Francesca and Vannozza saw the morning dawn, and not a bit of food of any description did they possess for themselves or for their inmates. They then went out to beg, as they had done before; but not merely as an act of humility, nor dressed as heretofore as became their rank, or in those places only where their names secured respect, and generally a favourable answer; but in the garb of poverty, in the spots where beggars were wont to congregate and the rich to bestow alms, they took their stand, and gratefully received the broken bits that fell from the tables of the wealthy. Each remnant of food, each rag of clothing, they brought home with joy; and the mouldiest piece of bread out of their bag was set aside for their own nourishment, while the best was bestowed on their guests.

In our own time, in our own rich and luxurious city, there is a counterpart to these deeds of heroic charity. There are young and well-educated women, who in their homes never lacked the necessaries or the comforts, nay perhaps the luxuries of life, who do the same; who receive into their abode the aged, the maimed, the crippled, and the deformed; lodging them in their best rooms, and themselves in cellars or garrets; tending them as their servants, and feeding them as their mothers; begging for them from door to door the crumbs from the tables of the rich, and carrying along their basket, rejoicing when it is heavy, even though their arms ache and their cheeks grow pale with the labour; like Francesca, feeding upon the remnants of the poor feast where the poor have sat before them.

Francesca was insulted in her career of mercy through the streets of Rome, when civil war and anarchy were raging there in the wildest epoch of lawless strife and fiercest passion; and the gentle sisters of the poor, the servants of the helpless, who have abandoned home and friends and comforts, and, above all, *respectability*, that idol of the English mind, that wretched counterfeit of virtue, for the love which they bear to Christ in His suffering members, have been insulted and beaten in the streets of London in the face of day, and only because of the habit they wore,—the badge of no common vocation,—the nun's black dress, the livery of the poor. The parallel is consoling to them, perhaps also to us; for is not Francesca now the cherished saint of Rome, the pride and the love of every Roman heart? And may not the day come when our patient, heroic nuns will be looked upon as one of God's best blessings, in a city where luxury runs riot on the one hand, and starvation and misery reign on the other? Will not the eye follow them with love, and many rise up to call them blessed? Their course is like hers; may their end be the same!

The historians of our saint relate that on one of the occasions above alluded to, when her only resource was to beg for her sick charges, she went to the Basilica of San Lorenzo without the walls, where was the station of the day, and seated herself amongst the crowd of beggars who, according to custom, were there assembled. From the rising of the sun to the ringing of the vesper-bell, she sat there side by side with the lame, the deformed, and the blind. She held out her hand as they did, gladly enduring, not the semblance, but the reality of that deep humiliation. When she had received enough wherewith to feed the poor at home, she rose, and making a sign to her companions, entered the old basilica, adored the Blessed Sacrament, and then walked back the long and weary way, blessing God all the while, and rejoicing that she was counted worthy to suffer for His dear sake.

Those who are well acquainted with Rome, who have frequented the stations and love the basilicas, and especially that venerable old pile of San Lorenzo, with its upper and lower chapel, its magnificent columns, its beautiful pulpit, its wide portico with half-effaced frescoes, and its rare mosaics—those paintings in stone which time itself cannot destroy; those whose eyes have gazed with delight on the glorious view as they approached it, and whose ears are familiar with the sound of the mendicant's voice, to whom the remembrance of Francesca's story may have won, perchance, an additional dole,—can form to themselves with ease a picture of the scene; and when they visit it again in reality, may be tempted to look out for some saintly face, for some sweet, angel-like countenance, amongst the sordid and suffering groups before them, and wonder if ever again such charity as Francesca's will animate a woman's heart. Not long ago, for a few short years, in Francesca's city, there was one who bade fair to emulate the virtues of the dear saint of Rome; but as she was rapidly treading in her footsteps, and her name was becoming every day more dear to the people amongst whom she dwelt, death snatched her away. Her memory remains, and the poor bless it even now. May God grant us such in our own land! Saints are sorely needed in these busy, restless, money-loving times of ours; as much as, or more than, in the wild middle ages, or the troubled centuries that followed.

Francesca possessed a small vineyard near the church of St. Paul without the walls; and in that time of scarcity, when every little resource had to be turned to account for the purposes of charity, she used to go there and gather up into parcels and faggots the long grass and the dry branches of the vines. When she had collected a certain number of these packets, she laid them on an ass, and went through the town, stopping at various poor dwellings to distribute the fruits of her labours. On one of these occasions her donkey stumbled and fell, and the wood which he was carrying rolled to a considerable distance. Francesca was looking about her in considerable embarrassment, not able to lift it up again, when a Roman nobleman, Paolo Lelli Petrucci, a friend of her husband's, chanced to pass by. Astonished at seeing her in such a predicament, he hastened to her assistance; and she received it with as much serenity and composure as if her occupation had been the most natural thing in the world.

By this time her virtues were destined to receive a wonderful reward, and God bestowed upon her the gift of healing to a miraculous degree. Many a sick person given over by the physicians was restored to health by the single touch of her hands, or the prayers which she offered up in their behalf. More than sixty of these cases were well attested at the time of her canonisation. Francesca was profoundly sensible of the blessedness of this gift, and grateful for the power it afforded her of relieving the sufferings of others; but at the same time her humility prompted her to conceal it as much as possible. She endeavoured to do so by making up an ointment composed of oil and wax, which she applied to the sick, whatever their disease might be, in the hope that their recovery would always be ascribed to its efficacy. But this holy subterfuge did not always succeed. The physicians analysed the ointment, and declared that it possessed in itself no healing qualities whatsoever. One day, upon entering the Hospital of the Trastevere, Francesca found a poor mule-driver, who had just been carried in, his foot having been crushed by the fall of a scythe; it was in such a horrible and hopeless condition, that the surgeons were about to amputate the limb. Francesca, hearing the cries of the poor wretch, bent over him, exhorting him to patience; and promising him a speedy relief, applied some of her ointment to his mangled foot. The wounds instantly closed, the pain vanished, and a short time after the mule-driver returned to his customary occupation.

Some days afterwards, the two sisters were returning home from the basilica of St. John Lateran; and passing by the bridge of Santa Maria, now the Ponte Rotto, (the very ancient little church opposite to the Temple of Vesta), they saw extended on the pavement a man whose arm had been severed by a sword-cut; and unable to procure medical assistance, the poor wretch had lain there ever since in excruciating tortures, which had reduced him to the last extremity. Francesca, full of compassion for his miserable condition, carried him with Vannozza's aid into her house, put him in a warm bath, cleansed his wound with the greatest care, and dressed it with her ointment. In a short time, and without any medical assistance, the severed limb was restored to its usual position, and a complete recovery ensued.

The bowl in which San Francesca compounded this miraculous remedy is preserved in the convent of Tor di Specchi. During the novena of the saint, when the doors are thrown open to crowds of devout persons, it stands on a table in the entrance-chamber, and is daily filled by the nuns with fresh sweet-smelling flowers—violets, primroses, anemones, and the like. The visitor may bear away with him some of these fragrant remembrances, and cherish them for her sake, the odour of whose virtues will last as long as the seasons return, and the spring brings back to our gladdened sight those

"Sweet nurslings of the vernal skies,
Bathed with soft airs and fed with dew."

A still more wonderful miracle than these occurred about this time. Francesca and her faithful companion Vannozza had been visiting several churches in that part of Rome which goes by the name of the Rioue de Monti. Passing before a mean-looking dwelling, they heard the most heart-rending sobs and cries. Stopping to inquire into the cause of this despair, they found a mother frantically weeping over the body of a child, who had died a few hours after its birth without having received baptism. Francesca gently reproved the woman for the delay which had endangered her son's salvation; then, taking the little corpse into her arms, she uttered a fervent prayer, and in a moment gave back the baby to its mother, fully restored to life and health. She desired her to have it instantly baptised, and then made her escape, trusting that she should remain undiscovered; and indeed the woman whose child she had been the means of saving had never seen her, and wondered awhile if an angel had visited her in disguise; but the description of her dress, and the miracle she had worked, convinced all who heard of it that the visitor was no other than the wife of Lorenzo Ponziano.

Compassionate to others, Francesca was mercilessly severe to herself; her austerities kept pace with her increasing sanctity. She was enabled to carry on a mode of life which must have ruined her health had it not been miraculously sustained. She slept only for two hours, and that on a narrow plank covered with nothing but a bit of rough carpet. The continual warfare which she waged against her body brought it more and more into subjection to the spirit; and her senses were under such perfect control, that natural repugnances vanished, and the superior part of the soul reigned supremely over the meaner instincts and inclinations of the flesh. Such was her spiritual proficiency at the early age of twenty-nine.

CHAPTER VII.

EVANGELISTA APPEARS TO HIS MOTHER-AN ARCHANGEL IS ASSIGNED TO HER AS A VISIBLE GUARDIAN THROUGHOUT HER LIFE,

EVANGELISTA had been dead about a year. His image was ever present to his mother's heart; she saw him in spirit at the feet of his Lord. Never, even in her inmost soul, was she conscious of a wish to recall him from the heaven he had reached to the earthly home which he had left desolate; but not for one moment could she forget the child of her love, or cease to invoke him as a celestial guardian akin to those who had so long hovered about her path. Her faith and resignation were richly rewarded. God gave her a sight of her child in heaven, and he was sent to announce to her one of the most extraordinary favours that was ever vouchsafed to a daughter of Adam. Francesca was praying one morning in her oratory, when she became conscious that the little room was suddenly illuminated in a supernatural manner; a mysterious light shone on every side, and its radiance seemed to pervade not only her outward senses, but the inmost depths of her being, and to awaken in her soul a strange sensation of joy. She raised her eyes, and Evangelista stood before her; his familiar aspect unchanged, but his features transfigured and beaming with ineffable splendour.

By his side was another of the same size and height as himself, but more beautiful still. Francesca's lips move, but in vain she seeks to articulate; the joy and the terror of that moment are too intense. Her son draws near to her, and with an angelic expression of love and respect he bows down his head and salutes her. Then the mother's feelings predominate; she forgets every thing but his presence, and opens her arms to him; but it is no earthly form that she encloses within them, and the glorified body escapes her grasp. And now she gains courage and addresses him,—in broken accents indeed, but with trembling eagerness.

"Is it you, indeed? (she cries) O son of my heart! Whence do you come? who are your companions? what your abode? Angel of God, hast thou thought of thy mother, of thy poor father? Amidst the joys of Paradise hast thou remembered earth and its sufferings?"

Evangelista looked up to heaven with an unutterable expression of peace and of joy; and then, fixing his eyes on his mother, he said, "My abode is with God; my companions are the angels; our sole occupation the contemplation of the Divine perfections,—the endless source of all happiness. Eternally united with God, we have no will but His; and our peace is as complete as His Being is infinite. He is Himself our joy, and that joy knows no limits. There are nine choirs of angels in heaven, and the higher orders of angelic spirits instruct in the Divine mysteries the less exalted intelligences. If you wish to know my place amongst them, my mother, learn that God, of His great goodness, has appointed it in the second choir of angels, and the first hierarchy of archangels. This my companion is higher than I am in rank, as he is more bright and fair in aspect. The Divine Majesty has assigned him to you as a guardian during the remainder of your earthly pilgrimage. Night and day by your side, he will assist you in every way. Never amidst the joys of Paradise have I for an instant forgotten you, or any of my loved ones on earth. I knew you were resigned; but I also knew that your heart would rejoice at beholding me once more, and God has permitted that I should thus gladden your eyes. But I have a message for you, my mother. God asks for Agnese: she may not tarry long with you; her place is ready in the New Jerusalem. Be of good comfort, nay, rather rejoice that your children are safely housed in heaven." Evangelista communed a short while longer with his mother, and then, bidding her tenderly farewell, disappeared; but the archangel remained, and to the day of her death was ever present to her sight.

She now understood the sense of the vision that had been sent her at the time of Agnese's birth. It was not for the cloister, but for heaven itself, that God claimed her young daughter; and during the few remaining days of her earthly life she waited upon her with a tenderness mingled with veneration; looking upon her as one who scarcely belonged to the rough world she was so soon to leave. And the chosen child of God, the little maiden on whom the mystic dove had rested in its flight, soon drooped like a flower in an ungenial air,—soon gave her fond mother a last kiss and a last smile; and then her gentle spirit went to seek her brother's kindred soul. They were buried together; and the day was now come for Francesca, when earthly happiness altogether vanishes, when life has its duties but has lost all its joys,— and then, what a lesson is in the story! God's angel henceforward stands visibly by her side, and never leaves her!

When Evangelista had parted from his mother, she had fallen prostrate on the ground, and blessed God for His great mercy to her, the most worthless of sinners, for such she deemed herself; and then, turning to the angel, who stood near her, she implored him to be her guide and director; to point out the way she was to tread; to combat with her against Satan and his ministers; and to teach her every day to become more like in spirit to his and her Lord. When she left the oratory, the archangel followed her, and, enveloped in a halo of light, remained always visible to her, though imperceptible to others. The radiance that surrounded him was so dazzling, that she could seldom look upon him with a fixed gaze. At night, and in the most profound darkness, she could always write and read by the light of that supernatural brightness. Sometimes, however, when in prayer, or in conference with her director, or engaged in struggles with the Evil One, she was enabled to see his form with perfect distinctness, and by Don Antonio's orders thus described him:—"His stature," she said, "is that of a child of about nine years old; his aspect full of sweetness and majesty; his eyes generally turned towards heaven: words cannot describe the divine purity of that gaze. His brow is always serene; his glances kindle in the soul the flame of ardent devotion. When I look upon him, I understand the glory of the angelic nature, and the degraded condition of our own. He wears a long shining robe, and over it a tunic, either as white as the lilies of the field, or of the colour of a red rose, or of the hue of the sky when it is most deeply blue. When he walks by my side, his feet are never soiled by the mud of the streets or the dust of the road."

Francesca's conduct was now directed in the most infallible manner. By a special privilege, a companion had been assigned to her from the heavenly hierarchy; and if she committed any faults, error could not now be pleaded in excuse. Her actions, her words, and her thoughts, were to be ever on a par with those of the sinless Being who was to be her guide throughout her earthly pilgrimage. It was an awful responsibility, a startling favour; but trusting in God's grace, though fully aware of her own weakness, she did not shrink from the task. Her greatest wish had always been to attain a perfect conformity with the Divine Will, and now this mysterious guidance furnished her with the means of knowing that Will in its minutest details. In her struggles with the Evil One, the archangel became her shield of defence; the rays of light which darted from his brow sent the demons howling on their way. Thus protected, she feared neither the wiles nor the violence of Satan.

The presence of her heavenly guide was also to Francesca a mirror, in which she could see reflected every imperfection of her fallen, though to a great extent renewed, nature. Much as she had discerned, even from her earliest childhood, of the innate corruption of her heart, yet she often told her director, that it was only since she had been continually in the presence of an angelic companion that she had realised its amount. So that this divine favour, far from exalting her in her own eyes, served to maintain her in the deepest humility. When she committed the slightest fault, the angel seemed to disappear; and it was only after she had carefully examined her conscience, discovered her failing, lamented and humbly confessed it, that he returned. On the other hand, when she was only disturbed by a doubt or a scruple, he was wont to bestow on her a kind look, which dissipated at once her uneasiness. When he spoke, she used to see his lips move; and a voice of indescribable sweetness, but which seemed to come from a distance, reached her ears. His guidance enlightened her chiefly with regard to the difficulty she felt in submitting to certain cares and obligations which belonged to her position as mistress and head of a family. She was apt to imagine that the hours thus employed were lost in God's sight; but her celestial guardian corrected her judgment on this point, and taught her to discern the Divine will in every little irksome worldly duty, in every trifling contradiction, as well as in great trials and on important occasions. The light of the angelic presence gave her also a marvellous insight into the thoughts of others. Their sins, their errors, their evil inclinations, were supernaturally revealed to her, and often caused her the Keenest sorrow. She was enabled through this gift to bring back to God many a wandering soul, to frustrate bad designs, and reconcile the most inveterate enemies. Francesca used sometimes, to say to Don Antonio, when she requested his permission for some additional austerities which he hesitated in granting, "Be not afraid, father; the archangel will not allow me to proceed too far in that course. He always checks me when I am tempted to transgress the bounds of prudence." And Don Antonio believed it, for his penitent always spoke the exact truth; and in the miraculous manner in which she over and over again read his most secret thoughts, and manifested them to him, he had a pledge of her veracity, as well as of her extraordinary sanctity.

CHAPTER VIII.

FRANCESCA'S ILLNESS AND RECOVERY— HER VISION OF HELL—RESTORATION OF TRANQUILLITY III ROME—RETURN OF FRANCESCA'S HUSBAND—HER POWER IN CONVERTING SINNERS.

Four long years had elapsed, during which Rome had been given up to dissensions and civil discord, while epidemics of various kinds were continually succeeding each other, and carrying off many of its inhabitants. At the opening of the year 1414, Sigismund, king of the Romans, and John XXIII., had agreed to convene a council at Constance; and the faithful were beginning to cherish a hope that the schism which had so long desolated the Church might be drawing to a close. But this distant prospect of relief was not sufficient to counterbalance the actual sufferings of the moment; and Francesca beheld with ever-increasing pain the amount of sin and of misery which filled the city of her birth. Her exertions, her labours, her bodily and mental trials, told at last upon her enfeebled frame, and about this time she fell dangerously ill. Almost all her acquaintances, and even her own family, fled from her, terrified, it would seem, by the idea of contagion. Vannozza alone remained, and never left her bed-side. Some there were who came to visit, but not for the purpose of consoling her; on the contrary, it was to reproach the dying saint with what they called her absurd infatuation, which had introduced the plague into her abode, and endangered her own life, for the sake of a set of worthless wretches. She listened with her accustomed gentleness, without attempting to defend herself from the charge. Her soul was perfectly at peace; she could joyfully accept the death that now appeared inevitable; she could thank God earnestly that the struggle was past, and Evangelista and Agnese safely lodged in His arms. She looked forward to a speedy reunion with these beloved ones; and marked the progress of her disease as the prisoner watches the process by which his chains are riven. A few words or love and faith she now and then whispered to Vannozza; at other times she remained absorbed in divine contemplation. Overshadowed by an angel's wing, calm in the midst of severe suffering, she performed her habitual devotions in as far as her strength permitted, and only gave up painful penances by the express order of her director. She who had healed so many sick persons cared not to be healed herself.

It was not, however, God's will that she should die so soon. After passing several months in prolonged sufferings, her health was suddenly restored. It was at this period of her life that she had the awful and detailed visions of hell which have remained on record, and in which many salutary and fearful lessons are conveyed. She was rapt in spirit, and carried through the realms of endless woe. What was once chosen by the genius of man as a theme for its highest poetic effort—a journey through "the mournful city, amongst that lost people"[1] —was given to the saint in mystic trance to accomplish. An angel led her through these terrific scenes; and an intuitive perception was given to her of the various sufferings of the condemned souls. So deep was the impression which this tremendous vision left on Francesca's soul, that never afterwards, as long as she lived, could she speak of it without tears and trembling; and she would often emphatically warn those persons who, trusting too implicitly to God's mercy, forgot in their reckless security the terrors of His justice. Some of the fresco paintings in the convent of Tor di Specchi represent this vision, and are visible to this day. The Pope John XXIII., and Sigismund, king of the Romans, had at last succeeded in forming a league, with the object of delivering Italy from the intolerable yoke of Ladislas, king of Naples. This tyrant had assembled a numerous army, and was marching upon Bologna; but the measure of his iniquities was now full, and the hand of death arrested him on his way. An illness, occasioned by his incredible excesses, seized him between Nurni and Perugia, and he died on the 5th of August, 1414. The sovereign Pontiff, free from the terrors which this fierce usurper had inspired, and yielding to the importuni-

---

[1] Per me si va nella città dolente, Per me si va tra la perduta gente."—
DANTE.

ties of the cardinal, set out for Constance, where he was to meet the Emperor Sigismund. This same Council of Constance was eventually to be the means of making void his election, and of ending the great schism of the West, by placing in the chair of St. Peter the illustrious Pontiff Martin V. The death of Ladislas restored peace to the states of the Church, and in particular to the city of Rome. With the cessation of civil broils the famine disappeared; and with it the grievous pestilence that had so long accompanied it. The fields were cultivated once more; the peasants gradually returned to their farms; the flocks grazed unmolested in the green pastures of the Campagna; and the whilom deserted provinces smiled again under the influence of returning prosperity.

The sufferings of the Ponziani were also at an end. They were recalled from banishment, and their property was restored. Lorenzo and his son—now his only son—Baptista. returned to their home, and to the wife and mother they had so longed to behold again. But mixed with sorrow was the cup of joy which that hour seemed to offer. Lorenzo, who a few years back was in the prime of life—strong, healthy, and energetic,—he who had met every foe and every trial without shrinking, was now broken by long sufferings; aged more through exile and grief than through years. We are told that when he entered his palace and looked upon his wife, deep sobs shook his breast, and he burst into an agony of tears. The two beautiful children which he had left by her side, where were they? Gone! never to gladden his eyes again, or make music in his home by the sound of their sweet voices. And Francesca herself, pale with recent illness, spent with ceaseless labours, she stood before him the perfect picture of a woman and a saint, with the divine expression of her beloved face unchanged; but how changed in form, in bloom, in brightness, in every thing but that beauty which holiness gives and time cannot efface!

Long and bitterly he wept, and Francesca gently consoled him. She told him how Evangelista had appeared to her; how their children were only gone before them, companions now of those angels they had so resembled upon earth. She whispered to him that one of these was ever at her side; and when he looked upon her, and remembered all she had been to him, doubtless he found it easy to believe. Taught by adversity, more than ever influenced by his admirable wife, Lorenzo henceforward adopted a more thoroughly Christian mode of life than he had hitherto followed. Not content with praising her virtues, he sought to imitate them, and practised all the duties of religion with the utmost strictness. On one point alone his conduct was inconsistent with the principles he professed, and this was, while it lasted, a source of keen anxiety to Francesca. There was a Roman nobleman who, several years before, had grievously offended the lord of Ponziano, and with whom he absolutely refused to be reconciled. This had formerly been, and was again after his return, an occasion of scandal to many. The more eminent were his virtues, the higher his religious profession, the more glaring appeared such an evident inconsistency. Francesca herself was blamed for it; and people used to wonder that she who was so often successful in reconciling strangers and promoting peace in families, had not the power of allaying an enmity discreditable to her husband and at variance with the dictates of religion. At last, however, by dint of patience and gentleness, she accomplished what had seemed for a long time a hopeless endeavour. The hearts of both parties were touched with remorse. Lorenzo, who was the aggrieved party, granted his enemy a full and free pardon, and a perfect reconciliation ensued. This triumph over himself on the one point where the stubborn natural will had so long held out, resulted, as is almost always the case, in a rapid advance towards perfection.

Lorenzo, from this time forth, withdrew more and more from public life, refused those posts of honour and of responsibility which a friendly government pressed upon him, and surrendered himself almost entirely to the duties and exercises of a strictly religious life. In his conversations with his wife, he daily gained a deeper insight into the secrets of the spiritual life. Far from complaining of the amount of money which she spent in charity, of the existence of an hospital within the walls of his palace, of her various and laborious works of mercy, or of the length of time which she spent in prayer, he renewed his request that she would, in every respect, follow what seemed to her the will of God, and the most perfect manner of life. Francesca gratefully complied with this his desire. She watched more strictly than ever over the conduct of those committed to her charge, and recommended to them by her example even more than by her precepts an exact observance of the commandments of God and of the Church. What money was exclusively her own, she regularly divided into two parts: with one-half she bought food for the poor, with the other clothing and medicine for the sick. Her own dress cost her next to nothing; she continued to wear her old green gown patched-up with any odd bits of cloth that fell in her way. Almost every day she went to her vineyard and gathered wood for the faggots which she gave away on her return. Her relations, her friends, and even her servants, were annoyed at her employing herself in such labour, and bitterly complained of the humiliation it occasioned them to meet her so meanly dressed and so meanly occupied. Lorenzo did not share those feelings; on the contrary, he used to look upon her on these occasions with an increase of affection and veneration; and supported by his approval, by the approbation of her director, and the dictates of her own conscience, she cared little for the comments of others.

The kind of apostolate which by this time she exercised in Rome was very remarkable; and her power over men's minds and hearts scarcely short of miraculous. There was a subduing charm, an irresistible influence in her words and in her manner, which told on every variety of persons. The expression of her countenance, the tones of her voice, her mere presence, worked wonders in effecting conversions, and in animating to virtue those whom she approached. Her gift of reading the thoughts of others, which had increased ever since the archangel had become her companion, enabled her in several instances to bring about conversions, several of which are related at length by her biographers.

Amongst them was that of a young woman who was lying dangerously ill in one of the hospitals of the city. Francesca had been distributing food to the sick, and was then attending the death-bed of a young man, who was about to receive the last Sacraments, when a piercing cry from one of the adjoining wards reached her ears. She hastened to the spot, and found a young woman stretched on one of the narrow beds, and dying in all the agonies of despair. No sooner had she looked upon the poor creature than her dreadful history was supernaturally revealed to her. She had some time before had an illegitimate child, and, under the pressure of shame and terror, had destroyed it. The consciousness of this crime was driving her to despair, and she had not courage to confess it. But now words were whispered in her ear, which went straight to the point on which the awful straggle turned; which spoke of the horrible misery of dying impenitent and unabsolved, and of the boundless mercy which has provided a remedy for the deepest stains of sin, the blood of Jesus applied to the soul by the grace of the Sacrament. For a long time the poor creature resisted, turned her head away, and refused to be comforted. But when Francesca, in still more pressing terms, alluded to the intolerable burden of an unacknowledged crime, of the life-giving humiliation of a sincere confession, of the dire confusion of an unforgiven soul on the day of Judgment; of the love of Jesus, of the tenderness of Mary, of the indulgence of the Church, the sweetness of pardon, the peace of reconciliation; then the stubborn heart yielded, the seared spirit was softened. Bursting into tears, the dying sufferer exclaimed, "A priest! a priest!" and one was at hand at the first call of contrition, and answered that expiring cry, as Matthew did the royal prophet's confession: "The Lord forgives; thou shalt not perish." And shortly after in Francesca's arms the pardoned sinner breathed her last.

About the same time, Francesca was the means of converting one who would doubtless have turned with contempt from the poor criminal on the hospital-bed with horror, from the guilty destroyer of her own child, and deemed that to breathe the same air as such a wretch was in itself contamination. And yet, in God's right, Gentilezza may have been as, or perhaps more guilty than the sorely-tempted, unprotected, miserable being, who in weakness first, and then in terror, almost in madness, had rushed into crime; for she was rich, noble, and beautiful; had been nursed in pomp and pleasure; hunger had never tempted, and scorn never pursued her. Her life had been one continued scene of amusement and of splendour. She cared for nothing but the homage of men, the incense of admiration, the intoxication of pleasure. There was not a duty that she did not neglect, nor one sacred obligation that she felt herself bound to observe. We are not told that she committed what men call crimes; but her husband she treated with open contempt, and ridiculed him on account of his attachment to religious duties; her children she altogether neglected, and abandoned them to the care of servants, while her days and nights were devoted to amusements and frivolities of every description. Several of the Roman ladies, who used to be her companions, had been induced, by Francesca's example and exhortation, to give up a life of dissipation, and adopt one better befitting the Christian profession; but Gentilezza laughed at her and at them, and used to say, with insolent derision, that she had no vocation for wearing rags and carrying faggots. Perfectly indifferent to the ridicule with which she sought to cover her, Francesca prayed incessantly for the vain and haughty woman, who seemed beyond the reach of reproach or of persuasion. One day, however, moved by a prophetic impulse, she thus addressed her: "You scorn my warnings, Gentilezza; you laugh at the advice of your confessor. But remember that God is powerful, and not to be mocked with impunity. The day is at hand when you will rue the stubbornness of your heart."

A few days afterwards, as Gentilezza, who was with child at the time, was descending the stairs of her palace, her foot slipped, and she fell headlong to the bottom. Her servants raised her in their arms, and found her all but dead. The physicians, who were summoned in haste, judged unfavourably of her case, and pronounced that her child must infallibly have been killed by the fall. The wretched woman burst into tears, but it was not so much her own danger, or the death of her infant which she deplored, as the ruin of her beauty, which had been her pride and her snare. Her features had been so injured by this accident, that her face was completely disfigured, and with rebellious anger she wept over her lost loveliness. Francesca, upon hearing of this event, hurried to the spot, and nursed the suffering woman with the tenderest care. With the utmost kindness she reminded her of the duties she had neglected, and of the means of grace she had despised, and exhorted her to recognise the hand of a merciful God in the chastisement she had received. She spoke to her of her husband, of her children, of the true and sweet vocations of a wife and a mother, of the transitory nature of all earthly enjoyments; and into the heart subdued by pain and disappointment her words made their way. It was as if scales had fallen from the eyes of the sufferer. "God is just," she exclaimed at last; "I deserved even a greater punishment than I have met with. Pray for me, Francesca Ponziano; pray for me; and oh, hear me promise, that if my life is spared, I will give up all my evil ways, and henceforward become a Christian wife and a Christian mother; so help me God, whom I have so grievously offended!" Francesca bent over her and embraced her; she saw that her repentance was sincere, and bade her be of good comfort, and that her penitence would be accepted. And so it turned out; for Gentilezza was safely delivered of a healthy little girl, and in time recovered not only her health but the beauty which she had once turned to such bad account; and, while faithful to her promise, she ceased to abuse the gifts of God, and devoted herself to the diligent performance of her duties, became a chosen friend of Francesca's, and one of the most pious and exemplary matrons in Rome.

Among the relatives of the saint, there was a young man whose name was Giovanni Antonio Lorenzi, whose temper was fierce and violent in the extreme. Having been, as he considered, insulted by another Roman nobleman, he vowed that he would take his life, and resolved to have him assassinated. Francesca's angel revealed to her his criminal design, which was as yet confined to his own breast. She instantly sent for the object of his enmity, and charged him, as he valued his existence, not to leave his own house for a certain number of days; and without informing him of the reason, obtained his promise to that effect. In the mean time she disclosed to Lorenzi her knowledge of his guilty project, and induced him to abandon all idea of revenge. Her influence over Angelo Savelli, on a similar occasion, was still more remarkable. He had quarrelled with a young man of his acquaintance, and a duel had ensued, in which he had been severely wounded. His anger was excessive; he did nothing but threaten and curse his adversary. Neither his own family nor that of his foe could succeed in appeasing him, and he was dying with vengeance in his heart, and accents of rage on his lips. Francesca was informed of his condition, and went, straightway to his bed-side. She had no sooner uttered a few words, than he bade her bring his enemy to him, that he might forgive and embrace him. He was himself astonished at the change thus wrought by her presence, and declared that the Holy Spirit had moved him by her means. He received the last Sacrament with the best dispositions, and died soon after, full of peace and hope, and repeatedly assured his family that God, in mercy to his soul, had sent the wife of Ponziano to save him from the ruin which was so nearly overtaking him.

One more instance amongst many of Francesca's powers of persuasion may be adduced, in addition to the preceding. She was, as we have seen, a constant attendant at the church of Santa Maria Nuova, where her confessor, Don Antonio Savello officiated. It so happened that one of the monks of his order, Don Ippolito, who subsequently played a part in the history of the saint, and who had been now residing ten years in the convent, was about this time appointed to the office of sacristan, although he had previously filled with distinction divers important functions in the monastery. He had accepted this appointment out of obedience and humility of spirit; but after a while the devil sorely tempted him to regret having done so; to repine at what he began to consider as an act of tyranny and injustice; and these reflections, gradually indulged in, made sad havoc of his peace of mind. An oppressive melancholy beset him; and at last he came to the resolution of abandoning his habit and the monastery, if the obnoxious appointment were not cancelled. But one day that he had been invoking Mary, our Lady of good counsel, he felt a sudden inspiration to go and communicate to Francesca his discontent, his restlessness, and the resolution he had formed. She listened attentively to his statement, and then quietly addressed to him some questions which placed the subject in its true light. She asked him with what purpose he had entered the religious state; whom he had intended to serve in doing so; which he preferred, the God who descends and dwells on the altar, or the servants who wait upon Him elsewhere? Which was the highest post, that of watching over the sanctuary, in company with the angels, or of ministering to men, however holy and eminent they might be, as would be his lot in another office? The wisdom and simplicity of this answer went straight to Don Ippolito's heart. He instantly acquiesced in its justice, and went directly to confession. With earnest benevolence he betook himself to the duties of his at once humble and exalted office, edified all his brethren by his unfeigned humility, and became in time the model of his order. He was afterwards successively named sub-prior, and then prior of the monastery of Santa Maria Nuova; and was later the associate and support of Francesca in the foundation of her congregation of the Noble Oblates of Tor di Specchi.

CHAPTER IX.

FRESH SUPERNATURAL EVENTS IN FRANCESCA'S HISTORY—HER OBEDIENCE TO HER HUSBAND AND TO HER CONFESSOR REWARDED BY TWO MIRACLES—MARRIAGE OF HER SON, AND ILL CONDUCT OF HIS WIFE—HER CONVERSION THROUGH FRANCESCA'S PRAYERS—FRESH MIRACLES WORKED BY FRANCESCA.

Francesca's obedience to her director in spiritual matters, and to her husband in other respects, continued to be exemplary. In both instances she received a miraculous proof that God regarded with especial favour that humble submission of spirit in one whom He endowed with such marvellous gifts. The story of these miracles might well furnish a subject to a painter or a poet. One day that she and Vannozza had asked permission to visit the shrine of Santa Croce in Gierusalemme, Don Antonio had given them leave to do so; on condition that, as an exercise of self-control, and a test of their obedience, they should walk there and back without once raising their eyes to look about them. He wished them to employ all the time of that long walk in mental prayer and meditation. They proceeded on their way without interruption, till, on approaching the hospital adjoining the church of St. John of Lateran, a sudden rush of people overtook them, and sounds of terror were heard on every side. A bull had escaped from its leaders, and driven frantic by the cries of the multitude, it was dashing savagely along. Francesca and Vannozza stood directly in his path. Loud shouts warned them to get out of the way; but, faithful to the obedience they had received, and probably inwardly assured that they would be protected against the danger, whatever it was, they advanced calm and unmoved with their eyes fixed on the ground. The bystanders, who were cowering at a distance, shuddered; for it seemed that the next moment must see them under the feet of the bellowing animal. But no; the same influence that tamed the lions in Daniel's den was at work with the savage beast. At sight of the two women, it suddenly stopped in its course, became perfectly tranquil, stood still while they passed, and then resumed its flight; while they proceeded to the church without having experienced the slightest emotion of fear. There is an ancient saying, that a wild beast is appeased by the sight of a maiden in her purity; and there can be no doubt that those saints who have regained in some measure, by mortification, penance, and heroic virtue, the purity of man's original nature, have at the same time recovered, in a certain degree, the power which Adam possessed over the animal creation. It is a fact of frequent occurrence in their lives, that mysterious homage paid to them by the wild inhabitants of the desert, or the gentle denizens of the grave. St. Francis of Assisi, and St. Rose of Lima, amongst others, were singularly endowed with this gift. There are few more touching thoughts, or any better calculated to make us understand the true character of sanctity, and the gradual restoration of a fallen nature to one akin to that of the angels.

The other miracle was one attested by Vannozza, who witnessed its occurrence. Francesca devoted all her leisure moments to prayer, but never allowed her delight in spiritual exercises to interfere with her duty as a wife. Her attention to Lorenzo's slightest wants and wishes was unceasing. She never complained of any amount of interruption or of trouble which his claims upon her time might occasion. One day that she was reciting in her room the office of the Blessed Virgin, he sent for her. Instantly rising from her knees, she obeyed his summons. When she had performed the trifling service he required, she returned to her prayers. Four successive times, for the most insignificant of purposes, she was sent for: each time, with unwearied good humour, she complied, and resumed her devotions without a shadow of discontent or annoyance. On resuming her book the last time that this occurred, great was her astonishment in finding the antiphon, which she had four times begun and four times left unfinished, written in letters of gold. Vannozza, who was present, witnessed the miracle; and the archangel whispered to Francesca, "Thus the Lord rewards the virtue of obedience." The gilded letters remained in the book to the day of her death.

Her prayers were frequent; her fervour in proportion. Beginning with the "Our Father" and the "Hail Mary," it was her practice to recite them slowly, and to ponder on each word as she pronounced it. The Office of the Blessed Virgin she repeated daily at the appointed hours, and almost always on her knees; the Rosary also, and a great number of psalms besides, as well as various devotions for the holy souls in purgatory. As to mental prayer, her whole life was one continued orison; ever in communion with God, she never lost the sense of His presence. From this time forward (she was now thirty-two years old), her life grew more and more supernatural. The mystical wonders that have manifested themselves in so many saints were displayed in her to an eminent degree. When she approached the tribunal of penance, but, above all, in going to communion, her body sometimes emitted a fragrant odour, and a halo of light surrounded her head. Often and often, after receiving the Bread of Life, she fell into a long ecstasy, and for hours remained motionless, and wrapt up in silent contemplation, unable to move from the spot but at the command of her director; the virtue of obedience overcoming even the mystical insensibility to all outward objects. Her intimate intercourse with heaven during those moments; the prophecies which she uttered; the manner in which distant and future occurrences were made manifest to her spiritual perceptions, testified to the supernatural nature of these ecstasies. An intimate union established itself between her and the objects of her incessant contemplation. When she meditated on the glorious mysteries, on the triumphs of Mary, or the bliss of the angelic spirits, an intense joy beamed in her face, and pervaded her whole person. When, on the other hand, she mused on the Passion of our Lord, or on the sorrows of His Mother, the whole expression of her face was changed, and bore the impress of an unutterable woe; and even by physical pains she partook in a measure of the sufferings of her God. The anxious torments of the Passion were rehearsed as it were in her body; and ere long a wound in her side manifested one of the most astonishing but indubitably established instances of the real though mystical share which some of the saints have had in the life-giving agonies of the Lord. None but Vannozza, who used to dress that touching and awful wound, and Don Antonio, to whom she revealed it in confession, were acquainted with this extraordinary token of union between the crucified Redeemer and His favoured servant. She suffered intense pain while it lasted, but it was a joyful suffering. Love made it precious to her. She had desired to drink of His cup, and be baptised with His baptism; and He destined her one day to sit at His side and share His glory. She had drunk to the dregs the cup of earthly sorrow; the anguish of bereavement, the desolation of loneliness, the torments of fear, the pangs of sickness and poverty. And now the most mysterious sufferings fell to her lot, of a nature too sacred for common mention, for man's investigation, but not the less real and true than the others. The relief was as miraculous as the infliction. In a vision she saw herself transported into the cave of Bethlehem, and into the presence of the Infant Jesus and of His Mother. With a sweet smile, the Blessed Virgin bade Francesca discover the wound which love had made, and then with water that flowed from the rock, she washed her side, and dismissed her. When her ecstasy was over, she found that the miraculous wound was perfectly healed.

It was at this time that she predicted in the most positive manner, and when appearances were all against such a result, that the papal schism was about to end. The Council of Constance was sitting, and new difficulties and conflicts continually arose. War was on the point of bursting out again, and every body trembling at the thought of fresh disasters. Contrary, however, to all expectations, the last weeks of the year 1415 saw the conclusion of the schism. The assembled fathers, with a courage that none had foreseen, and indifferent to the threats of Frederick of Austria on the one side, and of the King of France on the other, who were each advocating the cause of an anti-pope,—the former supporting John XXIII., the latter Benedict XIII.,—they deposed these two usurpers, obliged Gregory XII. to renounce his pretensions also, and on the 11th of November unanimously elected Otto Colonna, Cardinal Deacon of St. George in Velabro, who took the name of Martin V.; and by his virtues and his talents succeeded in restoring: peace to Rome itself, and to the whole Catholic world. It was generally supposed, even during her lifetime, and much more after her death, that Francesca's prayers, her tears and her sufferings, had accelerated that blessed event, and drawn down the mercy of God on His afflicted Church.

The son of Lorenzo and Francesca. Baptista Ponziano, had now arrived at the age of eighteen, and was considered the most promising of the young Roman noblemen. The excellent education he had received was bearing its fruits. In appearance and in manners, in talents and in character, he was equally distinguished. Lorenzo, anxious to perpetuate his family, and secure heirs to his large possessions, pressed his son to marry. It was with the greatest satisfaction that Francesca seconded his wishes. She longed to give up to a daughter-in-law the management of domestic affairs, and to be more free to devote her time to religious and charitable employments. The young person on whom the choice of Baptista and of his parents fell was Mobilia, a maiden of whom it is recorded that she was of noble birth and of singular beauty, but her family name is not mentioned. Immediately upon her marriage, according to the continental custom of the time, the bride came to reside under the same roof as her father and mother-in-law. She was received as a beloved daughter by Francesca and Vannozza; but she neither returned their affection nor appeared sensible of their kindness. Brought up by an excellent mother in a very strict manner and entire seclusion, her head was completely turned at suddenly finding herself her own mistress: adored by her husband, furnished with the most ample means of gratifying all her fancies, she was bent on making up for the somewhat austere life she had led as a young girl, and gave no thought to any thing but her beauty, her dress, and all the amusements within her reach. Wholly inexperienced, she declined to ask or to receive advice, and chose in every respect to be guided by her inclinations alone. Imperious with her equals, haughty with her superiors, she gave herself all the airs imaginable, and treated her mother-in-law with the most supreme contempt, hardly paying her more attention than if she had been the lowest menial in the house. In the gay societies which she frequented, it was her favourite amusement to turn Francesca into ridicule, to mimic her manners and her style of conversation; and she often declared herself perfectly ashamed of being related to a person so totally ignorant of the ways of the world. "How can one feel any respect," she used to ask, "for a person who thinks of nothing but the poor, dresses as one of them, and goes about the streets carrying bread, wood, and old clothes?" It was not that Mobilia's disposition was absolutely bad; on the contrary, she was naturally sweet-tempered; but never having been left before to her own management, and tasting for the first time the exciting pleasures of the world, the contrast which her mother-in-law's appearance, manners, and whole mode of life presented to that which seemed to her so attractive, irritated her beyond measure, till at last her dislike amounted to aversion; she could hardly endure Francesca in her sight. Vain were the remonstrances of her husband and of her father-in-law, vain their entreaties and their reproofs; unavailing also proved the interference of some mutual friends, who sought to convince her of the culpability of her conduct, and to persuade her that she was bound to show Baptista's mother at least the attentions of ordinary civility. The headstrong young woman persisted in exhibiting the utmost contempt for her. The Saint endured all her frowardness with unvarying gentleness and patience, never uttering a sharp or unkind word in return, and spending long hours in prayer that the heart so closed against her, and so given up to the world, might through God's mercy be softened and changed. One day, when she was renewing these petitions with more than common fervour, she heard the following words distinctly pronounced in her hearing: "Why do you grieve, Francesca? and why is your soul disquieted? Nothing takes place without My permission, and all things work together for the good of those who love Me." And her trial was even then about to end. It happened a few days afterwards, when all the inhabitants of the palace were assembled round the fire in the hall (for it was in the winter season), that Mobilia began as usual to attack her mother-in-law, and to turn her mode of life into ridicule, with even greater bitterness than usual; and turning to her husband and to his father, she exclaimed impatiently that she could not understand how they allowed her to follow her mean and degrading pursuits, to mix with the refuse of the rabble, and draw down upon the whole family not only merited disgrace, but intolerable inconveniences. She was going on in this way, and speaking with great violence, when all of a sudden she turned as pale as death, a fit of trembling came over her, and in a moment she fell back senseless. Francesca and Vannozza carried her to her bed, where, recovering her consciousness, she was seized with most acute pains. The intensity of her sufferings drew from her the most piteous cries. Then her conscience was roused; then, as if suddenly awakened to a sense of the enormity of her conduct, with a faltering voice she murmured: "My pride! my dreadful pride!" Francesca bent over her gently, entreated her to bear her sufferings patiently, assured her they would soon subside. Then Mobilia burst into an agony of tears, and exclaimed before all the bystanders, "They will subside, my dear mother, if you ask it of God; but I have deserved more, much more, by my horrible behaviour to you. Forgive me, dear mother; pray for me. I acknowledge my fault. Henceforward, if God spares my life, your daughter will be to you the most loving, the most obedient of handmaids. Take me in your arms, mother, and bless your child." Francesca pressed to her bosom the beautiful young creature in whom such a change had been suddenly wrought, and while she fervently blessed her, Mobilia felt that all her pains had left her.

From that day forward the whole tone of her mind was altered; her conversion was complete. Francesca became to her an object of the most affectionate veneration; she consulted her about all her actions, and communicated to her her most secret thoughts. Utterly despising the vanities of the world which had led her astray, she adopted her views and opinions, and set entirely at naught the seductions of worldly grandeur. The sanctity of Francesca was now so evident to her that she began to watch her actions, her words, every detail of her life, with a mixture of awe and of interest; and kept a record in writing of all that she observed, and of the miraculous occurrences which were so often taking place through her instrumentality, as well as in her own person. The forementioned particulars she attested upon oath after the Saint's death, when the depositions were taken which served at a later period for the process of her canonisation. The most intimate friendship established itself between Baptista's wife and his mother; nothing could exceed the devoted and affectionate reverence of the one, or the tenderness with which it was repaid by the other. Francesca, with the most watchful love, attended to Mobilia's slightest wants or wishes: nursed her assiduously in her confinements, and bestowed upon her grandchildren the same cares that she had lavished on her own children. It was a great relief to her that Mobilia, who was now only occupied with her duties, assumed at her request the management of the house, and the regulation of all domestic affairs. She was thus enabled to devote herself more unreservedly to the service of the poor and of the hospitals. The hospital which she visited most constantly was that which her father-in-law had founded near the Chiesa del Salvatore, called at a later period Santa Maria in Cappella. The miracles wrought by the laying on of her hands became more numerous than ever, and her fame increased in proportion. The degree in which her assistance was sought, her prayers implored, and the reputation of her sanctity extended, was painful to her humility; but her supernatural gifts were too evident to be concealed from others or from herself, and there only remained to her to humble herself more deeply at the feet of the God who thus showed forth His power in one whom she deemed the most worthless of His creatures.

A great work was preparing for her hand to do; the first stone of a spiritual building was to be laid; she was growing ripe for the work; and God was drawing men's eyes upon her with wonder and with awe, that when that day came they might listen to her voice. The warnings which she gave to persons threatened by secret dangers were innumerable; her insight into the condition of their souls marvellous. One day she sends word to her confessor that he will be "sent for on the following night to attend a sick person, but that he must on no account leave his house;" and it turns out that assassins were lying in wait for him in the street, and that the pretended sick man was a lure to draw him out. Another time a youth of sixteen, Jacopo Vincenzo, is lying dangerously ill in the Piazza Campitelli. His mother hastens to the Saint, who smiles when she enters the room, and bids her go in peace, for her son has recovered; and on her return she finds him in perfect health. She sees a priest at the altar, and he appears to her sight as if covered with a frightful leprosy. By her confessor's order she relates her vision to the object of it; and, confounded and amazed, the unhappy man acknowledges that he was celebrating in a state of mortal sin. He repents, confesses, and amends his life. Two men pay a visit together to the Ponziano Palace; one is the nephew of Vannozza, a pious and exemplary priest; the other a young man of twenty, whom he has adopted. Anger is working in the bosom of the youth; he has suffered from his benefactor some imaginary wrong, and he is planning his revenge, and is about to utter a calumny which will affect his character. Francesca takes him aside: what can she know of what is passing in his soul: how read what has not been revealed to any human creature? She tells him what he designs, and awakens him to a sense of his ingratitude, he no sooner has left the house than, falling at the feet of his companion, he confesses to him his crime, and implores his forgiveness. Cecca Clarelli, a relation of the Ponziani, is delivered of a little girl in such apparent good health that no one thinks of baptising her; a grand ceremony for the purpose is preparing in a neighbouring church, to take place the following day; but in the middle of the night Francesca arrives, and entreats that the child may be instantly baptised. The parents and the priest object, but the Saint is urgent; she will take no denial; with reluctance her request is complied with, and no sooner has the sacrament been conferred than the infant expires. A child of the same parents, a lovely little girl, is dumb; she is four years old, and not a single word has she ever pronounced. Andreozzo, her father, entreats his wife to carry her to the Saint, and implore her assistance. Francesca's humility cannot endure this direct appeal, and she tries to put them off; but, deeply affected by their tears, she at last touches with her finger the tongue of the little Camilla, and says, "Hope every thing from the mercy of God; it is as boundless as His power." The parents depart full of faith and comfort; and ere they reach their house, the child has uttered with perfect distinctness the blessed names of Jesus and Mary; and from that day forward acquires and retains the power of speech.

No wonder that the name of Francesca grows every day more famous, and that she is every day more dear to the people amongst whom she dwells; that hearts are subdued, sinners reclaimed, mourners consoled by the sight of her blessed face, by the sweet sound of her voice. Many rise about her and call her blessed; but children, and more especially her own spiritual children, are soon to call her mother. A new epoch is now at hand in her career. God had placed in her heart many years ago a hope which she had nursed in secret, and watered with her tears, and fostered by her prayers. Never impatient, never beforehand with God's providence, she waited: His time was she knew to be her time; His will was the passion of her heart, her end, her rule, and God had made her will His, and brought about by slow degrees its accomplishment. Permission to labour first,—the result far distant, but clear, the vision of that result, when once He had said to her, "Begin and work." To tarry patiently for that signal, to obey it unhesitatingly when once given, is the rule of the saints. How marvellous is their instinct! how accordant their practice! First, the hidden life, the common life; the silence of the house of Nazareth; the carpenter's shop; the marriage-feast, it may be, for some; and at last, "the hour is come," and the true work for which they are sent into the world has to be done, in the desert or in the cloister, in the temple or in the market-place, on Mount Thabor or on Mount Calvary; and the martyr or the confessor, the founder or the reformer of a religious order, comes forth, and in an instant, or in a few years, performs a work at which earth wonders and angels rejoice.

CHAPTER X.

FRANCESCA LAYS THE FOUNDATION OF HER FUTURE CONGREGATION—HER PILGRIMAGE TO ASSISI.

LORENZO PONZIANO'S admiration and affection for his wife had gone on increasing with advancing years; the perfection of her life, and the miracles he had so often seen her perform, inspired him with an unbounded reverence. His continual prayer, the ardent desire of his heart, was to have her by his side as his guide and his guardian angel during the remainder of his life and at the hour of his death. Perhaps it was to win, as it were, from Providence the favour he so earnestly implored, that he resolved in no way to be a clog on her actions, or an obstacle in the way of God's designs upon her. Taking her aside one day, he spoke to her with the greatest affection, and offered to release her from all the obligations imposed by the state of marriage, to allow her the fullest liberty of action and the most absolute control over her own person, her own time, and her own conduct, on one only condition,—that she would promise never to cease to inhabit his house, and to guide him in the way in which her example had hitherto led him. Francesca, profoundly touched by his kindness, did not hesitate to give this promise. She accepted his proposal joyfully and gratefully, in so much as it conduced to the accomplishment of God's will and of His ulterior designs upon her; but she continued to devote herself to her excellent husband, and with the most attentive solicitude to render him every service in her power. He was now in very declining health, and she rendered him by day and by night all the cares of the tenderest nurse. The religious life, the natural complement of such a course as hers had been, often formed the subject of her meditations;

and God, who destined her to be the foundress of a new congregation of pious women, suggested to her at this time the first steps towards its accomplishment.

It will be remembered that from her childhood upward she had been used to frequent the church of Santa Maria Nuova, on the Foro Romano; her mother had done so before her, and had intrusted her to the spiritual direction of one of the most eminent members of the order by whom that church was served. Santa Maria Nuova is one of the oldest churches in Rome. It had been destroyed and rebuilt in the eighth century; and in 1352 had been given up to the Olivetan monks of St. Benedict. As the congregation which Francesca instituted was originally formed on the model, and aggregated to that of the religions of Mount Olivet, it will not be irrelevant to give some account of their origin and the life of their illustrious founder.

Bernard Ptolomei or Tolomei, who was supposed to be descended from the Ptolemies of Egypt, was born in 1272. Distinguished by his precocious abilities, he became, at the early age of twenty-two, chief-magistrate (*gonfaloniere*) of his native town, Sienna; and at twenty-five attained to the dignity of doge. Soon after he was suddenly struck with blindness, and the material darkness in which he found himself involved opened his mental sight to the light of religious truth. He turned with his whole heart to God, and irrevocably devoted himself to His service and to a life of austerity and meditation. The Blessed Virgin miraculously restored his sight, and his purpose stood firm. Dividing his fortune into two equal parts, he bestowed one half on the poor, and the other to the foundation of pious institutions. With a few companions he retired into the mountainous deserts of Accona, about fifteen miles from Sienna, where they gave themselves up to a life of asceticism and prayer, which attracted to their solitude many devout souls from various parts of the world. Satan, as usual, set his batteries in array against the new anchorites, and trials of various sorts assailed them in turn. They were even denounced to Pope John XXII. as persons tainted with heresy; but Tolomei, with Piccolomini, one of his companions, made their way to Avignon, and there, in the presence of the sovereign Pontiff, completely cleared themselves from the calumnious imputation. Their order was approved, and they returned to Accona, where they took the name of "Congregation of Mary of Mount Olivet of the Benedictine Order." This was by the express desire of the Blessed Virgin, who had appeared to the saint, and enjoined him to adopt the rule of St. Benedict, promising at the same time her protection to the new order. On the 26th of March, 1319, the new religious received their habits; and Mount Accona took the name of Mount Olivet, in honour of the agony of our Lord. Terrible were the conflicts of the holy founder with the Evil One; but out of them all he came victorious. His expositions of Scripture were wonderful, and derived, it was said, from his mystical colloquies with the archangel St. Michael. The austerity of his life was extreme; his penances severe and continual. In 1348 St. Benedict appeared to him and announced the approach of the pestilence which was soon to visit Italy, and warned him of his own death, which speedily followed. Many of his disciples had visions of the glorious translation of his soul to heaven; and numerous miracles wrought at his tomb bore witness to his sanctity. His monks inhabited the church and the cloisters of Santa Maria in Dominica, or, as it is more commonly called, in Navicella, from the rudely-sculptured marble monument that stands on the grass before its portal, a remnant of bygone days, to which neither history nor tradition has given a name, but which has itself given one to the picturesque old church that stands on the brow of the Coelian Hill. As their numbers afterwards increased, they were put to great inconvenience by the narrow limits of their abode; and Cardinal Beltorte, titular of Santa Maria Nuova, obtained for them from Pope Clement VI. possession of the church of that name. They accepted the gift with joy; for not only did it owe its origin to the first ages of Christianity, but it contained many valuable relics; and amongst other treasures one of those pictures of the Blessed Virgin which tradition has ascribed to St. Luke the Evangelist; to this day it is venerated in that spot; and those who kneel at the tomb of St. Francesca Romana, on raising their eyes to the altar above it behold the sacred image which has been venerated for so many generations.

Through prosperity and adversity Francesca had never ceased to frequent that church. At its confessional and at its altars she had been a constant attendant. Other women, her friends and imitators, had followed her example; bound by a tender friendship, bent on the same objects, united by the same love of Jesus and of Mary, often and often they had been there together, those noble women who had resolved to glory in nothing but the Cross, to have no rank but that of handmaids in the house of the Lord. Francesca was their model, their teacher, their cherished guide: they clung to her with the tenderest affection;

they were, according to an Eastern poet's expression[1], a row of goodly pearls, and she the silken cord which bound them together. They were coming out of the church one evening, when Francesca gave them the first intimation of her hopes of their future destiny. They were not shown the distant scene, only the first step they were to take[2].

It was one of those small beginnings so trifling in men's sight, so important in their results,—the grain of mustard-seed hereafter to grow into a tree. Francesca spoke to them, as they walked along, of the order of St. Benedict, of the sanctity of its founder, of the virtues, the piety, the good works of its members, and submitted to them that by taking the name of "Oblates of Mount Olivet," and observing conjointly certain rules, such as might befit persons living in the world, they might participate in their merits, and enjoy their privileges. Her companions hailed this proposal with joy, and begged her to use all her efforts to carry it into effect. Don Antonio, to whom Francesca communicated their pious wishes, lent a favourable ear to the request, and in his turn brought it under the notice of the Vice-Prior Don Ippolito, who, in the absence of the superior, was charged with the government of the monastery. He was the same who at one time formed the project of leaving the order, and was deterred from so doing by Francesca's advice. He readily received their overtures, and obtained for her and for her companions from the General of the Order permission to assume the name of "Oblates of Mary," a particular aggregation to the monastery of Santa Maria Nuova, and a share in the suffrages and merits of the order of St. Benedict.

Greatly rejoiced at the happy result of their application, they gave themselves to fasting, prayer, and penance, in preparation for their special consecration to the Blessed Virgin. It took place on the Feast of the Assumption of the year 1425.

At break of day, in the church of Santa Maria Nuova, Francesca, Vannozza, Rita de Celli, Agnese Selli, and six more noble Roman ladies, confessed, received the pious instructions of Don Antonio, and communicated at a Mass which Don Ippolito said before the miraculous image of the Blessed Virgin. Immediately after the holy sacrifice,

---

[1] :"They a row of pearls, and I
   The silken cord on which they lie."
[2] :"Lead thou me on; I do not ask to see
   The distant scene: one step enough for me."
   Newman's *Verses on Religious Subjects*]

they dedicated themselves to her service, according to the formula used by the Olivetan monks; only that the phrase "me offero" was substituted for "profiteor;" and that instead of taking solemn vows, they were simply affiliated to the Benedictine Order of Mount Olivet. Such was the first beginning of the congregation of which Francesca was the mother and foundress. In these early times, Don Antonio, their director, did not assign them any special occupation, and only urged them to the most scrupulous obedience to the commandments of God and of the Church, to a tender devotion to the Mother of God, a diligent participation in the Sacraments, and the exercise of all the Christian virtues, and the various works of mercy. The link between them consisted in their constant attendance at the church of Santa Maria Nuova, where they received communion on all the Feasts of our Lady, and in a tender veneration for Francesca, whom they looked upon as their spiritual mother. They had incessant recourse to her advice; and her simplest words were as a law to them, her conduct their example. She assumed no power, and disclaimed all authority; but the sovereign empire of love was forced into her reluctant hands. They insisted on being governed by one they held in such affection, and gave up every pleasure for the sake of being with her, and sharing in her pursuits.

It was in the summer of the following year that Francesca decided on performing a pilgrimage to Santa Maria, or, as it is more commonly called "La Madonna degli Angeli," in honour of our Lady and of the seraphic Saint of Assisi. Vannozza and Rita eagerly agreed to accompany her; and they resolved to set out on the 2d of August, in order to arrive in time for the celebrated indulgence "del Perdono." It was in poverty, not only of spirit but of actual reality that they wished, to perform their journey to the tomb of the great apostle of poverty,—to go on foot, and unprovided with money, provisions, or comforts of any sort. Lorenzo and Parazza, who had readily consented to the proposed pilgrimage, demurred for a while at this mode of carrying it out; but Francesca prayed in her oratory that God would incline their hearts to consent to it; and soon, with a reluctant smile, they consented to all she proposed, and both only ejaculated, "Go on your way in peace; do as you list, and only pray for us." Out of the gates of Rome they went, through that country so well known to those who have often visited the Eternal City; up the hill from whence the first sight of its domes and its towers, of its tombs and of its pines, is hailed with rapture, from whence a long last lingering look of love is cast upon what the heart whispers is its own Catholic home. It was the first, and as it would seem the only occasion (at least none other is mentioned in her life) in

which Francesca left its walls, and trod other ground than that which
the steps of so many martyrs have hallowed, the blood of so many
saints has consecrated. The valleys of Veii on the one hand, the
heights of Baccano on the other, the beautiful and stately mountain of
Soracte, met their eyes as they do ours: would that we looked upon
them with the same earth-abstracted gaze as theirs! The Gothic towers
of Civita Castellana looked down upon the humble pilgrims as they
passed by in pious meditation. The sound of their sweet voices, reciting prayers or chanting hymns, mingled with the murmurs of the
stream that bathes the old walls of Nurni; and then through the wild
defile of Monte Somma into the lovely Umbrian Vale they went,
through that enchanting land where every tree and rock wears the form
that Claude Lorraine or Salvator Rosa have made familiar to the eye
and dear to the poetic mind; where the vines hang in graceful garlands,
and the fireflies at night dance from bough to bough; where the brooks
and the rivers are of the colour of the sapphire or the emerald, and the
purple mountains smile rather than frown on the sunny landscape;
where the towns and the convents, the churches and the cottages, are
set like white gems in the deep verdure that surrounds them. There is
no land more fair, no sky more tenderly blue, no breeze more balmy,
than the land where Spoleto and Toligno and Assisi rise in their picturesque beauty, than the sky which spreads its azure roof over the
Umbrian traveller's head, than the airs which are wafted from the
heights of Monte Falco, or the hill of Perugia. Beautiful is that country! fair these works of God!—but more beautiful still is the invisible
world which Francesca and her companions contemplated, the while,
with weary patient feet, in the sultry August weather, they trod the
lengthening road from one humble resting-place to another. Fairer the
inward perfection of a soul which God has renewed, than all the gorgeous but evanescent loveliness of earth's most lovely scenes.

At length their pilgrimage is drawing to a close; the towers of the
Madonna degli Angeli are conspicuous in the distance; half uncon-
sciously they hasten in approaching it; but the heat is intense, and their
lips parched with thirst; they can hardly speak, for their tongues cleave
to the roof of their mouths, when a stranger meets them, one of striking and venerable appearance, and clothed in the religious habit of St.
Francis. He hails the travellers, and straightway speaks of Mary and of
Jesus, of the mystery of the Passion, of the wonders of Divine love.
Never have such words of fire met the ears of the astonished pilgrims.
Their hearts burn within them, and they are ready to exclaim, "Never
did man speak like to this man." Francesca sees her angel assume his

brightest aspect. Hays of light seem to dart from his form, and to envelope in a dazzling halo the monk who is addressing them. She knows him now; and makes a sign to her companions. It is St. Francis himself. It is the seraphic saint of Assisi. He blesses the little troop, and touching a wild pear-tree by the road-side, he brings down to the ground a fruit of such prodigious size, that it serves to allay the thirst and restore the strength of the exhausted travellers.

That day they reached the shrine where they had so longed to kneel; that little hut, once the abode of the saint, which stands in its rough simplicity within the gorgeous church; where the rich and great of the world come daily to do homage to the apostle of poverty, the close imitator of Him who had not often where to lay His head. There they received communion the next morning; there they prayed for their absent friends; there Francesca had a vision, in which she was encouraged to persevere in her labours, to accomplish her pious design, and the protection of Jesus and His Mother was promised to her. Let us follow them in thought up the steep hill to Assisi—to the church where the relics of the saint, where his mortal remains are laid. Let us descend into the subterranean chapel, pause at every altar, and muse on the records of that astonishing life, the most marvellous perhaps of any which it has ever been permitted to mortal man to live. Let us go with them to the home of his youth, where his confessorship began in childish sufferings for the sake of Christ. Let us venerate with them the relics of St. Clare, the gentle sister spirit whose memory and whose order are linked with his; and for a moment think what prayers, what vows, what acts of faith, of hope, of charity, must have risen like incense from those devoted hearts in such scenes, amidst such recollections. Doubtless they bore away with them a host of sweet and pious thoughts. Their faces must have shone with heaven's own light as they retraced their steps to the home where loving hearts were awaiting them. Few such pilgrimages can have ever been performed, Francesca at the tomb of St. Francis of Assisi must have been a blessed sight even for an angel's eyes.

CHAPTER XI.

DEATH OF FRANCESCA'S FRIEND AND DIRECTOR, DON ANTONIO—TROUBLES IN ROME AND ITALY FORETOLD BY FRANCESCA—DEATH OF VANNOZZA, FRANCESCA'S SISTER IN LAW— FOUNDATION OF THE CONGREGATION OF OBLATES OF TOR DI SPECCHI.

THE extraordinary graces which had attended our Saint during her pilgrimage were the prelude of a trial which was awaiting her in Rome. Her earliest friend, her long-trusted guide, Don Antonio Savello, had died during her absence. Though she accepted this dispensation of God's providence with her habitual resignation, it cut her to the heart. She had deeply loved and reverenced her spiritual father; he had instructed her in childhood; directed her ever since with wisdom and faithfulness; and his loss was in one sense greater to her than that of any other friend. It occurred, too, at the very moment when she was about to carry out the Divine intimation with regard to the foundation of a new Congregation, when difficulties were every where staring her in the face, and the want of a powerful and willing auxiliary more than ever needful. She did not, however, lose courage, but prayed fervently that God would inspire her choice of a director; and much time she spent on her knees imploring this favour. No doubt the selection she made was the result of these prayers; and one of the proofs that God's ways are not as our ways, nor His thoughts as our thoughts. Her choice fell on Don Giovanni Mattiotti, the curate of Santa Maria in Trastevere, to whom she had already sometimes been to confession. He was a man of irreproachable character and distinguished piety, but of an irresolute and vaccillating disposition, easily disheartened; nor would he at first sight have appeared qualified for the direction of a person as far advanced in perfection as Francesca, on whom God had such great designs, and with whom He chose to deal in such wonderful ways. But the trials which Francesca had to endure from the irresolution of Don Giovanni; the patience with which she submitted to his varying commands; and the supernatural means through which he was taught to recognise her sanctity, and to assist in carrying out her designs, tended in the end to the glory of God, and the praise of the Saint, whose very humility was a trial to her, in those days of small beginnings, and often of painful doubts. Crosses of various kinds arose in connection with the undertaking. Some of the monks of Santa Maria Nuova, for instance, took occasion, on the visits of a father inspector, to complain of Don Ippolito, and to accuse him of transgressing the statutes, and going beyond his powers, in admitting a congregation of women to the name and the privileges of their order; especially considering that several of these women were married, and living in the world. But the visitor was a man of piety and prudence. He closely examined into the question, and satisfied himself that the institution tended to edification, and was pleasing to God; and he sanctioned it accordingly, as far as was in his power, and promised to advocate its cause with the father-general.

In the month of July of 1430 Francesca had a remarkable vision, which indicated to her the events that were speedily to follow, and which she prophesied with an accuracy, that, in the end, occasioned general astonishment. One night, after spending several hours in prayer, she saw a lurid light, through which a number of Satan's ministers were hurrying to and fro, shaking their torches, and rejoicing with dreadful glee over the impending calamities of Rome. The Saint fell on her knees, and besought the Lord to spare her unhappy country. Then falling into ecstasy, she beheld the Infant Jesus in His Mother's arms surrounded with angels, and St. Peter, St. Paul, and St. John the Baptist in the attitude of prayer, pleading for mercy to the Eternal City, which they seemed to protect by their fervent supplications. At the same time she heard a voice that said, "The prayers of the saints have stayed the arm of the Lord; but woe to the guilty city if she repent not, for great afflictions are at hand." Some days afterwards the lightning fell simultaneously on the churches of St. Peter, St. Paul, and on the shrine of St. John Baptist in the Lateran Basilica. Francesca shuddered when she heard of it; she felt at once that the day of grace had gone by; and in thrilling words described to her confessor, and to several other persons that were present, the misfortunes that were about to fall upon Rome.

The fulfilment of her predictions was not long delayed, though nothing at the time seemed to give them weight. The unwearied exertions of Martin V. had succeeded in healing the wounds of Christendom. In Rome he had repressed anarchy, recalled the exiled citizens to their homes, rebuilt the churches, given a new impulse to the government, to the administration of justice, to politics, to literature, to science, and to art. He had worked hard to promote a reformation in the manners of the clergy, and effected in many places the re-establishment of the discipline of the Church. The legates whom he sent to all the courts of Europe had restored some degree of union between the Christian princes, and preached a crusade against the Turks and the followers of John Huss. He had called together a council, which was first convened at Pavia, and afterwards removed, first to Sienna, and then to Basle. But before he could him self join the assembly, death overtook him. Worn out with his indefatigable labours for the welfare of Christendom, he went to receive his reward at an unadvanced age, in the month of February of the year 1431.

Gabriel Candalucero succeeded him under the name of Eugenius IV. The first Consistory which he held was marked by a fearful accident, which people chose to consider as an evil omen. The floor of the hall gave way, and in the midst of the confusion that ensued a bishop was killed, and many persons grievously wounded. A discontented monk put about the report that Martin V. had died in possession of a considerable treasure; and the Colonnas, catching eagerly at this pretext, took up arms to make good their claims to this supposed heritage. Once more the adverse factions rose against each other, and blood flowed in the streets of Rome. The Colonnas were constrained to fly; and the monk, convicted of having conspired to deliver up the Castle of St. Angelo to the rebels, and to get the Pope assassinated, was condemned to death and executed. A temporary reconciliation was effected between Eugenius IV. and the too powerful family of the Colonnas; but their haughty and violent temper soon brought about a rupture. They advanced upon Rome at the head of their troops; a bloody engagement took place under the walls of the city, in which the pontifical troops had the upper hand, but many of the nobles perished in the affray.

Conflicts of a still more harrowing nature now arose between the Pope and the Council of Basle. Duke Philip of Milan availed himself of this opportunity to retrieve the sacrifices he had made in a treaty which the Pope had led him to sign with the Venetians. He forged a decree which, purported to proceed from the fathers of the council, appointing him lieutenant-general of the Church in Italy; and armed with this assumed title, he despatched to the Roman States Francesca Sforza and Nicholas Fortebraccio, two famous adventurers in his pay. The latter advanced upon Rome, and began to devastate its neighbourhood. The Pope, wholly unprepared for defence, warded off the danger by sowing dissension between the two generals, which he effected by giving up to Sforza, for his lifetime, the possession of Ancona, and of the provinces which he had conquered in the states of the Church. Sforza, in consequence, took part with Eugenius, and defeated Fortebraccio at Tivoli; but in the meantime a general insurrection broke out in Rome itself. The Ghibelline party attacked the Pope, laid siege to the church of the Holy Apostles, where he had taken shelter, and from whence he escaped with difficulty disguised as a monk, embarked on the Tiber, and found a refuge first at Pisa and then at Bologna. Rome was given up for five months to all the horrors of anarchy, the pontifical palace pillaged, and new magistrates chosen in lieu of those appointed by the Pope; the garrison of the castle of St. Angelo alone remaining firm in its allegiance to the sovereign Pontiff. Weary at last of so much disorder, the city of its own accord submitted itself to lawful authority. Eugenius sent a legate, who in some measure succeeded in re-establishing peace; but he himself remained in the north of Italy, engaged in convoking a council, wherewith to oppose the irregular decrees of that assembled at Basle.

These events, which spread over several years, are related in confirmation of the prophetical gifts of Francesca, who accurately foresaw and foretold them when nothing presaged their occurrence. At the time when this storm was about to burst over Italy, and the beginning of sorrow was at hand, she was doomed to experience another of the heavy afflictions that life had yet in store for her. Vannozza, her cherished companion, her sister, her counsellor, her bosom friend, was summoned to receive her heavenly crown; and she herself to add to all her virtues a more perfect detachment from all earthly ties. They had been united by every link that affection, sympathy, and similarity of feeling, tastes, and opinions can create between two hearts devoted to God, and through Him to each other. Their union had not been obscured by the smallest cloud. Together they had prayed, suffered, and laboured; and in trials and joys alike they had been inseparable. Francesca had been warned in a vision of the approaching end of her sister-in-law; and at length, strong in faith, she stands by her dying-bed; and when the Evil One, baffled in life, makes a final effort to disturb the departing soul, she prays for the beloved of her heart, sprinkles holy water on that much-loved form, reads aloud the history of the Passion of our Lord; and Vannozza, supported by those sacramental graces which Satan cannot withstand, followed almost beyond the verge of life by that watchful tenderness which had been her joy on earth, sees the evil spirit retire before the might of Francesca's angel, and breathes her last in perfect peace. The soul which had served and loved God so fervently upon earth was carried up to heaven in a form visible to the eyes of her friend; a pure flame, enveloped in a light transparent cloud, was the symbol of that gentle spirit's flight into its kindred skies.

The mortal remains of Vannozza were laid in the church of the Ara Coeli, in the chapel of Santa Croce. The Roman people resorted there in crowds to behold once more their loved benefactress,—the mother of the poor, the consoler of the afflicted. All strove to carry away some little memorial of one who had gone about among them doing good; and during the three days which preceded the interment, the concourse did not abate. On the day of the funeral, Francesca knelt on one side of the coffin, and, in sight of all the crowd, she was rapt in ecstasy. They saw her body lifted from the ground, and a seraphic expression in her uplifted face. They heard her murmur several times with an indescribable emphasis the word, "When? when?" (*Quando? quando?*) When all was over, she still remained immovable; it seemed as if her soul had risen on the wings of prayer, and followed Vannozza's spirit into the realms of bliss. At last her confessor ordered her to rise, and to go and attend on the sick. She instantly complied, and walked away to the hospital which she had founded, apparently unconscious of every thing about her, and only roused from her trance by the habit of obedience which, in or out of ecstasy, never forsook her.

From that day her visions grew more frequent and more astonishing. She seemed to live in heaven; and during those hours of mystical intercourse with saints and angels, and with the Lord of angels and of saints, to obtain supernatural lights which guided her in the foundation of her new congregation. The Blessed Virgin revealed to her that St. Paul, St. Benedict, and St. Mary Magdalene were to be its protectors; and that Don Giovanni Mattiotti, her director, Fra Bartolommeo Biondii, of the order of St. Francis, and Don Ippolito, of the Olivetan Obedience, were to co-operate with her in its establishment. To Don Giovanni a particular message was sent to confirm him in the intention of forwarding the work, and to warn him against discouragement from the many difficulties it would meet with. Wonderful were the sights which it was given her to see in those long ecstasies, during which her soul seemed to absent itself from her all-but spiritualised body. Sometimes a speechless contemplation held all her faculties in abeyance; at others, in burning words, she described what passed before her mental sight. At times her motionless attitude almost wore the semblance of death; while often she moved about and performed various actions in connection with the subjects of her visions. In the churches which she frequented,—in Santa Croce in Gerusalemme, in Santa Maria in Trastevere, in the Chapel of the Angels in Santa Cecilia, in her own oratory,—she is favoured with the presence of celestial visitants. The various ecclesiastical feasts of the year bring with them analogous revelations; she spends her time in the cave of Bethlehem and the house of Nazareth, on the mountains, where Jesus was wont to pray, where He was transfigured, where He agonised, and where He died. She adores with the shepherds and the wise men; she listens to His voice with the disciples and the devout multitude; she suffers with the Mother of sorrows, and weeps with the Magdalene at the foot of the Cross. The beauties of the New Jerusalem, the lovely pastures, the fresh waters, the bright flowers, the precious stones, which typify the glories of the world to come, are spread before her in those mystic trances. Deeper and more mysterious revelations are vouchsafed, wonderful secrets disclosed to her under expressive symbols, and St. Paul is her guide through those regions where he was ravished in spirit while still, like her, an inhabitant of earth. One day that she was in ecstasy a voice of more than common sweetness addressed to her these words—"Thy path is strewn with thorns, Francesca, and many an obstacle will stand in thy way, ere thy little flock can be gathered together in our abode. But remember that hail does not always follow upon thunder, and that the brightest sunshine often breaks through the darkest clouds."

Encouraged by this intimation, the Saint began in earnest to consider of the means of establishing her congregation. During a short absence which her husband made from Rome, she invited all the Oblates to her house, and having made them share her slight repast, she assembled them around her, and spoke to them to the following effect: "My dear companions, I have called you together in order to impart to you the lights which I have received from the Lord and His blessed Mother with regard to our congregation. For seven years we have been especially consecrated to her service, and have bound ourselves to live in chastity and obedience, and to observe the rules prescribed to us; and I have long thought that as we have been united in spirit and in intention, so ought we to be in our outward mode of life. For a while I fancied that this my desire might only be the result of my maternal affection for you, and of my solicitude for your advancement. But the Lord has at last revealed to me that it is His will that I should found a new spiritual edifice in this city, the ancient stronghold of religion and of faith. It will form an asylum for those persons of your sex and of your rank who have conceived the generous resolution of forsaking the world and its allurements; I have tagged of the Lord to select for His purpose one less unworthy than myself, but I dare no longer withstand the manifestation of His will. I am prepared to accomplish His bidding; but without you, my sisters what can I do? You are the foundations of the building, the first stones of the new spiritual house of His mother. You are the seed from which a plentiful harvest is to spring. Earthly cares, the temporal affairs of life, must no longer take up your time. He summons you to a retreat, where you will live in His presence, imitate His example, and copy the virtues of Mary, where you will pray for Rome, and turn away His wrath from the degenerate and guilty city. Have you not heard how two years ago the thunderbolts fell on her sacred towers? Do you not see how every day fresh miseries are gathering on the devoted heads of her people? But God is full of mercy; when most incensed at our sins, He casts about for souls that will appease His anger. He has turned His eyes upon us. He bids us unite, and stand in the breach between Him and the daring sinners who each day defy Him. Why tarry we longer? why further delay? The arms of the Blessed Virgin are wide open to receive us. Shall we draw back from her embrace?—No, rather let us fly to her feet."

As she pronounced these last words Francesca fell into an ecstasy, which lasted for some time, and during which she pleaded with God for those who were to belong to the new institute. Her companions gazed upon her with silent veneration; and when she came to herself, all with one accord, and with tears of joy, professed themselves ready to make every sacrifice which God might require of them, and to adopt the mode of life and the rule which Francesca might suggest. But their assent was only a preliminary step in the undertaking. It was necessary to find a house suitable to their purpose, to obtain the consent of the still existing parents of some of the Oblates, to fix in a definitive manner their rule and constitutions, and finally to procure the sanction of the Holy Father, and his approval of the new order. Francesca attended in turn to each of these objects. To the first place she consulted her three coadjutors on the choice of a house; and difficulties without number arose on this point. The priests were alarmed at the sensation which this undertaking would produce, and were quite at a loss to find money for the purchase. Francesca had long since given away almost all that she possessed. What little remained was devoted to works of charity which could not be abandoned, and all agreed that she was on no account to have recourse on this occasion to her husband or to her son. While they were deliberating, Francesca was favoured with a vision, in which the divine assistance was promised to the Oblates, and their protectors (Don Giovanni in particular) exhorted to perseverance. Encouraged by these assurances, they looked out for a house adapted to the requirements of a religious community; and after many researches Don Ippolito proposed to Don Giovanni a building in the Campitelli district, on the spot where the old tower, known by the name of "Tor di Specchi," used to stand, directly opposite to the Capitol, and not far from the Santa Maria Nuova. Various obstacles arose to the purchase of this house, which was neither as large nor as convenient as might have been wished; but they were finally overcome, and the acquisition completed towards the end of the year 1432. This house, which was at first considered only as a temporary residence, was subsequently added to, and has remained to this day the central house of the order; and in the pontifical bull the congregation is designed by the name of "Oblates of Tor di Specchi." This matter once arranged, Francesca succeeded in dissipating the objections raised by the parents of some of the younger Oblates, and to reconcile them to the proposed alteration in their daughters' mode of life. It was doubtless a trial to her that while she was removing all the difficulties in the way of the more perfect life which her companions were about to lead, she herself could only, like Moses, look on the promised land of spiritual seclusion which they, her disciples and her children, were entering on, and after which she had yearned from the days of her childhood. But she never hesitated as to her line of duty; it was clear before her. Lorenzo had released her from all obligations but one— that of residing in his house and watching over his old age. His infirmities were increasing, and her attentions indispensable to his comfort. No one could supply to him Francesca's care. She offered up to God the daily self-denial of her existence; and by fresh tokens of His favour He rewarded her obedience.

Her next anxiety was the formation of the constitution and of the rules which were to govern the infant congregation; and in frequent conferences with her pious coadjutors the subject was discussed. After many deliberations, during which they could arrive at no conclusion, it was agreed that the matter should be laid before God in prayer; and their hope was not deceived. In a series of visions,—in which St. Paul in the first instance, and on other occasions the blessed Virgin and St. John the Evangelist, appeared to Francesca,—directions were given her so ample and so detailed as to the rule which her spiritual daughters were to follow, that there remained no room for hesitation. The several fasts which they were to observe; the length of time which they were to devote to prayer, to work, and to sleep; the manner in which their actions were to be performed; the vocal prayers they were to recite; the solitude, the silence they were to keep; the poverty, the community of goods which they were to practise; their dress, their occupations, their separation from the world, their detachment from all earthly ties of interest and kindred which they were at all times to be inspired with; the precautions to be taken in procuring the consent of parents, and securing the free action of the Oblates who might hereafter join the order, were all indicated with the greatest precision; and instructions were transmitted to Don Giovanni and his co-operators to enlighten them as to the guidance and government of the congregation. The miraculous manner in which the Saint had often read their most secret thoughts, the miracles they saw her perform, and the admirable tenour of her life, in which the most active virtues were combined with the deepest humility, and supernatural favours received with the most profound self-abasement, were to them a warrant of the genuineness of her revelations, the substance of which, condensed and reduced into a series of rules, are to this day observed by the Oblates of Tor di Specchi.

CHAPTER XII.

PROGRESS AND TRIALS OF THE YOUNG COMMUNITY—IT IS CONFIRMED BY THE POPE—TROUBLES IN ROME AND THE CHURCH TERMINATED THROUGH FRANCESCA'S INTERCESSION AND THE COUNCIL OF FLORENCE.

It was on the 25th of March, the Feast of the Annunciation, in the year 1433, that the Oblates, ten in number, met in the church of Santa Maria in Trastevere, where their holy foundress had so long been in the habit of resorting. They all heard Mass, and went to communion with the utmost fervour, and then in procession proceeded to the house they were henceforward to inhabit. That house, which now-a-days is thrown open during the Octave of the Feast of San Francesca, where young women come with their little children, and point out to them the room which they inhabited in their own childhood, when under the gentle care of the Oblates of Mary. It is no gloomy abode, the Convent of Tor di Specchi even in the eyes of those who cannot understand the happiness of a nun. It is such a place which one loves to see children in; where religion is combined with every thing that pleases the eye and recreates the mind. The beautiful chapel; the garden with its magnificent orange-trees; the open galleries, with their fanciful decorations and scenic recesses, where a holy picture or figure takes you by surprise, and meets you at every turn; the light airy rooms where religious prints and ornaments, with flowers, birds, and ingenious toys, testify that innocent enjoyments are encouraged and smiled upon, while from every window may be caught a glimpse of the Eternal City, a spire, a ruined wall,—something that speaks of Rome and its thousand charms.

On Holy Thursday no sepulchre is more beautiful than that of Tor di Specchi. Flowers without end, and bright hangings, all sweet and costly things, do homage to the Lord in the hours of His loving imprisonment.

But on the day when Francesca's companions first entered those walls, there was nothing very fair or beautiful to greet them, though they earned there, however, in their hearts, from the altar they had just left, the source of all light and love; and to the eyes of faith the scene must have been a bright one. With delight they exchanged then ordinary dress for that which the rule prescribed: Francesca alone stood among them no nun in her outward garb, but the truest nun of all, through the inward consecration of her whole being to God. Agnese de Sellis, a relation of hers, and a woman highly distinguished for virtue and prudence was elected superior of the house. There was a truly admirable spectacle presented to the people of Rome; these women were all of noble birth, and accustomed to all the comforts and conveniences of life. Most of them had been wealthy; some of them were still young; and for the love of God they had given op every thing, and made over their possessions to their relations; for it was not to lead a life of ease, of religious quietude, of holy contemplation alone, that they had separated themselves from the world. It was to imitate the poverty of Christ, to place in the common stock, as the first Christians did, the little they had reserved, and to endure all the privations incident on poverty. Their exact and spontaneous obedience to the gentle Agnese was as remarkable as the sweetness and humility with which she ruled. Seldom seen abroad, their hours were divided between prayer, meditation, spiritual reading, and works of mercy[1]. Francesca, obliged to be absent from them in body, was ever present with them in spirit. She was the tenderest mother to the little flock that had gathered under her sheltering wing: ministering to their necessities; visiting them as often as she could leave her husband's side; exciting them on to perfection by her words and example; consoling the weak, and confirming the strong.

---

[1] The rule which they then adopted remains the same to this day. The Oblates of Tor di Speechi are not, strictly speaking, nuns: they take no vows, and are bound by no obligations under pain of sin; they are not cloistered, and their dress is that which was worn at the period of their establishment by the widows of the Roman nobles.

It was not to be expected that the infant congregation could be free from evil reports, and from the kind of persecution which ever attends the undertakings and tries the courage of God's most faithful servants. The mode of life of the Oblates became the general subject of conversation; and though the wiser and better portion of the community were filled with respect and admiration for their virtues, there were not wanting persons to raise a cry against them and against their foundress, and to complain that women should be allowed to lend an existence which was strictly speaking neither secular nor religious; a monastery without enclosure, without vows, without revenues, without any security for its permanent support. Their comments were not without effect on the naturally irresolute mind of Don Giovanni Mattiotti and Fra Bartolommeo Biandii. The former, in particular, grew discontented and desponding. The direction of the order was a heavy burden to him; and his faith in Francesca's revelations was shaken by the many worldly difficulties which he foresaw. The miraculous manner in which the Saint read his thoughts, and transmitted to him and his companion the reproofs and encouragements which were supernaturally addressed to them through the medium of one of her visions, opened their eyes to a sense of their pusillanimity, and made them ashamed of their misgivings.

Another threatened trial was, by the mercy of God, turned into a consolation. One of the youngest of the Oblates, Augustina Coluzzi, was the only child of her mother, who was a widow. This mother had made a generous sacrifice to God in gladly surrendering this beloved daughter to the exclusive service of Him who had called her to that high vocation; but she had miscalculated her sacrifice, or, perhaps, trusted too much to her own strength. When the sacrifice was made, the human feelings rose in her heart with terrible violence, and life appeared to her as one dreary blank, now that her home was shorn of its light, now that the beloved child of her heart had ceased to gladden her eyes. Self-reproach for their vain repinings heightened her misery, and misery at last grew into despair. In an instant of wild recklessness she seized a knife, and was about to destroy herself, when, like an angel at the hour of her utmost need, her daughter was at her side, and arrested her arm. It was so against all rules and all probabilities that she should have come to her at that moment, that she gazed on her in silent astonishment. Francesca was in prayer at the moment, when Satan had been tempting the unfortunate woman; and the dreadful danger she was in was miraculously revealed to her. She instantly ordered Augustina to leave what she was about, and hurry to her mother. The young girl arrived in time; and so great was the impression which this merciful interposition produced on the mother, so deep her sense of the peril to which her soul had been exposed, that she hastened to throw herself at Francesca's feet, and with blessings on her and on her daughter, she expressed her gratitude for Augustina's vocation, and her earnest wish that she should remain faithful to it.

Another trial arose in those early days at Tor di Specchi from the resolution formed by a wealthy young heiress to join the order. She belonged to one of the noblest families in Rome, and was bent on employing her fortune in supporting the infant congregation. Francesca was reluctant to receive her; but, over persuaded by the opinions of others, she gave way. A violent opposition immediately arose; and there was no end to the calumnies and vituperations which were employed on the occasion. Francesca, again enlightened by a divine intimation, insisted on restoring the young person to her family; and a rule was henceforward made that none but persons of a more advanced age should be admitted into the order.

These and many other difficulties rendered it very desirable that the approval of the Holy Father should set its seal on the work, and furnish it with a shield against the malice of the world. The permissions which they sought were as follows: 1st, that the Oblates should be allowed the rights to live in community, and to admit other persons into their society; 2d, that they might elect for themselves a superioress; 3d, that this superioress should have the power of choosing a confessor for the house; 4th, that they should have a chapel in which to hear Mass, to go to confession and to communion, and be exempted from the jurisdiction of the parish and the parish priests. This scheme was fully approved of by the three coadjutors; but it was some time before Don Giovanni could be induced to lay it before the sovereign Pontiff. He alleged that the disturbed state of Rome, and the many distracting cares which were besetting the Holy Father, held out no prospect of success in such a mission; but, urged by various irresistible proofs that God willed that he should undertake it, he at last consented. The petition was framed in the name of the Oblates, Francesca absolutely refusing to be mentioned as the foundress. While he bent his way to the pontifical palace, the Oblates of Tor di Specchi and the monks of Santa Maria Nuova joined in fervent prayer to God for the success of his application. Eugenius IV. received Francesca's messenger with great kindness, and bade him carry back to her assurances of his favourable disposition towards the congregation, recommending himself at the same time to her prayers and to those of her sisters. He commended the examination of the case to Gaspard, Archbishop of Conza, and enjoined him to verify the facts recited in the petition, and to communicate on the subject with the prior and the monks of Santa Maria Nuova; and if satisfied with the result, to grant the privileges therein requested. The archbishop applied himself with diligence to the execution of these orders; and the original document in which this authorisation is recorded still exists amongst the archives of the monastery. It stipulates that the Oblates shall be subject to the jurisdiction of the superior and of the monks of Santa Maria Nuova, and that they may continue to inhabit the house of Tor di Specchi until such time as they shall have made purchase of another. A short time afterwards the Oblates, full of gratitude and joy at the favours which had been granted them, and every day more satisfied with their abode, solicited and obtained permission to remain in it in perpetuity. This last transaction took place at the very time when Rome was given up to anarchy, and frightful disorders reigned within its walls; when the pontifical magistrates had been thrust aside, and furious demagogues installed in their places. The Pope had taken refuge in Bologna, and it is from that town that is dated the last-mentioned decree. The congregation was successively confirmed by three of the generals of the Olivetan order; and in 1444 Eugenius IV. extended still further the privileges and franchises of the Oblates.

Francesca was deeply impressed with the responsibility she had incurred in the establishment of her congregation, and felt herself bound to advance more and more in virtue herself, as well as further the piety of her spiritual daughters. During her visits to the convent she used to work indiscriminately in the kitchen or in the parlour; waited at table, and cleaned the plates, as it might happen; and could not bear to be treated with the least distinction. In coming in, and in going away, she always reverently kissed the hand of Agnese de Sellis the superioress, and asked for her blessing. She sometimes accompanied the sisters to her vineyard near St. Paul without the Walls, where they gathered wood, and carried it back to Rome bound in faggots for burning. She gently reproved one of the Oblates who, on one of these occasions, sought to screen her from observation when an illustrious personage was passing by. She took them with her to visit the hospitals and the poverty-houses in the city: and the miraculous cures which she performed in their presence confirmed their faith, and inflamed them with the most ardent desire to imitate her example.

At the time that the misfortunes of Rome were at their height, Francesca appeared one morning at the monastery, and gathering around her her spiritual daughters, she thus addressed them: "What shall we do, my children? The wrath of God is warring fierce against our unhappy country; Rome is in the hands of cruel and lawless men; the Holy Father in exile; his ministers prison, his life sought after as if he were an odious oppressor, and we know not when to look for his return. Immorality is increasing, vice triumphant, hell yawning for souls which Christ's blood has redeemed, and those who ought to extinguish do but excite the flame, and draw upon us the just judgment of God. The Blessed Virgin requires at our hands more fervent prayers, more tears, more penances. We must supply for the great dearth of love. Mortifications and prayer are the weapons we are furnished with; our hearts are the victims which must he slain for men's sins; our tears must quench those unholy fires; we shall not be true Oblates until we have made a complete sacrifice of ourselves, of our souls and of our bodies, to the Lord. We are few; but do not doubt the strength of prayer. Let us be fervent and persevere, and soon we shall reap the fruit of our intense supplications, of our long-continued pleadings; and liberty, peace, and all God's blessings, will be restored to Rome." Francesca's exhortations had their effect, and the fervent prayers they drew forth had theirs also; for in the same year the Bishops of Recaunti and of Turpia reassumed, in the Pope's name, possession of the city; and the Romans, wearied with anarchy, gladly welcomed their rule.

A more terrible evil, a more appalling danger now threatened not only Rome but the whole Catholic world. The undutiful conduct of the Council of Basle, with the violence of their language with regard to the Holy See, brought matters to such a point that a deplorable schism appeared inevitable. Pope Eugenius was divided between the fear of hurrying it on, and that of compromising by undue concessions the legitimate authority of the Chair of Peter. It was at this juncture that the Blessed Virgin appeared one night to Francesca, surrounded by saints and apostles, serenely beautiful, and with a compassionate expression in her countenance. After some preliminary spiritual instructions, she intimated to the Saint that God was waiting to have mercy, and that His wrath had to be softened by assiduous prayers and good works. She named certain religious exercises, certain penitential practices; which were to be observed on the principal feasts of the ensuing year; and recommending to the faithful in general, and more particularly to the Oblates, a great purity of heart, a sincere contrition for past sin, and a spirit of earnest charity, she charged Francesca to see that her orders were complied with; and disappeared after bestowing her blessing. It was in vain, however, that this revelation was communicated by Don Giovanni to the clergy of Rome. They rejected it as the dream of a pious and sickly woman; and even the most earnest amongst them absolutely declined to attach to it the slightest importance. Not so the Vicar of Christ, when Francesca's confessor carried to him at Bologna the message of the saint; he listened to it with reverence and gratitude, and sent back by his means all the necessary mandates for the execution of the orders which the Blessed Virgin had given. When he arrived at Tor di Specchi, Francesca met him; and before he could open his mouth, she gave him an exact account of all that had taken place on his journey, and of the very words which the Holy Father had used during their interview. The Pope's directions were attended to, the appointed Masses said, the processions organised; and in a short time it was seen that a favourable result ensued. The Pope was happily inspired to convene the council that met at Ferrara, and subsequently continued its labours at Florence. This at last put an end to the pretensions of the illegal assembly at Basle, and the wounds of the Church were gradually healed. There was but one opinion at the time as to the cause of this favourable change in the aspect of affairs. It was unanimously ascribed to the prayers of Francesca and to the Pope's compliance with the orders she had received; and in the process of her canonisation this point is treated of at length, and satisfactorily established; and those who are acquainted with the extreme caution observed on these occasions in admitting evidence on such a subject, will he impressed with the conviction that she was used as an instrument of God's mercy towards His suffering Church.

CHAPTER XIII.

DEATH OF FRANCESCA'S HUSBAND—SHE GOES TO RESIDE WITH THE COMMUNITY OF TOR DI SPECCC—HER LIFE AS SUPERIORESS.

FRANCESCA had been forty years married to Lorenzo Ponziano; and through her married life, the heart that had been consecrated to God from the first dawn of existence had been faithful in its love to him whom God Himself had appointed to be her chief earthly care: and blessed had been the course of that union; blessed by the tender affection which had reigned between the husband and the wife, and by the exercise of no common virtues, multiplied by the pursuits of one common object. Francesca had led the way; in meekness, in humility, in subjection; but with a single aim and an unwavering purpose. Many and severe trials had been their portion at different epochs of their lives; but the latter part of Lorenzo's existence had been comparatively tranquil. Lorenzo was the first to be called away. God spared him the trial he had probably dreaded. We seldom are called upon to suffer the particular grief that fancy has dwelt upon. His health had been breaking for some years past, and now it utterly failed, and his disease assumed an alarming character. Francesca, though apparently worn out with toil, with abstinence, and mental and bodily labours, found strength for every duty, and energy for every emergency. During Lorenzo's prolonged and painful illness, she was always at his side, nursing him with indefatigable tenderness, and completing the work which her example had wrought. His passage from life to eternity appeared but a journey. The efforts of Satan to disturb him on his deathbed, though often repeated, were each time frustrated. Lorenzo had been a just man, and his death was the death of the righteous. Few men would have shown themselves as worthy as he did of such a wife as Francesca. From the moment of his marriage he had appreciated her virtues, rejoiced in her piety, encouraged her good works, and to a great extent shared in them. No mean feelings of jealousy, no human respect, no worldly sentiment of expediency had influenced him. When he saw her renouncing all the pleasures and vanities of the world, dressing like a poor person, wearing herself out in the zeal of her charity, turning the half of his palace into a hospital, he did not complain, but rather rejoiced that she was one of those "whom fools have for a time in derision, and for a parable of reproach; whose life is esteemed madness, and their end without honour; but who are numbered amongst the children of God, and whose lot is amongst the saints." He had his reward; he had it when his sight failed him and his breath grew short, when he felt that his hour was come. He had it when in his dying ears she whispered words of peace; and Satan, with a cry of despair, for ever fled away from his couch; and when the everlasting portals opened, and the sentence was pronounced at the immediate judgment that follows death. Masses, prayers, fervent communions, and pious suffrages followed him beyond the grave; and when the saint, who had been the model of wives, stood by that grave a widow, her earthly task was, in one sense, done: but work remained; but it was of another sort. From her earliest youth she bad been a nun in spirit; and the heart which had sighed for the cloister in childhood yearned for its shelter in these her latter days. She must go and live in the shade of the tabernacle; she must be alone with her Lord during the few remaining years of life. This must have been foreseen by her children; and yet, like all trials of the kind, however long looked forward to, it came upon them at last as a surprise. When she said, "I must go," there was a loud cry of sorrow in the Ponziano palace. Baptista, the only son of her love, wept aloud. Mobilia threw herself into her arms, and with impetuous grief, protested against her leaving them. "Are you not afraid for me?" she exclaimed, "if you abandon me, you who have taught me to love God and to serve Him I What am I without you? Too much, too tenderly you have loved me. It cannot be that you should forsake me. I cannot endure existence without you." Her grandchildren also, whom she was tenderly attached to, clung to her, weeping. Moved by their tears, but unshaken in her resolution, she gently consoled them; bade them recollect that she was still to inhabit Rome; that her affection for them would be unchanged, and that she would always be at hand to advise and to aid them; but that her vocation must now he fulfilled, and the sacrifice completed. Then turning to Mobilia, as to a dearly-beloved child, she fondly said, "Do not weep, my daughter; you will survive me, and bear witness to my memory." This prediction was fulfilled; for Mobilia was alive at the time that the process for Francesca's canonisation was commenced, and the testimony she gave to her virtues and to her miracles was on that occasion most important, and the most detailed.

After this, Francesca took leave of her family, and went straight to the Tor di Specchi. It was on the 21st of March, the festival of St. Benedict, that she entered its walls, not as the foundress but as a humble supplicant for admission. At the foot of the stairs, having taken off her black gown, her veil, and her shoes, and placed a cord around her neck, she knelt down, kissed the ground, and, shedding an abundance of tears, made her general confession aloud in the presence of all the Oblates; described herself as a miserable sinner, a grievous offender against God, and asked permission to dwell amongst them as the meanest of their servants; and to learn from them to amend her life, and enter upon a holier course. The spiritual daughters of Francesca hastened to raise and to embrace her; and clothing her with their habit, they led the way to the chapel, where they all returned thanks to God. While she remained there engaged in prayer, Agnese de Sellis the superioress, assembled the sisters in the chapter-room, and declared to them, that now that their true mother and foundress had come amongst them, it would be absurd for her to remain in her present office; that Francesca was their guide, their head, and that into her hands she would instantly resign her authority. They all applauded her decision, and gathering around the Saint, announced to her their wishes. As was to be expected, Francesca strenuously refused to accede to this proposal, and pleaded her inability to the duties of a superioress. The Oblates had recourse to Don Giovanni, who began by entreating, and finally commanded her acceptance of the charge. His orders she never resisted; and accordingly, on the 25th of March, she was duly elected to that office.

She was favoured with a vision which strengthened and encouraged her in the new task she had before her. The angel who for twenty-four years had been by her side, defending and assisting her on all occasions, took leave of her now with a benignant smile, and in his place another, more refulgent still, was ordained to stand. By day and by night he was continually weaving a mysterious woof, the threads of which seemed to grow out of the mystical palm which he carried. St. Benedict appeared to Franceses on the day of her election, and explained to her the meaning of those symbols. Gold was the type of the love and charity which was to govern her dealings with her daughters, while the palm implied the triumph she was to obtain over human weakness and human respect. The unceasing labours of the angel was to mark the unwearied efforts she was to use for the right ordering and spiritual welfare of the community intrusted to her care; and truly she laboured with indefatigable zeal in her new vocation. She had ever before her eyes the words of St. Paul to Timothy and to Titus: "Preach the word. Be patient in season and out of season. Entreat, rebuke, in all patience and doctrine. In all things show thyself an example of good works, in doctrine, in integrity, in gravity." Preaching far more by her actions than by her words, she gave an example of the most heroic virtues. It would be difficult to imagine any thing mom perfect than her life in the world; but the new duties, the new privileges of her present vocation added each day new splendour to her virtues. She appointed Agnese de Sellis her coadjutress, and begged her to share her room, and watch over her conduct, entreating her at the same time to warn her of every fault she might commit. Her strictness with her spiritual children, though tempered by love, was extreme. She never left a single imperfection unreproved, and allowed of no infractions, however slight, of the rule. Sometimes, when through shyness or false shame, they concealed some trifling offence which they were bound to confess, she read their hearts, and reminded them not to give Satan a hold upon them by such reserve. She was most careful of their health, and sought to procure them as often as she could some innocent recreation. They used occasionally to go with her to one or other of her vine-gardens without the walls, to take exercise in the pure open air. Francesca's gentle gaiety on these occasions increased their enjoyment; and the labour of gathering wood and grass, of making up faggots, and carrying away their spoil on their heads at night, was a part of their amusement. The conversation that was carried on between them the while was as merry as it was innocent. These young persons, born in palaces and bred in luxury, worked like peasants, with more than a peasant's lightness of heart.

One fine sunny January day—and those who have inhabited Rome well know how fine a January day can be—Francesca and seven or eight of her companions had been since early dawn in the vine-gardens of Porta Portese. They had worked hard for several hours, and then suddenly remembered that they had brought no provision with them. They soon became faint and hungry, and above all very thirsty. Perna, the youngest of all the Oblates, was particularly heated and tired, and approaching the Mother Superior, with a wearied expression of countenance, she asked permission to go and drink some water at a fountain some way off on the public road.

"Be patient, my child," Francesca answered; "the fountain is too distant." She was afraid of these young persons drinking cold water, heated as they were by toil and exposure to the sun. They went on with their work; and withdrawing aside, Francesca knelt down, clasped her hands, and with her eyes raised to heaven, said, "Lord Jesus, I have been thoughtless in bringing my sisters here, and forgetting to provide food for them. Help us in our need."

Perna, who had kept near to the Mother Superior, probably with the intention of urging her request, overheard this prayer, and, a little irritated by the feverish thirst she was enduring, said to herself with some impatience, "It would be more to the purpose to take us home at once."

Francesca read the inward thought, and turning to the discontented girl she said, "My child, you do not trust enough in God. Look up and see." Perna obeyed, and following the direction of Francesca's hand, she saw a vine entwined around a tree, from whose dead and leafless branches were hanging a number of the finest bunches of grapes, of that purple and burnished hue which the fervid sunbeams of August and September impart to that glorious fruit.

"A miracle! a miracle!" exclaimed the enraptured Perna; and the other Oblates assembled round the tree in speechless astonishment, for they had seen all day the bare and withered branches. Twenty times at least they had passed and repassed before it; and at all events the season for grapes had long gone by.

After kneeling to give thanks to God for this gracious prodigy, they spread a cloth on the grass, and gathered the precious fruit. There were exactly as many bundles as persons present; and with smiling faces and joyful hearts Francesca's children fed on the supply which her prayer had obtained for them. Obedience was a virtue of which the Saint herself gave a most perfect example, and which she unremittingly required of others. One of the Oblates having refused one day to comply with an order she had received, Francesca fixed her eyes upon her with an expression of so much severity, that the person in question suddenly fainted away, and remained afterwards speechless and in a state of insensibility. The doctors were sent for, and declared that her life was in imminent danger. This was a severe trial to the Saint; she could not reproach herself for a severity which had been a matter of duty, not of passion, but at the same time she trembled for the soul of one who had apparently lost the use of reason at the very moment she was committing a serious fault. After addressing a fervent prayer to God, and invoking the Blessed Virgin, she went straight to the bedside of the sister, and taking her by the hand with great solemnity, addressed to her these words: "If it be true that our congregation is approved of God, and has His Holy Mother for its foundress, in the name of Holy Obedience, I command you to speak to me." The Oblate seemed to awake from a long dream, and opening her eyes, she distinctly said, "Mother, what would you have me to do?" From that moment she rallied, and was soon restored to health.

Another time, when an aged member of the congregation was dying, and every moment expected to be her last, Franceses prayed that she might not be allowed to depart in the absence of Don Giovanni, the director of the house. For six days and six nights the sick woman lingered between life and death. On the arrival of her spiritual father she revived, went to confession, and received the last Sacrament Then, as she again sank into insensibility, Francesca bent over her and said, "Sister Catherine, depart in peace, and pray for us;" and in that instant the aged woman expired.

The poverty of the congregration was extreme. The slender means of the first Oblates had been exhausted by the purchase of the house and the erection of a small chapel. Francesca had indeed made over to it her two vineyards of Porta Portese and of St. Paul without the Walls; but the trifling revenue they furnished was wholly inadequate to the support of fifteen persons; and moreover the religions were so endued with the spirit of their foundress, that they never could bring themselves to turn away a beggar from their doors as long as they had a slice of bread to bestow. They often went a whole day without eating, rather than deny themselves the happiness of feeding the poor. Francesca, happy in the virtues of her children, but tenderly anxious for their welfare, was indefatigable in her efforts to procure them the necessaries of life. She used on these occasions to beg of her relations, or even of strangers; and Almighty God allowed her sometimes to provide for them in a miraculous manner.

One day that the sister whose turn it was to attend to the victualling department found herself unable to put upon the table any thing but two or three small fragments of bread, she went to consult the Saint, who immediately proposed to go out with her and beg. According to her invariable custom, she asked Agnese de Sellis, her coadjutoress, for permission so to do. Contrary to her habit on such occasions, Agnese refused, and said, that if it was necessary for any one to beg, she, with another of the sisters, would undertake it. Then Francesca, after a moment's thought, replied, "I think that God will provide for us without any one going out of the house;" and calling the Oblates to the refectory, she asked a blessing on the bread, and distributed it in minute portions amongst them. Each on beginning to eat her share saw it multiply apace; and not only were their wants thus supplied at the moment, but enough remained when they had done to furnish them with food for the next day.

The gift of prophecy she also exercised more frequently than ever at this period. Once, when she was praying in her cell, the nuns heard her exclaim, "O King of Heaven, support and comfort that poor unhappy mother;" and some hours afterwards, they heard that at that very moment a young nobleman, Jacobo Maddaleni, had been thrown from his horse and killed on the spot, to the inexpressible grief of his mother. Lorenzo Altieri was dying, and his wife Palozza overwhelmed with sorrow; she had several young children, and was almost in despair at the idea of losing her husband. The physician had declared his case hopeless; and when she sent for Francesca her heart was breaking. The Saint came up to her, and said compassionately, "Dear sister, give up the love and the vanities of the world, and God will take pity upon you. Lorenzo will yet recover; he will be present at my burial." The prediction was fulfilled, and Lorenzo, restored to health, assisted, as she had said, at the funeral of the Saint; and Palozza, whose heart had been entirely converted at that moment, and who had vowed in case of his death to retire into a convent, whenever her children could spare her, led henceforward, in every respect, the life of a Christian wife and mother.

The Superioress of the Sisters of the third order of St. Francis consulted her one day on the admission of a young girl, who had requested to be admitted among them. Francesca had not seen or known any thing of the candidate, but unhesitatingly answered, that the vocation was not a real one, and she recommended that she should be refused. "She will enter another monastery," she added, "and after remaining in it a short time, will return to the world, and soon after she will die." It happened exactly as the Saint had foretold: Francesca da Fabrica went into the convent of Casa di Cento Finestre, on the shores of the Tiber, gave up the habit before the end of the year, and a sharp fever carried her off soon after her return. Gregorio and Gentilesca Selli had a little girl of four years old, who was paralysed, and up to her waist her frame appeared completely withered. They had often been urged to have recourse to the spells or charms then so much in vogue, but had always refused to seek a blessing through such means.

They were carrying the little child to Francesca, full of faith in her prayers, which they were coming to ask, when she exclaimed at the first sight of them: "Happy are you who have not sought your child's recovery in unlawful ways. In three days, my friends, she will be restored to health;" and the prediction was fulfilled to the letter.

It would be useless to multiply such recitals as these. As she advances in years, especially since her retirement at Tor di Specchi, more and more frequent become the exercise of those supernatural gifts with which God had endowed the gentle Saint of Rome. No day elapses that some new prodigy does not call forth the grateful enthusiasm of the warm-hearted and devout Trasteverini. If a child is trodden under foot by a runaway horse, Francesca is sent for, and at the sight of the Saint he revives. If a young boatman, in the prime of youth, is thrown into the Tiber, and curried away by the stream under the arches of the Ponte Rotto, from whence his afflicted mother receives him into her arms without a symptom of life, she calls out to her friends, "Run, ran to the servant of God: go to Francesca dei Ponziano, and bid her pray for the boy." And when they return, the mother is weeping still over her apparently lifeless child; but they shout from a distance, "The servant of God says he will not die;" and in a few instants, Paul Guidolini opens his eyes, and smiles on his mother, who some years later becomes one of the Oblates of Tor di Specchi. If Francesca sits down for a moment to rest on the steps of a church, as she did one Good Friday, after the service at St. Peter's, a paralytic woman kneels at her feet, and obtains that she should lay her hand on her withered limbs, which are instantly restored. There is no illness on record which her prayers, or the touch of her hand, does not dispel and subdue. She restores sight to the blind, the dumb speak, the deaf hear, the lame walk at her bidding; pestilence and madness and fits and wounds and possession itself disappear before the power with which Almighty God has endued her; and she walks this earth of ours dispensing blessings, as the faithful handmaid of Him who went about doing good.

At the same time, more and more ecstatic grew her prayers, more visible to all eyes the indwelling of the Holy Spirit in her soul, more removed from the natural conditions of existence the tenour of her life. At the hours of meals, which she observed in obedience to the rule, her companions notice that she hardly ever eats, but that her face is turned to the window, and her eyes fixed on the sky, while rays of light seem to play around her, and her countenance grows dazzling from the celestial brightness which overspreads it. Longer and longer became her orisons; often in visiting a church she falls into an ecstasy, which lasts till night. The sublimity of her vision, the glimpses of heaven which she enjoys, the sight of angels, and of the Lord of angels, is occasionally exchanged for the terrific apparitions, the renewed assaults of Satan, who attack her at times with redoubled violence, now that her ultimate triumph is at hand, and the crown about to descend on a brow which already shines with the mystic radiance of sanctity. The old frescoes of the original chapel of Tor di Specchi represent some of these mysterious struggles between Francesca and the Evil One; and her cell bears the impress of that strange violence which Satan is permitted to exercise at certain moments, and which is the type of the warfare which is ever waged between him and God's Church. He can shake it at times by the storms he raises; but vain are his attempts to overthrow it. The mark of Satan's fury is stamped on the roof of Franceses's lowly cell; but the relics of the canonised Saint now fill the chamber which, in his impotent rage, the tempter once sought to destroy. But this life of wonders, of trials, and of miracles, was drawing to a close. She who had been the holiest of maidens, of wives, and of widows, had all but finished her course, and many were the intimations she received of her approaching end.

On one of these occasions she selected one of the chapels in Santa Maria Nuova as a place of sepulture for the Oblates, and obtained from the Olivetan Monks that it should be reserved for that purpose. She often spoke of her death to the sisters, and told Rita, one of the companions of her youth, that she would succeed her in the government of the congregation. Don Ippolito, one of her coadjutors in the foundation of the order, had often implored two favours of her, that she would look upon him as her spiritual son, and that she would summon him to her death-bed. She assured him that the prayers of such a worthless sinner as herself were not deserving of a thought; but, moved by his importunities, she promised in the end to comply with his request. Accordingly, towards the end of the year 1439, when he was in Sienna on business, he received a letter from Francesca, in which she reminded him of his desire to be present at her last moments, and in consequence exhorted him to conclude his affairs, and return to Rome as soon as possible, which he accordingly did. On Christmas-day and on the Feast of St. Stephen she had visions of the Blessed Virgin and of the infant Jesus, which she communicated to Don Ippolito in the church of Santa Maria Nuova, where she had gone on her way back from San Lorenzo without the Walls and St. John of Lateran, which she had successively visited. The religious said to her with emotion: "Mother, you will now grant me the favour I have so often asked of you."

"Yes," replied the Saint, who had been all day in a kind of ecstasy, though she moved from one place to another; "yes; I look upon you now as my father, as my brother, and as my son." And so saying she left him, and returned to Tor di Specchi, still absorbed in contemplation.

Don Ippolito followed her with his eyes till she had disappeared from his sight, and joy and sorrow were struggling in his heart; for he felt that the time was come for her great gain and her children's unspeakable loss.

CHAPTER XIV.

FRANCESCA'S LAST ILLNESS AND DEATH.

FRANCESCA was fifty-six years old. Her frame, worn out with labour, with fastings, and austerities, was enfeebled also by frequent illnesses; but her activity, her indomitable energy, was still the same. She never flagged, never wearied, never gave way under the pressure of physical or moral sufferings. It was probably a trial of the latter description, one which she had always been keenly alive to, that hurried her end.

A fresh schism broke out in the Church, to the scandal and grief of all the faithful. The refractory bishops assembled at Basle, ventured to decree the deposition of Pope Eugenius, and to elect as anti-pope the aged Amadeus, Duke of Tuscany, who had abdicated in favour of his son, and was living as a hermit on the shores of the Lake of Geneva. The usurper took the name of Felix V., and this unhappy schism lasted ten years. Francesca turned to heaven her weary eyes—she besought her Lord to take her away from this scene of trial: too keenly did she feel the woes of the Church; too deeply did she sorrow over these renewed conflicts, and the consequent dangers to which the souls of Christians were exposed. Perhaps it was given to her in that hour to foresee the fearful storm that was lowering over the Church,—the monster heresy that, in less than a century, was to rise against the Mystical Bride of Christ, and rob her of her children.

On the 3d of March, 1440, Francesca was sent for by her son Baptista, who was laid up with a sharp attack of fever. She instantly obeyed the summons; and, on arriving at the Ponziano palace, found him already much better, and able to leave his bed; but, at the earnest request of the whole family, she agreed to spend the whole day with them, the Oblate Augustina, who had accompanied her, also remaining to return with her at night. Towards evening she grew so weak that she could hardly stand; and Baptista and Mobilia implored her to stay at the palace, or else to let herself be carried in a litter to the convent; but she persisted in setting out on foot. Stopping on her way at the church of Santa Maria in Trastevere, she went in to ask, for the last time, her spiritual father's blessing, and found Don Giovanni in the Chapel of the Angels—that spot where she had so often been favoured with divine revelations. As he was inquiring after Baptista, he was struck with the more than habitual paleness of her face, and the evident exhaustion she was labouring under, and commanded her, as a matter of obedience, instantly to return to the Ponziano Palace, and to spend the night there, This order was a severe trial to Francesca, for she felt at once that if she was not now to return to Tor di Specchi, she would never again enter those hallowed walls; but, faithful to the spirit of perfect obedience, she meekly bowed her head in token of submission, and went back to her son's house.

In the course of the night a virulent fever came on, and in the morning she was as ill as possible. Francesca's first care was to send for her director, and to request him to apprise her spiritual daughters of her illness. Four of them (Agnese, Rita, Catherina, and Anastasia,) hurried to her side; and when they heard her entreat Don Giovanni not to omit any of the necessary precautions for her soul's welfare, they all burst into tears, and seemed at once to understand that their beloved mother was about to leave them. Francesca gently consoled them, and dismissed them towards the evening, only keeping with her Augustina, who watched her during the night, and witnessed the ecstasy during which the following vision was vouchsafed to the sufferer:—Our Lord appeared, surrounded with angels and with saints, and announced to her that in seven days she would die, and receive the crown which was prepared for her in heaven. Sister Augustina saw her face shining with supernatural brightness; a radiant smile playing on her lips, and heard her say with ineffable unction: "Be Thou eternally praised and blessed, O my dear Lord Jesus Christ! Thanks be to Thee for the unmerited favours I have received at Thy hands. To Thee, to Thee alone, do I owe all the blessings I have, and have yet to receive." When Don Giovanni saw her afterwards, he imagined she was rallying; but she related to him her vision, and bade him tell her daughters that her end was approaching. Their tears and their sobs choked their utterance; and the Saint gently reproved that excess of sorrow, and bade them rejoice with her, and bless the Divine goodness for the great mercy that was shown to her. During the next two days she suffered much; but no word or sound of complaint escaped her. Her face was as serene as if her body had been perfectly free from pain; and to those who expressed a hope that she would yet recover, she only answered with a sweet smile, "God be praised, my pilgrimage will end from Wednesday to Thursday next." She asked for the Sacraments, confessed, went to communion, and received Extreme Unction. Ardent ejaculatory prayers, devout aspirations, burning expressions of love, were ever rising from her heart to her lips. Each day she repeated, as if she had been in perfect health, the Office of the Blessed Virgin, the Rosary, and all her usual prayers. The Oblates watched by her in turns, and Mobilia hardly ever left her side; so that the smallest particulars of that wonderful death-bed were carefully recorded. Francesca allowed all those who wished to see her to come in. She had words of advice, of warning, and of consolation for all.

When the news of her illness was spread in Rome, the heart of the great city was stirred to its very depths, and a mournful, anxious, loving multitude beset the palace and the very bed of the dying Saint. Nowise disturbed or annoyed at this oppressive testimony of their affection, she had a smile, or a look, or a kind word for each. No cloud obscured her understanding; no irritability affected her temper. Peace was within and around her, and heaven's own calm on her brow and in her heart. The evil spirits, the arch-enemy himself—who, for her sanctification and the glory of God, had been permitted so often to haunt her path and assault her during life—are banished now, and stand at bay, gazing, no doubt, from afar, with envious rage, on that peace which they may no longer mar. Don Giovanni, who had known so well her former trials, often inquired, during her last illness, if Satan's ministers were molesting her. "No," she would answer, with a smile; "I see them no more. God has conquered; His foes have fled." But the bright archangel, whose task is nearly at an end, is still at his post; he weaves the last threads of the mystic woof, and seems to make haste to finish his work. The halo of light which surrounds him grows brighter and brighter, and Francesca's dying form reflects that splendour.

On the Monday morning she is still in the same state. Glorious visions pass before her; divine forms bend over her, and whisper words of welcome. During Mass, which her confessor says in her room, the Lord Himself appears to her again; and from the consecrated Host He speaks to her entranced soul. The Blessed Virgin and the angels surround her, and the voices of the blest make sweet music in her ears. Late on that day, when her ecstasy was over, the weeping Oblates surround her bed, and with suppliant accents implore her to ask of God yet to leave her upon earth, for the sake of the souls intrusted to her care. It was a hard request: to have had a glimpse of heaven, and to turn back; to have tasted the cup of celestial bliss, and to draw back from its sweetness! Full of love, of pity, of resignation, of holy indifference, she exclaims: "God's will is my will; His good pleasure mine. If He Chooses me to tarry yet on earth, so be it then. I am ready to remain in this miserable world, if He commands it."

But it was not ordained. The next day she grew rapidly worse, and from that time slept not again. "I shall soon rest in God," she replied to those who were urging her to repose. The Oblates once more kneel around her to receive her last instructions: one of them alone, Francesca del Veruli, is kept away by a severe illness, which confines her to her bed. Touching were the last words of the dying mother to her spiritual children; sweet the words of blessing she pronounced on their heads. *Love, love*, was the burden of her teaching, as it had been that of the beloved disciple. "Love one another (she said), and be faithful unto death. Satan will assault you, as he has assaulted me; but be not afraid. You will overcome him through patience and obedience; and no trial will be too grievous, if you are united to Jesus; if you walk in His ways, He will be with you." Then with earnest accents she thanked Don Giovanni, in her own name and in that of the order, for all he had done to them; and commended the Oblates to his fatherly care.

At that moment her son Baptista entered the room. His mother sat up in the bed, and gazing upon him with an expression of anxious scrutiny, she said: "And can it be that you quarrel with poor shepherds? And do you rob God of His glory by unlawful dealings with hell?" The persons who were standing around the bed looked at each other in surprise, and imagined that Francesca was delirious; but Baptista's countenance and actions soon undeceived them. Tears rushed into his eyes, and with great emotion he publicly acknowledged that he had been guilty of striking, in his anger, some peasants who had injured his fields, and had gone to consult in secret one of the persons who dealt in occult sciences, as to the possibility of his mother's recovery. No one but himself knew of his twofold sin; and the rebuke of the dying Saint came upon him as a direct reproof from God, and an awful warning for the rest of his life. As the day advanced, Francesca grew weaker and weaker; but the flame of love was burning more brightly, as that of life was waning. "What are you saying?" asked Don Giovanni at one moment, on seeing her lips move. "The Vespers of the Blessed Virgin," she answered in a scarcely audible voice. As an infant almost she had begun that practice; and on the eve of her death she had not yet omitted it. On the seventh day of her illness, as she had herself announced, her life came to a close. A sublime expression animated her face; a more ethereal beauty clothed her earthly form. Her confessor for the last time inquires what it is her enraptured eyes behold, and she whispers, "The heavens open! The angels descend! The archangel has finished his task. He stands before me. He beckons to me to follow him." These are the last words that Francesca utters; a smile of indescribable brightness beams from her face. The eyes that have so long been closed to the vanities of life are now closed in death, and her spirit has taken its final leave of earth.

CHAPTER XV.

FRANCESCA'S FUNERAL, AND HER SUBSEQUENT CANONIZATION.

THE body of the Saint remained during a night and a day at the Ponziano palace, the Oblates watching by turns over the beloved remains. Their grief was tempered with joy, for they felt she was in heaven; though the pang of separation was keen, and their home on earth desolate. Don Giovanni, Don Ippolito, and Don Francesco dello Schiano recited the prayers of the Church over the corpse; and though deeply affected themselves, strove to console the bereaved sisterhood, chiefly by extolling the rare merits and the heroic virtues of their departed mother. Almighty God vouchsafed, even during the first night of their loving watch, to give them a proof of that sanctity which was so soon to be triumphantly demonstrated. Sister Margaret, of the third order of St. Frances, had been present at Francesca's death, and remained by her side during the night that followed. Her arm had been paralysed for six months, and to all appearance withered. Inspired with a lively faith, she touched the body of the Saint, and was instantaneously cured. The Oblates all fell on their knees at the sight of this miracle, and blessed God for the earnest He thus gave of the wonders which Francesca's intercession was to accomplish. Each moment they were confirmed in the blessed assurance of her immediate admission into heaven; each moment brought with it a new occasion for joyful exultation. The sweet perfume, the "odour of sanctity," which expression is so often supposed to be simply metaphorical, whereas it often indicates an actual physical and miraculous fact, soon pervaded the room and filled it with fragrance. Francesca's face, which had recently borne the traces of age and of suffering, became as beautiful again as in the days of youth and prosperity; and the astonished bystanders gazed with wonder and awe at that unearthly loveliness. Many of them carried away particles from her clothes, and employed them for the cure of several persons who had been considered beyond the possibility of recovery. In the course of the day, the crowd augmented to a degree which alarmed the inhabitants of the palace, and Baptista took measures to have the body removed at once to the church and a procession of the regular and secular clergy escorted the venerated remains to Santa Maria Nuova, where they were to be interred.

The popular feeling burst forth on the occasion; it was no longer to be restrained: a sort of pious insurrection, which the Church smiles upon, even though it refuses to sanction it; as a mother can scarcely rebuke a somewhat irregular action in one of her children when it springs from a generous feeling, even though she feels herself bound to check it. "Francesca was a saint—Francesca was in heaven." Francesca was invoked by the crowd, and her beloved name was heard in every street, in every piazza, in every corner of the Eternal City. It flew from mouth to mouth; it seemed to float in the air, to be borne aloft by the grateful enthusiasm of a whole people, who had seen her walk to that church by her mother's side in her holy childhood; who had seen her kneel at that altar in the grave beauty of womanhood, in the hour of bereavement, and now in death; carried thither in state, she the gentle, the humble Saint of Rome, the poor woman of the Trastevere, as she was sometimes called at her own desire.

Francesca del Veruli, the Oblate whom illness had detained from the death-bed of her beloved mother, hears from her sick-room the confused hum of voices, the sound of hurrying feet, which indicate the approach of the procession. Full of faith, she starts up, and with clasped hands exclaims, "Oh, my mother! oh, Francesca! I have not seen you die; I have not received your last blessing; obtain for me now that I may visit your remains." With a violent effort, and leaning on one of her sisters, she contrives to rise and to make her way to the bier. The very instant she has touched it, her health and strength return. Meanwhile the crowd augments, and hurries into the church. They press round the precious body; they refuse to let it be buried. As a favour, as a boon of the greatest price, they obtain that the obsequies be put off to the Saturday; and in the meantime, day and night, there is no limit to the concourse of people that assemble in the chapel. Still the saintly body exhales its perfume; still the sweet features retain their beauty; and to that spot, in an apparently never-ending succession, come the blind, and the lame, and the halt, and the sick, and the suffering; and each of those who touch the bier, or to whom is carried something that has belonged to Francesca, is instantaneously cured. Truly God was wonderful in this His Saint, and wonderful are the details of the miracles wrought during those days; and not only were the ills of the body relieved by contact with the holy corpse, but grace reaches the souls of many who have been hitherto steeled against its entrance.

Amongst others, two young men of dissolute lives and irreligious spirits, on hearing of the miracles at Santa Maria Nuova, begin to jeer and laugh on the subject, and, moved only by curiosity, go to the church, approach the bier with mock demonstrations of respect. But no sooner have they knelt before it, than their hearts are simultaneously touched; a sudden change comes over them. Having come to scoff, they remain to pray,—they rise from their knees only to seek a confessor; and return home that night converted to God, and ever after lead the lives of pious Christians. The miracles wrought before and after Francesca's burial are so multifarious, that it might be tedious (a strange word to use on such an occasion, but nevertheless correct) to attempt to relate them all. Great was the moral effect of this singular outpouring of God's powers through His servant. Faith grew more timid, and hope more strong; charity burned in the hearts of many with an ever-increasing fervour; and the examples which the Saint had given, and which were now dwelt upon with affectionate veneration, induced many to walk in the same path, and look to the same end. It was in Lent that she had died; and from every pulpit in Rome her praises were heard. The most eminent ecclesiastics of the time all foretold her canonisation; and the public voice and the public devotion ratified the burst of popular enthusiasm that had hailed her as a Saint on the very day of her death, and long preceded the formal recognition of her sanctity by the authority of the Church.

A few months after her death, her tomb was opened in order to remove the corpse into a monument which Baptista, Mobilia, and several Roman noblemen had erected in her honour. It was found in a state of perfect preservation, and still exhaling the same fragrance as before. The most exact and detailed examinations were taken in the year of her death, both as to all the particulars of her life, and as to the supernatural and miraculous events which had marked its course, as well as those which had succeeded her death.

From time to time earnest endeavours were made to hasten her formal canonisation. The materials were ample, and the evidence complete; but a variety of circumstances interfered with the conclusion of the process; and though several Popes, namely, Eugenius IV., Nicholas V., Pius II., Innocent VIII., and Julius II., promoted the question, it was not much advanced till the accession of Clement VIII., who had a great devotion to the Saint, and brought the matter nearly to a close; but his death occurring in the meantime, and his successor, Leo XI, only outliving him twenty-seven days, it was Paul V. (Borghese) who decreed the canonisation of Francesca, to the joy of the Oblates of Tor di Specchi, of the monks of Santa Maria Nuova, and of the whole people of Rome. Her festival was appointed to be kept on the 9th of March; and those who have been in Rome on that day can tell how vivid is the devotion that still exists,—the worship that is yet paid to the holy Francesca, the beloved Saint of the Trastevere, the model of Christian matrons; and in the church of Santa Francesca Romana, as the old Santa Maria Nuova is now called, and in the Casa dei Esercizii Pii (the old Ponziano Palace), and in the time-honoured walls of Tor di Specchi, a tribute of love and of devotion is yielded, which touches the heart, and carries the mind back to the days when, amidst the strife of war and the miseries or anarchy, faith, fresh, strong, and pure, asserted its power, and wrought wonders through such feeble instruments as a woman's heart and a woman's works.

On the 29th of May, 1608, in the church of St. Peter, then lately erected, and adorned for the occasion with the utmost magnificence, after a pontifical High Mass, in the presence of the Sacred College, and of an immense affluence of strangers as well as of Romans, the decree was proclaimed which placed Francesca amongst the canonised saints, and sanctioned the worship which a devout people had paid her, with but few interruptions, since the day of her death. Rome was illuminated that night; the fiery cupola of St. Peter, and the sound of innumerable bells, told the neighbouring plains and hills that "God had regarded the lowliness of His handmaiden," and that, in her measure, all generations were to call her Blessed.

In 1633, the tomb of Francesca, which, in consequence of some alterations in the church, had remained out of sight for a great number of years, was, through the pious exertions of the Oblates, assisted by the abbot of Santa Maria Nuova, and the Cardinals Borghese, Barberini, and Altiere, discovered in the spot where it had been placed two centuries before. Her bones were exposed to the veneration of the faithful, and a number of religious processions and services took place on the occasion. Various miracles again gave testimony to the virtues of those holy relics, and a magnificent monument was erected beneath that altar where the Saint had so often prayed.

BLESSED LUCY OF NARNI.

IT was towards the latter end of the 15th century that Lucia Broc-coletti was horn in the ancient city of Narni, in Umbria, where her father's house had long held a noble and distinguished rank. Even as a baby in the cradle, there were not wanting signs which marked her as no ordinary child; and if we may credit the account given us by her old biographers, both her nurses and mother were accustomed to see her daily visited by an unknown religious dressed in the Dominican habit, whose majestic appearance seemed something more than human, and who, taking her from her cradle, embraced her tenderly, and gave her her blessing. They watched closely, to see whence this mysterious visitor came and whither she went, but were never able to follow her; and the mother becoming at length alarmed at the daily recurrence of this circumstance, it was revealed to her that her child's unknown visitor was no other than St. Catherine of Sienna, to whom she was given as an adopted daughter.

The accounts that have been preserved of Lucia's childhood have a peculiar interest of their own. Whilst the early biographies of many saints present us with instances of extraordinary graces and favours granted to them in infancy, quite as numerous and remarkable as those bestowed on Blessed Lucy, yet in her case we find them mixed with the details of a characteristic vivacity of temperament, which give them a lifelike reality, and show her to us, in the midst of her super-natural visitations, with all the impetuosity of an imaginative child. When she was only four years old, her mother's brother, Don Simon, came on a visit to his sister's house, and brought with him from Rome various toys and presents for the children. Lucy was given her choice; and whilst the others were loudly clamouring for the dolls and pup-pets, she selected a little rosary with an image of the Child Jesus; and this being given to her, she took it in her arms, bestowing every name of childish endearment on it, kissing its hands and feet, and calling it her dear Christarello, a name which continued to be given to it ever afterwards. The rest of the day she spent in her own little room, where she arranged a corner for the reception of the Christarello, and was never tired of seeing and caressing her new treasure. Henceforth it was here that she spent the happiest moments of the day. If ever she got into any trouble in the house, it was here she came to pour out all her sorrow; and the innocent simplicity of her devotion was so pleasing to God, that more than once He permitted that the Christarello should wipe away the tears which she shed on these occasions with His little hand, as was several times witnessed by her mother, who watched her through the half-open door. As she grew a little older, she began to accompany her mother to church; and they frequently went to visit the great church of St. Augustine, which was close to the house where they lived. Now it happened that in this church, among other devout images, there was a small has-relief of the Blessed Virgin holding her Divine Son in her arms, which took the child's fancy the first time they entered, so that she stopped to look at it. Her mother observed her as she lingered behind: "Lucy," she said, "do you know who that beautiful lady is whom you see there? She is the Mother of your Christarello; and the little Child whom she carries in her arms is the Christarello also. If you like, we will come here sometimes; and you shall bring the rosary you are so fond of, and say it before her image." Lucy was delighted at the idea; and whenever she could escape from her nurse's hand, she found her way to the church, to admire this new object of her devotion. One day, being thus occupied, the thought came into her head, how much she would like to hold the Christarello for once in her own arms, as she had learnt to hold her little baby brother. She therefore prayed to the Blessed Virgin with great earnestness that her request might be granted, and immediately the marble figure of the little Jesus was extended to her by His Mother, and placed in her arms. Nor was this all: no sooner had she received her precious burden, than she felt the cold marble become a living Child; and, full of delight, she ran home still carrying Him; and though she met many people on the way, who stopped her as she hurried along, and tried to take Him from her, she succeeded in getting safe to her own room at home, where she shut herself up with her treasure, and remained with Him for three days and nights without food or sleep, insensible to all the entreaties and remonstrances of her astonished mother. Conquered at length by fatigue, on the third day she fell asleep; and when she woke she became sensible of the truth that God abides only with those who watch with Him; for, on opening her eyes, the first thing she perceived was that the Christarello was gone. Her cries of distress were heard by her mother, who, to console her, carried her once more to the church; and there they found the marble child restored to the image as before, although for the three previous days its place in the arms of the Virgin's figure had been empty.

She was accustomed from time to time to pay a visit to the uncle before mentioned, and when about seven years old she went as usual to spend some time with him at his country house. She remembered, on the occasion of a former visit, to have seen a room in some part of the house where there were some little angels painted on the walls, as it seemed to her, holding their hands and dancing; and the first morning after her arrival, she determined to set out on a diligent search after the dancing angels. The room in which they were painted was in a wing of the house which had fallen out of repair, and was no longer used by the family; a staircase had led to the upper story, but this was now fallen and in ruins; and though Lucy, as she stood at the bottom, could see the little angels on the wall above her head, all her efforts were unavailing to climb the broken staircase and reach the object of her search. She had recourse to her usual expedient, prayer to the Christarello, and instantly found herself in the empty room, without well knowing how she came there. But her thoughts were soon busy with the angels. There they were; little winged children, their heads garlanded with flowers, their mantles floating as it seemed in the air; and they danced with such an air of enjoyment and superhuman grace, that Lucy sat on the ground before them, absorbed in admiration. As she sat thus, she heard her own name called from the window. She turned round, expecting to see her uncle or some of the servants of the house; but a very different spectacle met her eye. A glorious company of saints and angels stood round the Person of Jesus Himself. On His right was His Virgin Mother; on His left, St. Catherine and the great Patriarch St. Dominic, with many others. Then those mystic espousals were celebrated which we read of in so many other tales of the Saints of God: the Divine Spouse receiving the hand of the delighted child from His Blessed Mother, placed a ring on her finger, which she preserved to the hour of her death; after which He assigned her to the special guardianship of St. Dominic and St. Catherine, whom from that day she always was used to call her "father and mother." "And have you nothing to give Me?" He then asked of His little Spouse; "will you not give Me that silk mantle and pretty necklace?" Lucy was dressed in the rich fashion of the day, with a crimson damask mantle over her other garments, and a necklace of gold and coral beads about her neck; but at these words of her Spouse, she hastily stripped them off, and lay them at His feet. He did not fail, however, to give her a richer dress in their place; for she had no sooner taken off the silk mantle, than St. Dominic clothed her with the scapular of his order, which she continued to wear during the rest of her life under her other clothes. When the vision had disappeared, Lucy found herself full of a new and inexpressible joy. She turned to the little angels on the wall, the only companions left her after the last of the heavenly train had faded from her eyes, and with the simplicity of her childish glee, she spoke to them as though they were alive. "You dear little angels," she said, "are you not glad at what our Lord has done?" Then the angels seemed to move from the wall, and to become, indeed, full of life; and they spoke to her in reply, and said they were very glad to have her for their queen and lady, as the Spouse of their dear Lord. And they invited her to join in their dance of joy, and sang so sweet and harmonious a music, and held out their hands so kindly and graciously, that Lucy would have been well content never to have left her happy place of retreat; nor would she have done so, if she had not been found by her uncle, and carried against her will back to the house.

The death of her father, left her whilst still young, to the guardianship of her uncle. All her own wishes were fixed on a life of religion, but her uncle had different views for her; and after long resistance on her part, he succeeded in inducing her to accept as her husband Count Pietro of Milan, a young nobleman of considerable worth and abilities. The marriage was accordingly celebrated; but not until, in answer to earnest prayers, Lucy had received a divine revelation that a life so contrary to all her own wishes and intentions was indeed God's will regarding her.

Doubtless it is one of those cases in which it is not easy for us to follow the ways of Divine Providence. The marriage was followed by much suffering to both parties; yet, if we be willing to take the Saints' lives as they are given us, without seeking to reduce the supernatural elements we find in them to the level of our own understanding, we shall not be disposed to doubt the truth of the revelation which commanded it, or to fancy things would have been much better if Blessed Lucy had never been placed in a position so little in harmony with her own wishes. On the contrary, we must admire the grace of God, which would perhaps never have been so amply manifested in His servant, had she been called to a more congenial way of life. We are accustomed to admire the wonderful variety of examples which are

150

presented to us in the lives of the Saints: that of Blessed Lucy offers us one of a soul with all her sympathies and desires fixed on the higher life of religion, yet fulfilling with perfect exactitude the minutest duties of a different vocation. She sanctified herself in the will of God, though that will was manifested to her in a position which the world is used to call the hardest of all to bear—an ill-assorted marriage. She found means to practise the humiliation of the cloister, without laying aside the duties, or even the becoming dignity, of her station.

Her first care, on finding herself the young mistress of a house full of servants, was with them, whom she ever looked on less as menials than as a cherished portion of her family. And in the beautiful account given us of her intercourse with them, we must remember that at the period in which she lived, it was considered nothing uncommon or unbecoming for ladies of the highest rank to join in the household occupations, and take their part in the day's employment, working with their servants, and presiding amongst them with an affectionate familiarity, which, without rendering them less a mistress, gave them at the same time almost the position of a mother. Blessed Lucy delighted in the opportunities, which the simple manners of the day thus afforded her, of laying aside her rich dress and ornaments, and assisting in her own kitchen, where she always chose the meanest and most tiresome offices. What was with others only done in compliance with the ordinary habit of the day, was with her made the occasion of secret humiliations. One of her servants, a woman of very holy life and disposition, she took into her confidence, submitting herself to her direction, and obeying her as a religious superior. On Holy Thursday, she washed the feet of all her domestics; and that with so touching a devotion as to draw tears from the eyes of the rudest and most indifferent among them. So perfect was the discipline she succeeded in introducing among them, that, far from presenting the spectacle of disorder so common in households filled with a crowd of feudal retainers of all kinds, her palace had the quietude and serenity of a monastery. Never was an oath or licentious word heard among them; the name of God was honoured; and habits of devotion became cherished and familiar, where before they had been too often an occasion of mockery. All the family dined at the same table; and during the repast the Lives of the Saints, or the Holy Scriptures, were read aloud. If any fault were committed by any of the household, Blessed Lucy knew how to punish it so rigorously as to prevent a repetition of the offence; and in this she was often assisted by the gift of prophecy, which she enjoyed in a remarkable degree. We read an amusing account of two of her maidens, who took the opportunity of their mistress's absence at church to kill two fine capons, which they resolved to dress privately for their own eating. The birds were already on the spit, when their mistress was heard entering the house. Fearful of discovery, they took the half-roasted capons from the fire, and hid them under a bed. Blessed Lucy, however, knew all that had happened. "Where are the capons," she said, "that were in the court this morning?" "They have flown away," said the two women, in great confusion: "we have been looking for them every where." "Do not try to deceive God, my children," replied Blessed Lucy: "they are both under your bed; if you will follow me, I will show them to you." The servants followed her in silent dismay; but their astonishment was still more increased, when not only did she lead them to the very place where they had hidden their spoils, hut calling the birds to come out, they flew out alive, and began to crow lustily.

In another story of her life, we find her represented with her women washing the linen of the house by the side of a river that flowed by the castle. Whilst so engaged, one of them fell into the river and sank to the bottom; but Blessed Lucy made the sign of the cross over the water, and immediately the drowning woman appeared on the surface safe and sound, close to the river's bank.

And in the midst of these simple and homely occupations, the supernatural life of prayer, and ecstacy, and communion with God, was never for a moment interrupted. Strange and beautiful sights were seen by many of those who were present in the church when she communicated: sometimes a column of fire rested on her head; sometimes her face itself shone and sparkled like the sun. Once two little children, whom she had adopted as her own, saw, as they knelt behind her, two angels come and crown their mother with a garland, of exquisite roses. But the children began to weep; for they said one to another, "Certainly our mother cannot have long to live, for the angels are even now crowning her with flowers."

The beauty of her face, and its extraordinary brilliancy at these times, had a singular power in controlling those who beheld it. Even Count Pietro himself was tamed and conquered by a glance from her eye, when it shone with this more than human splendour.

This mention of Count Pietro's name reminds us that it is tune we should say something of him, and of his share in a story which has in some parts, as we read it, the character of a romance. He was not a bad man; he seems indeed to have had many good qualities, and to have been possessed in some respects of a degree of refinement beyond what was common at the time. He was sincerely attached to his saintly wife; but he could not understand her. They were beings of different worlds; and the very qualities which extorted his respect and admiration often sadly perplexed and worried him. Her very affection for himself was above his comprehension; his own feelings were too much made up of the ordinary selfishness of the world, for him to know how to measure the love of one whose love was in God. He felt her power over himself; and whilst he yielded to it, it irritated him, and not the less because there was nothing of which he could complain. This irritation showed itself in a morose jealousy, sometimes varied by fits of passionate violence; in which he went so far as to confine his wife to her room, and once even to threaten her life.

All this, and the yet more wearing trial of their daily intercourse, was borne by Blessed Lucy with unvarying sweetness and gentleness. But though she accommodated herself in every thing to his sullen temper, and even showed him a true and loyal obedience, the desire after those heavenly espousals to which she had been promised whilst still a child never left her heart; and as time went on, she began to look about for some opportunity of carrying her wishes into effect. In those days it was no uncommon spectacle to see a wife or a husband, in obedience to the interior call of heaven, abandon every tie of flesh and blood for the retirement of the cloister; nor was the propriety of such a step ever questioned. Society, as a body, in the ages of faith, acknowledged the principle, that one whom Christ calls should leave all and follow Him. When, therefore, we hear that Blessed Lucy at length resolved to leave her husband's house, and take the habit of religion in the Order of St. Dominic, we must remember that she was no more acting contrary to the custom of the age, than when she worked with her servants in the kitchen. It is not an easy matter at any time for us to judge of the vocation or conscience of another; but when we have to carry back our investigation four hundred years, we can hardly hope that the whole history of a resolution of this nature,—why it was carried out now, and why it was not carried out before her marriage,— should be laid open before us like the pages of a book. Of one thing only we cannot doubt,—God's will had been very clearly and sufficiently declared; both at first, when she consented to give up her own wishes, and now, when the time was come for them to be granted. She contented herself at first with receiving the habit of the third order, and remaining in her mother's house for a year; during which time she had to endure much from the indignation of her husband, who expressed his own disapproval of her step in a very summary way, by burning down the monastery of the prior who had given her the habit. But her uncles at length took the case into their own hands; and after considering the very extraordinary signs of a divine call which had been made manifest in her life, they decided that she should be suffered to follow it without further molestation, and placed her in the monastery of St. Catherine of Sienna at Rome.

Within a year from her entrance there, the fame of her sanctity had become so universal, that Father Joachim Turriano, the General of the Order, being about to found a new convent of nuns at Viterbo, selected her as the prioress of the new foundation; on which office she accordingly entered in the year 1496, being then exactly twenty years of age. So great was the reputation she enjoyed, that though the number of religious sent with her to Viterbo by the general was only five, the crowds that applied for admission as soon as her presence was known was so great that the convent had to be enlarged; and she soon saw herself at the head of a numerous and flourishing community.

Meanwhile, her unhappy husband had not abandoned all hopes of inducing her even yet to return to the world. He had followed her to Rome, and made vain efforts to see and speak with her: he now followed her also to Viterbo; and though unsuccessful in his attempts to obtain the slightest answer to his continual applications and appeals, he continued to linger about the convent, in the restless mood of one who would not give up his design as hopeless. Every tongue around him was busy with the fame of Lucy's saintliness; from one he heard of her almost continual prayer, from another, of the glory which was seen to hover over her face in the presence of the Blessed Sacrament: but soon, in the February following her removal to Viterbo, the interest of all was absorbed in a new report,—that she had received the sacred stigmata; and that in so remarkable a manner as to put all doubt on the subject out of the question. For it was hi the choir, with the other religious, that, being engaged in profound meditation on the Passion, she was observed by one of the sisters to look pale and as if suffering acute pain. The sister went up to her to support her, and was struck with the appearance of her hands, the bones of which seemed dislocated, and the nerves torn. "Mother of God!" she exclaimed, "what is the matter with your hands?" "Nothing," was the faint reply; "they are only gone to sleep." But within a few moments the agony she was enduring and endeavouring to conceal overpowered her, and she became perfectly senseless. They carried her from the choir and restored her to consciousness, so that she was able to return within an hour and receive Holy Communion; but the same sister who had first observed her, being convinced something very extraordinary had happened, continued to watch her, and followed her to her cell. She then remarked that her hands were livid, and the skin raised and much inflamed; and by the end of the week the wounds became large and open, and shed so great an abundance of blood that it could no longer be concealed. The excitement which followed, when these circumstances became generally known, can hardly be described. A minute investigation was first made by the Bishop of Viterbo; after which three successive commissions of inquiry were appointed by the command of the Pope to examine the affair, and each of these inquiries terminated in the declaration that the truth of the miracle was beyond all dispute. Multitudes flocked to the convent to see and touch the sacred wounds, and came back full of the wonders which their own eyes had witnessed. Duke Hercules of Este, the Pope's nephew, made earnest applications to his uncle to suffer her to be removed to his own city of Ferrara; and whilst all these things were going on, Count Pietro still remained in Viterbo.

The world about him was echoing with his wife's renown, but none knew his own connection with her. Each marvel that he heard did but seem to widen the gulf between them; yet still he stayed and lingered within sight of the walls that shut her from him for ever: now bitterly accusing himself for the blindness of his own conduct towards her; now striving to keep alive a kind of despairing hope that, could he but once gain admittance to her presence, he might even yet regain possession of a treasure which, when it was his, he knew not how to value. At length his desires were granted. A sudden inspiration induced Lucy to consent to an interview: it was the first that had taken place since she had fled from his house, and it was the last they ever had in this life.

It must have been a singular meeting: the two years of their separation had altered both. As to the Count, his restless despair had worn him to an old man. He had never seen Narni since the day of her departure for Rome, whither he had followed her; and had spent the long days of those two years hanging about the convent-gates like some miserable beggar. And the same two years had placed Lucy far beyond his reach, as it were in a supernatural world above him. When she stood before him at the grate, and he beheld her marked with those sacred and mysterious wounds, and bearing in her whole appearance the air of one whose sympathies were for ever removed from the affections of humanity, his heart failed him. He had thought to speak to her of her home, and the claims which should recall her to the world; he saw before him something a little lower than the angels; and falling on his knees, he bent his eyes to the ground, and remained silent. Then she spoke; and heaven seemed to speak to him by her voice. The mists of earthly passion rolled away from his heart as he listened; the world and its hopes died in him at that moment; an extraordinary struggle tore his very soul, then passed away, and left it in a profound calm. For the first time he caught a glimpse of that reality which till now he had treated as a dream; the world and its unquiet joys were now themselves the dream, and heaven opened on him as the reality. All life fell away from him in that hour; and when his wife ceased speaking, she had won his soul to God. He dragged himself to her feet, and bathed them in his tears; he conjured her pardon for all the persecutions and violence of the past, and renounced every right or claim over her obedience for ever. Then, leaving her without another word, he obeyed the voice which had so powerfully spoken to his heart; for within a few weeks he took the habit of the Friars Minor of the strict observance; and persevering in it for many years, died a little before his wife, with the reputation of sanctity.

Were this a romande, the story of Blessed Lucy might well end here. But her life was yet scarcely begun. Shortly after the interview with her husband just spoken of, Duke Hercules obtained the Pope's orders for her removal to Ferrara. This was only done by stealth; for the people of Viterbo having got intelligence of the design, guarded the city night and day; so that, in order to gain possession of the Saint, the duke was reduced to the expedient of loading several mules with large baskets, as if full of goods; and in one of these Blessed Lucy was concealed and carried off, under the guardianship of a strong body of armed men. Being arrived at Ferrara, the duke received her with extraordinary honours, and built a magnificent convent for her reception, to which Pope Alexander VI. granted singular privileges, by a brief wherein he declared her to have "followed the footsteps of St. Catherine of Sienna in all things." In this convent she gave the habit to her own mother, as well as to many noble ladies of Ferrara.

It were too long to tell of all the signs of Divine favour which were granted to her during the first years of her new government; of the miracles wrought by her hands, the visions of marvellous beauty that were given to her gaze; and the familiarity with which she seemed to live among the saints and angels. Thus one day, passing into the dormitory, she was met by the figure of a religious, whom she knew to be St. Catherine of Sienna. Prostrating herself at her feet, she prayed her to bless the new monastery, which was dedicated in her name. The saint willingly complied, and they went through the house together; Blessed Lucy carrying the holy water, whilst St. Catherine sprinkled the cells, as the manner is in blessing a house. Whilst they went along, they sang together the hymn *Ace Maris Stella*; and having finished, St. Catherine left her staff with Blessed Lucy, and took her leave. And another time they saw in the same dormitory a great company of angels, and the form of one of surpassing beauty, and clad in an azure robe in the midst of them, standing among them as their queen. Then she sent them hither and thither, like soldiers to their posts, and bid them guard the various offices of the monastery; "for," she said, "we must take possession of this house."

One lingers over this period of her story, unwilling to pass on to the sorrowful conclusion. God, who had elevated her so highly in the sight of the world, was about to set upon her life the seal of a profound humiliation. Hitherto she had been placed before the eyes of man as an object of enthusiastic veneration: her convent gates were crowded by persons of all ranks, who thronged only to see her for a moment. Duke Hercules of Este applied to her for counsel in all difficulties of state. The Pope had issued extraordinary briefs to enable the religious of other convents and orders to pass under her government, and even to leave the second order to join her community, which belonged to the third,—a privilege we shall scarcely find granted in any other case. But now these triumphs and distinctions were about to have an end. Blessed Lucy was about twenty-nine years of age. The honour in which she was held, and the public celebrity she enjoyed, were a continual source of sorrow and humiliation to her; and with the desire to escape from something of the popular applause which followed her, she ceased not earnestly to implore her Divine Spouse to remove from her the visible marks of the sacred stigmata, which were the chief cause of the veneration which was paid her by the world. Her request was in part granted, the wounds in her hands and feet closed; but that of the side, which was concealed from the eyes of others, remained open to the hour of her death. Whether the withdrawal of these visible tokens of the Divine favour was the cause of the change in the sentiments of her subjects, we are not told; but we find shortly after, that some among them, disgusted at her refusal to allow the community to become incorporated with the second order, rose in rebellion, and even attempted her life. The scandal of this crime was concealed through the exertions of Lucy herself; but on the death of her great protector, Duke Hercules, in 1505, the discontented members of the community recommenced their plots against her authority and reputation. Then—

designs were laid with consummate art; and at length they publicly accused her of having been seen in her cell endeavouring to re-open the wounds of her hands and feet with a knife, in order to impose on the public. Their evidence was so ably concocted, that they succeeded in gaining over the heads of the order to their side. Hasty and violent measures were at once adopted; every apostolic privilege granted by Pope Alexander was revoked; she was degraded from her office of prioress, deprived of every right and voice in the community, and placed below the youngest novice in the house. She was, moreover, forbidden to speak to any one except the confessor, kept in a strict imprisonment, and treated in every way as if proved guilty of an infamous imposture. Nor was this disgrace confined within the enclosure of her own monastery; it spread as far as her reputation had extended. All Italy was moved with a transport of indignation against her; the storm of invective which was raised reached her even in her prison; her name became a proverb of reproach through Europe; and the nuns who had been professed at her hands made their professions over again to the new prioress, as if their vows formerly made to her had been invalid.

One can hardly picture a state of desolation equal to that in which Blessed Lucy now found herself. It was as if this token of deep abjection and humiliation were required as a confirmation of her saintliness. If any such proof were indeed needed, it was furnished by the conduct which she exhibited under this extraordinary trial. During the whole remaining period of her life, a space of eight-and-thirty years, she bore her heavy cross without a murmur. Perhaps its hardest suffering was, to live thus among those whom she had gathered, together with her own hands, and had sought to lead to the highest paths of religion, compelled now to be a silent witness of their wickedness. Her life was a long prayer for her persecutors, and we are assured that no sorrow or regret ever seemed to shadow the deep tranquillity of her soul. So far as it touched herself, she took it as a more precious token of her Spouse's love than all the graces and favours He had ever heaped on her before. But it is no part of saintliness to be indifferent to the sins of others; and we can scarcely fathom the anguish which must hourly have pierced her heart, at the ingratitude and malignity of her unworthy children.

And so closed the life which had opened in such a joyous and beautiful childhood. God indeed knew how to comfort one whom the world had utterly cast out; and though cut off from the least communication with any human being, she could scarcely be pitied whilst her neglected and solitary cell was the resort of celestial visitants and friends. The reader is possibly a little tired of such tales; yet we ask his indulgence whilst referring to one of these last incidents in the life of Blessed Lucy, which we can scarcely omit. There lived at the same time, at Caramagna in Savoy, another beatified saint of the same illustrious order, Blessed Catherine of Raconigi. She had never seen Blessed Lucy; but had heard of her saintly fame, and the lustre of her life and miracles, and then also of her sufferings and disgrace. But the saints of God judge not as the world judges; and Catherine knew by the light of divine illumination the falsehood of the charges brought against her sister. She had ever longed to see and speak with her; and now more than ever, when the glitter of the world's applause was exchanged for its contumely and persecution. The thought of her sister, never seen with mortal eye, yet so dearly loved in God, never left her mind; and she prayed earnestly to their common Lord and Spouse, that He would comfort and support her, and, if such were His blessed will, satisfy in some way her own intense desire to hold some kind of intercourse with her even in this life. One night, as she was thus praying in her cell at Caramagna, her desires were heard and granted. The same evening Lucy was also alone and in prayer; and to her in like manner God had revealed the sanctity of Catherine, kindling in her heart a loving sympathy with one who, though a stranger in the world's language, had been brought very near to her heart in the mysteries of the Heart of Jesus. We cannot say how and in what way it was, but they spent that night together; but when morning came, and found her again alone as before, Lucy had received such strength and consolation from her sister's visit, that, as her biographer says, "she desired new affronts and persecutions for the glory of that Lord who knew so well how to comfort and support her in them."

Her last illness came on her in her sixty-eighth year: for eight-and-thirty years she had lived stripped of all human consolation; and the malice of her enemies continued unabated to the last. None came near her, as she lay weak and dying on her miserable bed. Like her Lord and Master, they hid their faces from her, counting her as a leper. The ordinary offices of charity, which they would have done to the poorest beggar in the streets, they denied to her; she was left to die as she had lived, alone. But if the world abandoned her, God did not. Her pillow was smoothed and tended by more than a mother's care. Saint Catherine did not neglect her charge. It is said she was more than once seen by the sick-bed, having in her company one of the sisters of the community, who had departed a short time before, with the reputation of sanctity; and together they did the office of infirmarians to the dying Saint. When the last hour drew nigh, she called the sisters around her bed, and humbly asked their pardon for any scandal she had given them in life. We do not find one word of justification, or remonstrance, or even of regret; only some broken words of exhortation, not to be offended at her imperfection, but to love God and be detached from creatures, and abide steadfastly by their rule. At midnight, on the 15th of November, 1544, she felt the moment of release was at hand; and without any death-struggle or sign of suffering, she raised her hands and cried, "Up to heaven, up to heaven!" and so expired, with a smile that remained on the dead face with so extraordinary a beauty, that none could look on it without a sentiment of awe, for they knew it was the beauty of one of God's Saints.

The truth could not longer be concealed; one supernatural token after another was given to declare the blessedness of the departed soul. Angelic voices were heard singing above the cell by all the sisters; an extraordinary perfume filled the cell and the whole house; and the community, who had probably for the most part been deceived by one or two in authority, without any malice on their own part, now loudly insisted on justice being done to the deceased. It was done, so far as funeral honours can make amends for a life of cruelty and calumniation. The body was exposed in the church; and the fickle crowds who had called her an impostor while living, crowded now to see and touch the sacred remains. The wound in her side was examined, and found dripping with fresh wet blood; the sick were cured, and evil spirits cast out, by cloths which had been placed on the relics.

Four years after the body was taken from its grave, and found fresh and beautiful as in life. Then it was again exposed in the church to the veneration of the faithful, who crowded once more to pay it honour, and were wonder-struck at the perfume, as of sweet violets, which issued from it, and attached to every thing which it touched. And it was again disinterred, little more than a century ago, in 1710, when it presented the same appearance as before, and the sacred stigmata were observed distinct and visible to all. On this occasion a part of the body was translated to Narni, where it now reposes in a magnificent shrine, and receives extraordinary honours, amid the scene of her childish devotion to the Christarello. Perhaps, as we read of these honours to the dead, we may feel they were but poor reparation for the calumnies and injuries heaped on her while living: or, if we seek to measure these things in the balance of the sanctuary, we can believe that to her blessed spirit now, those long years of abandonment and desolation, which cut her off from all communion with this earth for more than half her mortal life, were a far more precious gift than all the shrines, and funeral honours, and popular veneration, which the world in its tardy repentance was moved to give her.

She was finally beatified by Benedict XIII. towards the middle of the last century.

DOMINICA OF PARADISO.

About four hundred years ago there lived at a small country village near Florence, called Paradiso, a poor gardener and his wife, whose names were Francis and Costanza. They had several children, of whom the youngest was named Dominica, who was brought up to the life of labour and hardship ordinary among the poorer peasantry of Italy, and whose daily task it was to help in the cultivation of the garden on which the whole family depended for support. Beyond the first rudiments of the Christian faith, Dominica received no education; for her parents were in no way superior in intelligence to others of their class in life. Nevertheless, from her very infancy she showed signs that the few instructions which they were able to give her had made a wonderful impression on her heart; and as her soul received each new religious idea, it was cherished and meditated on; so that she gathered materials enough out of these simple elements to build up a life of the highest contemplative prayer. Among all the biographies of the saints which have been preserved to us, there are few which so vividly illustrate the growth of a profound and supernatural devotion in the heart of an uneducated child as that before us. Nor will it be thought that the extreme simplicity which mingles with some of the passages of her life which are here selected, lessens the beauty of a narrative whose incidents charm us like a poem.

Dominica was marked in a special way as the child of Mary, even from her cradle. The first occasion when we read of the Blessed Virgin appearing to her was one day when she was lying on her poor little bed, being then only four years old. The presence of the Divine Mother with a train of shining angels then first awoke in her little heart a longing after God and heaven; and she began to pray-though scarcely knowing the meaning of the words she uttered-that she might be taught the way to reach that glory, the vision of which had captivated her imagination. Then she came to understand that fidelity to God's precepts, and contrition for sin, was the path of saintliness; and so were traced out on her soul the first lineaments of perfection. Now she had learnt that contrition was a sorrow for sin; and the simple sort of catechism which her mother was accustomed to teach her spoke also of the heart being full of sin, and how tears of penitence were necessary to wash it from its corrupt steins. A metaphor of any kind was far beyond the reach of Dominica's comprehension; she therefore took these expressions in a very straightforward way, and wept heartily to think her heart should be so defiled and dangerous a thing. And the handkerchief which was wet with her childish tears she laid over her breast, thinking that this must be the way to wash away the stains they talked of.

All day long she revolved in her mind the one idea which had been revealed to her soul,—perfection, as the road to God's presence; and thinking incessantly of these things amid the various occupations in which she was engaged, she came to make every part of her day's work associated with the subjects of her meditation. To her eye, all untaught by man, but enlightened by the Divine light, the invisible things of God were clearly seen by the things that were visible. Once she was helping an elder sister to make some cakes mixed with poppy-seeds, to give to her brother who was ill and suffering from want of sleep. As she baked the cakes, her thoughts were, as usual, busy finding divine meanings in the things before her. The interior voice, whose whispers she as yet scarcely understood, seemed to speak to her of another kind of food which should satisfy the soul, so that it should slumber and repose in the sleep of Divine love. Then she prayed very earnestly to be given this wonderful food; and the voice spoke in answer, and said, "Daughter, the food of which I spake is none other than My love, with which when the saints in heaven are filled and satisfied, they sleep so sweetly, that they forget all created things, and watch only unto Me." And Dominica wondered how the saints took this marvellous slumber, and whether it were on beds made like her own straw mattress, or in the bosom of God, even as her mother was wont to rock the little baby to sleep. When she was at work, in the garden, she would raise her eyes to heaven, and think how she could make her heart a garden of flowers for the delight of God. And once, as she so mused, He who had undertaken the office of teacher and director to her soul appeared to her, and taught her that prayer would keep that soul ever fresh and green before Him; and that He would open in that garden five limpid and crystal fountains to refresh it, even the five wounds of His Sacred Passion; and that she, on her part, must keep it free from weeds, daily plucking up evil passions, and the idle thoughts of vanity and the world; that so it might be beautiful to the eye, and abundant in all-pleasant fruits. If she ran upstairs, her thoughts ascended to heaven; if she came down, she abased herself in the depths of lowliness and humility. The oxen ploughing in the field reminded her to bear meekly the yoke of obedience; and as she stood in her father's wine-press she taught herself to tread under her own will and nature, if she would taste of the sweetness of divine consolations. Once the sight of a hen with her brood of chickens so vividly brought before her the mystery of the Incarnation, and that wonderful love which gave its life to cover our sins and shield us from the wrath of God, that she was rapt in a state of ecstasy, and so remained in the garden all that day and the following night. And again, as she gathered the ripe apples which her mother was hoarding for the winter, she became absorbed in contemplating the beauty of that soul wherein the fruits of virtue are brought forth, making it pleasant in the eye of God. And she sighed deeply, and said, "Oh, that I knew how to store my soul with these precious fruits! how happy should I then be!" And the Spouse of her heart came swiftly to her, and showed her how for every apple she gathered for the love of Him, there was brought forth a glorious fruit within her soul, more gracious and beautiful in His sight than the fairest apples of her garden. All this was going on in her mind whilst yet not six years old; and so her life divided itself between the homely exterior labour and rough discipline of a peasant life, and an interior of spiritual contemplation, wherein were revealed to her many of the profoundest secrets of mystic theology. The world became to her a book written within and without with the name of God; all creatures talked to her of Him. And this was sometimes permitted to be manifested in extraordinary ways; as once, when walking by the side of a lake near their cottage, the thought suggested itself that the fish, being creatures of God, must be obedient to Him, and ready to do Him service. Therefore she stood by the water-side, and called them to come and help her whilst she sang His praises; and the fish, swimming to the shore, did so after their kind, leaping and jumping about out of the water; while she sat on the grass, and sang a little song which she had learnt, and was fond of repeating to herself over her work in the garden.

One day she was ill, and her mother desired her to eat some meat, which she did, although it was Friday; and afterwards felt great scruples, fearing she had committed a great sin. She had never yet been to confession, being under the age when it is usual for children to confess. But she now felt very anxious to relieve her conscience of this weight; only, being confined to her bed, she could not get to the church; nor did she dare to ask her mother to send for the priest. She therefore considered within herself what she should do; and she remembered to have seen the people in the church not only kneeling in the confessionals, but also before the crucifixes and devout images on the altars; and in her simplicity, she thought that they were likewise confessing their sins to them. Now there was a little picture of the Madonna holding the Holy Child in her arms, which hung in her room, and Dominica thought she could confess to this; therefore, getting out of bed, she knelt down devoutly before it, and confessed her fault in eating the meat with many tears, praying the little Jesus to give her absolution for her fault, which she thought He would do by placing His hand on her head, as she had seen the old priest do to the little children of the village. But when she had knelt a long time, and saw that the image did not move, she became very unhappy, and prayed all the harder that He would not deny her absolution, but would give her the sign she asked for. Then it pleased our Lord to grant her the answer which her simple confidence extorted from Him; and the figures of the Mother and the Son raised their hands, and placed them on the child's head, who remained filled with delight at the thought that her sins were now forgiven her, and her conscience at rest.

After this her mother took her once a year to confession in the church. It grieved her much not to be able to go oftener; but her angel-guardian taught her to submit in this matter to her mother's pleasure, and to supply the place of more frequent confession by every evening examining her conscience, and confessing her daily faults before the same picture as before. Nor was this the only teaching which she received from him; he taught her that the path to Paradise was a way of suffering; and that they who aspired to the mystic nuptials of Christ were careful to clothe themselves with the livery of the cross. And Dominica, in obedience to these instructions, began to afflict her body with fasts and other austerities, and gave the food which she saved from her own dinner to the poor. She ever showed great devotion to the Blessed Virgin, especially after the circumstances narrated above; and made it her particular duty to light the lamp before her picture every Saturday, and to garland it with flowers on that day, as being specially dedicated to her. On one of these occasions, Mary appeared to her with her Divine Child in her arms, and promised her that in reward for her devotion she should one day become His spouse, but not until she had grown further in perfection and in His love. This promise became thenceforth the absorbing subject of her thoughts; and at seven years of age she consecrated herself to Him, whom from that hour she considered her Spouse, by a solemn vow, cutting off her beautiful golden hair, as she understood the custom was, and offering it to her Lord. When her mother saw her hair cut off, she was greatly displeased, and commanded her to suffer it to grow again, and not to attempt to cut it a second time. Dominica obeyed; but she secretly prayed that God would send her some infirmity of the head, which might prevent the growth of the hair. And this indeed happened; so that the head remained closely cut until her fifteenth year, when it was cured, and miraculously crowned, as we shall see, by God.

Our Blessed Lady very often favoured her with her visible presence; but on these occasions she appeared alone, and without her Son. Dominica was greatly grieved at the absence of her Lord, and at length one day resolved to ask the Blessed Virgin the reason why He never came. "O Divine Lady," she said, "you come very often to see me and talk to me; but you never bring Him who is to be my Spouse; why is this, for it grieves me that I never see Him?" Then our Lady, smiling on her, showed her the Holy Infant sleeping in her bosom. Dominica was delighted at the sight. "But how very small He is!" she exclaimed "He will grow," replied Mary, "when you will, and as much as you will; and as she spoke, Dominica perceived that He was already much larger. "Ah! He is already growing," she exclaimed; "now He is twice the size He was!—how is that?" "He grows with your growth," again replied Mary; "and your growth must be not in the flesh, but in the spirit: when you have attained to your full growth in holiness, He will come and celebrate those espousals which you desire so much." Then the Child extended His hand to Dominica as a token of His renewed promise; and the vision disappeared. She remained very sad and disconsolate; and her grief, when she thought of the loveliness of Jesus, and the long time that was yet to elapse before His promise could be fulfilled, became so poignant, that she fell ill, and spent eight days in continual tears and sorrow of heart. This abandonment of her soul to grief was by no means pleasing to the Blessed Virgin, who appeared again at the end of the eight days, and gave her a sharp reproof for her want of resignation. "Daughter," she said, "you grieve for the loss of sensible consolations; but know this, that to those who attach themselves to such things, visions, and revelations, and the sensible presence of the Beloved, are not blessings but evils: wherefore put away your sorrow, and serve God with a joyful and contented heart." "But how can I be joyful," said the weeping child, "whilst I am so far from my Spouse and His palace, and still kept a prisoner in this vale of tears?" Then the merciful heart of Mary was moved with pity, and she said, "Follow me with your eyes, and you shall see a glimpse of the country where He dwells;" and so saying, she rose towards heaven before her eyes. Dominica watched her as she had said, and she saw how the heavens opened to receive their queen; and caught through the parted doors of those celestial regions something of the glory of the New Jerusalem. She saw her pass on through the countless choirs of the angels, till she came close to the throne of God; and in the midst of the unapproachable light she saw the Child Jesus, more beautiful and glorious than she had ever seen Him before; and then, even as she gazed on Him, forgetting all beside, the golden gates closed on the scene, and shut it from her eyes. Now when Dominica looked round, and saw that it had all passed away, she remained full of an unspeakable longing to reach that glorious country, or at least to see it once again. She kept her eyes constantly fixed on the sky, for she thought perhaps it might once more open; and in her simplicity she thought she should be nearer to her Lord, and to the beauty amid which He dwelt, on high places: therefore, at night, when all the family were asleep, she rose softly, and taking a ladder, mounted to the roof, where she spent the night in prayer, looking wistfully at the stars, which she thought were at least little sparks of that great glory which had been revealed to her. And having repeated this several times, it pleased God more than once to open the vision of heaven to her again; so that she came to have a familiarity with that blessed place, and to know the choirs of angels one from another, and to tell the different degrees of the blessed by the crowns they wore, and many ether mysteries which, whilst she beheld, she as yet did not fully comprehend.

When Easter came, her mother took her to church, and she saw all the people going to Communion, and grieved much to think she was too young to be suffered to approach with them. It seemed also very strange to her that they should come to so wonderful a banquet, and go away again, just as if nothing had happened to them; and she thought it would not be so with her: for, indeed, whenever she was present at Mass, and the priest elevated the Sacred Host before her eyes, she saw the visible person of her divine Spouse, adorned with so wonderful a beauty that it seemed marvellous to her that no one else seemed moved by the sight; and she thought that all saw what she saw, and never dreamt that it was a revelation granted to her eyes alone. And once, as she thus reasoned within herself, and looked sorrowfully on the crowds who were going to receive a happiness which was denied to her, the Lord of her soul Himself drew near to comfort her with a fore-taste of His presence, and Dominica felt on her tongue a drop of His precious Blood.

Autumn brought the harvest, and with it hard work in the fields for Dominica, whose prayers and visions never interrupted her life of dai-ly labour. She was one day in the fields watching them burn the stubble, and helping to heap the loads of straw and rubbish on to the fire. With childlike glee, she danced and clapped her hands to see the flames leaping high into the air; and she thought to herself that the fire was like Divine love, and longed that her own heart could be con-sumed in its flames like the worthless straw. Then the voice of her Spouse spoke within her and said, "What would you do, Dominica, if you saw your Spouse in the midst of those flames?" And she an-swered, "I would run to Him and embrace Him." "But," replied the voice, "would you not fear the fire? do you not remember how terrible was the pain when your sister burnt her hand?" And even at that mo-ment Dominica saw through the flames, how a beautiful lady entered the field on the other side of the fire, leading a child of surpassing loveliness by the hand. As she looked at them the lady spoke to her: "Dominica," she said, "why are you here, and what do you seek?" And Dominica replied, "I am looking at the flames, and I am seeking for God in them!" "God." answered the lady, "is very near you, and yet you do not know Him." Then her eyes opened, and she knew that she had been speaking to no other than Jesus and Mary; and forgetting the fire and her own danger, and all but the presence of her Beloved, she ran through the flames to the other side, and cast herself at His feet. In doing this she was severely burnt, for her legs and arms were bare like other peasant children; but Dominica did not feel the pain, for she was gazing on her Lord. And the glorious Child took her lovingly by the hand, and said, "O Dominica, thou has conquered flames for the love of Me; therefore shall thou ever abide in My grace, and shalt dwell with Me for ever." Then he blessed her; and disappearing from sight, Dominica was again alone. On looking round her, she found that it was quite dark, and the stars were shining brightly; for the moments that had seemed to her to fly so quickly had indeed been hours, and it was now night. She began to be very frightened; knowing that her ab-sence would cause great alarm; but we are assured that, on returning in the morning, she found she had not been missed, her angel-guardian having taken her form, and discharged all the household offices which it was her duty to perform.

On another occasion, she was as usual at work in the garden, whilst her brothers were bringing in a load of manure which smelt very offensive. The habit of drawing spiritual meanings from all external objects had become so completely second nature to Dominica, that her thoughts seem to have shaped themselves into these analogies on all occasions. The bad smell therefore suggested to her mind an image of mortal sin, and she prayed that she might be taught in some way how it appeared in the eyes-of God. At that moment a soldier entered the garden for the purpose of purchasing some vegetables, and Dominica perceived that his soul was very offensive in the sight of God. She looked in his face, and it seemed to her so disfigured by foul and monstrous deformity, that she was moved with a deep compassion for him; she prayed therefore very earnestly, that God would give him the grace of conversion, and save him from his miserable state. She longed to say something to him; but not daring to address him, she remained before him, still looking up in his face, and weeping bitterly. Her manner at length drew his attention, and he asked her what was the matter, and why she kept thus looking at him and weeping. "I weep," she answered, "because your soul is so ugly; you must certainly be very unhappy. How is it you do not remember the Precious Blood which redeemed you from the power of the devil? Do you not see the bow bent, and the arrow ready to fly?" "What bow, and what arrow, are you talking of?" said the astonished man. "The bow," replied the child, "is divine justice, and the arrow is death and the judgment, which will certainly overtake you if you do not change your wicked life and become a good man." As she spoke, the simplicity of her words fairly conquered the obdurate heart to which they were addressed. With tears rolling down his cheeks, he knelt before her, and confessed he was indeed an enormous sinner, who deserved nothing but hell; but that if she would help him with her prayers, he would go that very day to confession, and begin a new life; and with this promise he left her. For eight days Dominica continued in very earnest prayer for him, in spite of unheard-of troubles and persecutions of the devils; but on the eighth she knew that her prayers had been heard, for she saw his soul white and clean like that of a newly-baptised child; and he himself came to thank her for the grace she had obtained for him, and by means of which he had been enabled to make a good and contrite confession. He told her, moreover, that he was resolved to leave the world and retire to a hermitage, to spend the remainder of his life in penance; but prayed her, before he went, at least to give him her blessing. This request puzzled Dominica; and she replied she would readily oblige him, but she did not know how. Then her angel raised her little hand, and guided it to sign the sign of the Cross above his head; and a voice which was not hers said for her, "May God bless thee in this world and in the world to come." Fourteen years after, this man died in his hermitage, with the reputation of sanctity.

This first conversion awoke in her soul an ardent thirst for the salvation of sinners. It was a new feeling, and to her quick and sensitive soul one which soon became wholly absorbing. Happening about this time to see a little picture representing the sufferings of the souls in hell, she was greatly touched with compassion, and innocently prayed God to relieve them and set them free. Then her faithful guardian instructed her on this matter, and taught her that the only way to save souls from hell was, to prevent sin and convert sinners by her prayers. And to increase her zeal he showed her, not a picture, but the real sufferings of the lost souls; and the sentiments of pity which these excited were so lively, that a desire awoke within her to suffer something in her own body, in order to save other souls from these terrible flames. And with the idea of experiencing something of a like kind of suffering, she took a lighted torch, and courageously held it to her shoulder till the flesh was burnt, which caused her agonies of pain for many days. These, however, she had self-command enough to conceal, in spite of some emotions of very natural alarm, which determined her to find out if possible some other less dangerous method of afflicting her body. She even prayed God to teach her in what way she should do this; and one day seeing a picture in the church of St. John Baptist clothed in his garment of camel's hair, the thought was suggested to her mind of forming some such garment for herself out of horsehair; which she accordingly did, and wore it for nine years. And here one can hardly fail to admire the means by which, step by step, she was led on in the path of a saintly life. Human teaching she had none; she had probably never seen a book: but yet we see how the commonest incidents and accidents, being accompanied by God's grace, were enough to reveal the secrets of His counsels to her soul. A picture, or a chance word, or the thought which rose spontaneously out of some image of the visible things around her, were food enough for a soul which literally "waited continually upon God;" it drew sustenance and life out of what seemed the very barrenest desert.

From this time commenced a new life of austerity, so rigorous and continual, that extraordinary strength must have been supplied to have enabled her to live under the perpetual tortures she inflicted on her innocent flesh. And though in the details of these austerities we find many things precisely similar to those related of other saints, yet it is certain that their lives and examples were wholly unknown to her, and therefore that in this matter she must have followed the instinct of her own devotion, guided by the Spirit of God. But, again, we observe how she was directed by that quick and watchful eye of the soul which let nothing escape its vigilance;—a coarse and common print of the Scourging of our Divine Lord, once seen, was enough to teach Dominica those sharp disciplines to blood in which she persevered during the remainder of her life.

We pass over the account of many temptations and apparitions of evil spirits, to give the story of one vision with which she was favoured, whose beauty can perhaps scarcely be equalled by any similar incident to be met with in the Lives of the Saints. It has been said that she was accustomed to observe Saturday as a day of special devotion in honour of the Madonna, whose image on that day had its garland of fresh flowers hung up, and its little lamp brightly burning in the midst. Now it happened that one Saturday Dominica had taken unusual care in the decoration of her little image; she had picked her choicest flowers, and hung them in wreaths and bunches which took her some little time to arrange. But her trouble was well rewarded; for the Blessed Virgin reached out her hand and took some of the flowers, and smelt them, and then gave them to her Son, that He might smell them likewise. Dominica, full of delight, besought them ever thus to smell her flowers, and to forget the unworthiness of her who offered them. And then she remembered that she could not stand there looking at her beloved Madonna any longer; for it was the hour when she was accustomed to go to the cottage-door with the scraps she had saved from her dinner, that she might give alms to any poor beggar who should be passing by. Accordingly, she ran to the door with her basket of broken bread, and waited patiently till some object of charity should pass that way. At length she perceived a woman approaching, leading a child by the hand. By their dress she saw that they were very poor; yet there was an air of dignity, almost of majesty, in the manner and appearance of both. They came up to the spot where she stood; and the child, addressing himself to her with a certain gracious sweetness, held out his hands, as if begging, and said, "You will certainly give me something, my good little peasant girl?" And as he did so, she perceived that in either hand there was a large open wound; and that his dress was likewise covered with blood, as from a fresh wound in his side. Touched with compassion, she bade them wait whilst she entered the house for something to give them; but she had scarcely done so, when she perceived that they were by her side. "Ah!" said Dominica, "what have you done! if my mother knows I have let any one in, she will never forgive me." "Fear nothing," said the woman; "we shall do no harm, and no one will see us." Then Dominica saw that the child's feet were likewise bleeding; and pitying him very much, she said, "How can your son walk on the rough roads with those wounded feet of his?" And his mother replied, "The child's love is so great, he never complains of himself." Now as they were thus talking, the child was looking at the image garlanded with the lovely fresh roses; and with a winning and innocent grace he held up his little hands and asked for some of the flowers: and Dominica could not refuse to give them to him; for spite of their poor rags, there was something about her strange visitors which captivated her heart. And the mother took the roses, and smelt them, and gave them to her son; and turning to Dominica, she said, "Why do you garland that image with flowers? it would seem as if you cared for it very much." "It is the Madonna and the Holy Child Jesus," answered Dominica; "and I give them my flowers because I love them dearly." "And how much do you love them?" continued the woman. "As much as I can," said Dominica. "And how much is that?" said the woman again. "Ah!" replied Dominica, "it is as much as they help me too." But still as she spoke she could not take her eyes off the child; for his extraordinary grace and beauty filled her with an emotion she could not comprehend. "Why do you stand thus gazing at my son?" said the woman; "what do you see in him?" "He is such a beautiful child," said Dominica; and she leant over him to caress him. But she started back with surprise, for those wounds gave forth a wonderful odour, as of Paradise; and turning, to the woman, she exclaimed, "Mother of God! what is this? with what do you anoint your son's wounds, for the odour of them is sweeter than my sweetest flowers?" "It is the ointment of charity," said the mother; but Dominica scarcely heard the reply: she was still gazing at the child, and trying to attract his notice, as the manner is with children. "Come to me, my child," she said, "and I will give you this piece of bread." "It is of no use," said the mother; "tell him of Jesus, and how you love Him, and the child will come readily enough." And at the words he did indeed come; and looking up sweetly into Dominica's face, he asked, "And do you really love Jesus?" And that sweet odour became so marvellously powerful, that she was yet more filled with surprise; and she said, "O beautiful child, what wonder is this? if your wounds give forth this delicious perfume, what will the perfume of Paradise be like?" "Do not wonder," said the mother, "that the perfume of Paradise should be where God is;" and then the blindness fell from her eyes, and she knew that she was talking to none other than to Jesus and Mary. And even at that moment the poor rags fell off them, and she saw them dressed in royal robes of surpassing splendour; and the Child Jesus grew to the stature of a man, whilst over the wound of His side there gleamed the radiance of a brilliant star. Dominica fell prostrate at their feet as they rose into the air; and taking the roses from His mother's bosom, the Divine Spouse scattered them over the head and garments of His beloved, and said, "O My spouse! thou hast adorned My image with garlands and roses, and therefore do I sprinkle thee with these flowers, as an earnest of the everlasting garland with which I will crown these in Paradise;" and so saying, they both disappeared. Dominica strove in vain to follow them with her eyes; but for eight days after there remained the perfume of the wounds, and her head and dress were seen covered with flowers.

At length she arrived at the age when it is customary for children to make their first Communion; and her mother, therefore, took her during Lent to the priest, that he might examine and prepare her for that purpose. A very few words satisfied him that she was full of Divine grace, and he accordingly desired her to go to communion at the approaching Easter, which was considerably sooner than her mother had intended. "How can I do so?" said Dominica; "I am only eleven years old, and my mother is used to say, 'Children should not go to Communion till they are twelve.' Moreover, there are but three weeks to Easter, and in that short time I can never prepare fitly to receive our Lord;" and so saying, she began to weep. Nevertheless, the priest laid her under obedience to do as he had said, and sent her away; and Dominica returned home with her thoughts full of this weighty matter of the three weeks of preparation. Now the dignity of the Holy Sacrament appeared to her so very great, that she thought a year would be too little to make ready the chamber of her heart; and thinking how she could make the most of the short time allowed her, she determined not to go to bed for that time but to remain in prayer and meditation all night, that she might make the weeks longer; for indeed, she was so simply impressed with the conviction of her own vileness, that she dreaded lest the Sacred Host should disappear, or some other token of Divine displeasure should be evinced, if she approached without much preparation and examination of heart. So, as we have said, she never went to bed; but remained kneeling and praying all night, examining her innocent conscience, and going over a world of resolutions and forms of preparation, which she believed were necessary to be got through in the time. It was a child's simple thought;—we love Domini-ca all the better for the childishness that forgot that its excellent resolve was an impossible one for flesh and blood to keep;—for very often the poor little girl was conquered by weariness, and fell asleep in the midst of her long prayers, and in spite of her manful efforts to keep awake; and then she would try to rouse herself with the thought of her preparation for Communion, and begin all over again, with a kind of nervous terror that the time would be too short after all.

At length Holy Week came, and her mother took her to Florence to hear the preaching of the Passion at the great church of St. Reparata. It was a new life to Dominica: seated by her mother's side, she drank in every word of the impassioned eloquence of the preacher; and with her usual innocence, believed that Christ would really visibly appear, and suffer before the eyes of the people as He did on Calvary. And when the preacher said, "yesterday He was betrayed," and "to-day He is led to death," she believed he spoke literally; for she had not learnt to un-derstand metaphors better than when, a child of four years old, she had desired to know the kind of bed that the angels slept on. And, indeed, the spectacle was given to her eyes, and she saw the scene of the Cru-cifixion, and how Mary stood beneath the Cross, and how Nicodemus took down the Sacred Body and laid it in her arms. She saw it, as it were, in the midst of the crowd of people who stood round her, and wondered how they looked so unconcerned; and she herself longed to push her way through them to get nearer to her dying Lord; but the crowd kept her back. Then, when she got back to her own room at home, she knelt down to think of what she had witnessed; and the Blessed Virgin appeared to her, and taught her that it had been but a vision, and one revealed to her alone, and not to the people. Dominica then told her all her fears that her preparation had been too short; that our Lord would certainly never allow her to come to Him; and that she was so unworthy and unfit to communicate, she should drive Him out of the church. But Mary comforted her, and assured her that the tears of contrition she had shed were all the preparation He required.

When Dominica heard this she was a little consoled; yet her fear lest the Sacred Host should indeed fly from her as unworthy was so great, that she spent Holy Saturday in incessant prayer, promising pil-grimages, fasts on bread and water, and every devotion she could remember, if only our Lord would deign to remain with her on the fol-lowing day. Thus the whole night passed, and in the morning she went, pale and trembling to the church to receive Holy Communion with her mother.

Her agitation increased every moment; but at length it was her turn to go up to the alter steps. She did so, and the priest came to her and pronounced the customary words; but she did not seem to hear him: he bent down over her to rouse her from her stupor; and it was not till he had shaken her by her dress that she was sufficiently recovered to receive. Yet this was not an emotion of terror, but an ecstasy of joy; for at that moment her fears and scruples had been removed by the sight of the Sacred Host, not flying from her as she had feared, but shining like a glorious sun, whose brilliant rays overpowered her by their excessive lustre.

It would be tedious to give in detail any thing like a faithful narration of the ecstasies with which from this time she was favoured every time she communicated. They were so wonderful and so numerous, that we are assured she made a vow by which she obliged herself never to move from the spot where she knelt; and that she did this in order to control the impulse which urged her to cast herself at the feet of her Lord, whom she saw in so glorious a shape whenever the Sacred Host was elevated before her eyes.

Time went on, and Dominica was no longer a child. With womanhood came the cares and charge of the entire family; for her mother, seeing her grave, diligent, and prudent, left every thing in her hands, and troubled herself with none of the household duties. With unmurmuring obedience Dominica accepted every thing that was laid on her; she swept and washed the house, cooked the food, washed the clothes, looked after the garden and the horses, and saw to every thing which was sent to the market. Long before break of day she had to be up to load the mules, and give them in charge to her brother Leonard. When they came home late in the evening, it was she, tired with her innumerable labours, who had to take them to the stable and make up their stalls. Not a moment of her time but was filled up with hard bodily work and fatigue; yet, thanks to the habits of her childhood, she knew how to infuse into all these the spirit of prayer; and her incessant occupations never put a stop to the devotions and austerities which she had accustomed herself to practise; nay, she found means to make them assist her in her mortification. She contrived two crosses of wood garnished with sharp nails, which she constantly wore in such a way, that at every movement of the body, in washing, sweeping, and working in the garden, the nails pressed into the flesh; and so constantly reminded her of the sufferings of her Lord, even when externally engaged in the commonest employments of her peasant life.

But in spite of the way in which she strove to do all in and for God, she secretly sighed after the retirement of the desert or the cloister, and for space and time to pour out her soul in that fulness of contemplation and love which swelled like a deep ocean within it. When she was fifteen, she accidentally heard the history of St. Mary Magdalen for the first time; and the account of her retirement and long penance in the desert of Marseilles made an impression on her mind which was never effaced. She longed to imitate her, and to find some secret place where she might commence a similar life. Believing this desire to be the vocation of God, she accordingly determined on the experiment; and secretly leaving her mother's house one night, she went on foot to a neighbouring mountain, and entered a thick wood, where she hoped to find some cavern where she might take up her abode. Her first adventure was the meeting with a wolf; but Dominica knelt down on the earth, not without some secret emotions of terror, and recommended herself to God; after which she rose, and commanded the animal in God's name to depart without hurting her, which he did, and she pursued her way without further alarm. At length, near the Valle del Monte, she found such a spot as she was in search of. There was a grotto sunk in the rocky side of the mountain, and near its mouth ran a stream of crystal water. It was the very picture of a hermitage; and Dominica's happiness was complete. She immediately prepared to take up her night's lodging in her grotto. But alas! picturesque and inviting as it seemed, it was very small; so small, that when the fervent little devotee had crawled into it, and knelt down to give vent to her joy and thankfulness, she found it impossible to get her whole body into its shelter; but her feet remained outside, and what was worse, dipping into the cold water of the stream. These inconveniences, however, were neither cared for nor even noticed by Dominica. She was alone with God, and that was enough for her. Three days and nights she spent in her little cavern, absorbed in ecstatic contemplation, and without food of any kind; but on the third day a voice spoke to her, and roused her from her long trance of silent happiness. "Dominica," it said, "rise and come forth; I have already forgiven thee thy sins." At these words she rose and left her cavern, and beheld a beautiful sight. The Valle del Monte was before her, at she had seen it the evening of her arrival; there was not a human habitation to be seen, nothing but the green woods which clothed the mountain side, and the clear waters of the little stream, and the rocky summits of the hills which rose above the trees. But all these objects were now lit up by a wonderful light, brighter than that of the sun which fell on them from heaven. It grew every moment more and more dazzling, and then she saw in the midst the form of her Divine Lord, attended by his Blessed Mother and a vast company of angels. He spoke again, "Dominica, what seekest thou here, amid these rocks and woods?" "I have been seeking Thee, O Lord," she replied, "and it seems to me that I have found Thee." "But," returned her Spouse, "when I chose thee for my divine espousal, it was not to do thine own will, nor to enjoy aught else than My good pleasure, in doing which thou shalt alone find peace. I have not called thee to the quietude of the desert, but that thou shouldst help me to bear My cross in the great city yonder,—the heavy cross which sinners make for Me by their sins. Hereafter shalt thou see My face in heaven and contemplate Me there for ever; but for the present moment, return to thy mother's house, and wait for the manifestation of My will." "I go," said Dominica; "yet I know not what I can do for Thee in the world; I am nothing but a poor peasant girl, who have been brought up among beasts and oxen. Moreover, if I go back, my mother will certainly beat me, for I have been away three days." "Fear nothing," was the answer; "for an angel has taken thy form, and they do not know of thine absence."

Then Dominica found herself transported, she knew not how, back to her own little room in her mother's house; and whilst she still wondered, she heard her brother's voice calling hastily to her from below to come and help unload the mules. Dominica obeyed; but she was not a little confused, when on coming down he began to ask her about some money which he had given her the evening before. She knew of no money,—for, indeed, it had been given not to her, but to the angel in her likeness; and she would have been sorely puzzled how to satisfy his demands, if the angel had not discovered to her the place where the money was placed. And so her absence remained a secret to the family; nor were the circumstances ever revealed, until many years after, when, a short time before her death, her confessor obliged her under obedience to reveal all the graces with which God had favoured her.

At length, in her twentieth year, Dominica resolved to leave the world altogether and enter religion. Her wish was not opposed by her mother, and she entered as lay-sister in the Augustinian convent at Florence. The sisters received her very warmly, for her character for holiness and her discretion and industry were well known to them; and they immediately employed her, much to their own satisfaction, in the garden and kitchen; and kept her so constantly and laboriously occupied, that poor Dominica found that she had even less time for her exercises of prayer than when at home. She endeavoured to make up for the loss by secretly rising at night; but when this was discovered, the Superior, with a mistaken charity, would send her to bed again, saying that after all her hard day's work she needed rest; not perceiving that the real rest she required was time for her soul to commune with God. Dominica, therefore, became very unhappy; and one day as she was digging in the garden she heard a mournful voice speak plainly and articulately by her side, saying, "Ah, My spouse! why hast thou left Me thus?" And it seemed to her that it was the voice of her Lord, who tenderly expostulated with her for suffering the intercourse which had so closely bound them together to be broken and interrupted by so many occupations. She threw the spade on the ground, and sitting down, covered her face with her hands and wept bitterly. Was it never to end, this life of many cares? It seemed as though her soul, which was struggling to rise into the serene and quiet atmosphere of contemplation, was ever destined to be kept down amid cares and labours from which she could not escape, and which yet seemed, as it were, to separate her from her Lord. So long as it had been His will, she had never resisted nor complained; but now it was not His will. He had said so; and the sweet sorrowful tone pierced her very heart, as she dwelt on the words, and the accent in which they were uttered,—"Ah! why hast thou left Me thus?" And as she wept and prayed and sorrowed, yet saw no way of escape, the same voice spoke again; but now they were words of comfort and encouragement: "Be at peace, Dominica; God will follow His own will, and you shall be comforted." And, indeed, a short time after she was attacked by a sickness, which compelled the sisters to send her back to her mother's house; and though on recovering she returned to them, yet she was again taken ill, and again forced to leave. A third time her mother took her back to the convent; but Dominica knew that it was not God's wish that she should receive the Augustinian habit: and the nuns themselves seemed to feel that this was the case; though, as they well knew her worth and sanctity, it cost them many regrets before they could consent to her finally leaving their community. She returned home, therefore; and now, with the advice of her confessor, entered on a life of strict religious retirement in her mother's house, until the designs of God regarding her should be more plainly manifested.

The manner of this new life was not a little remarkable. Next to the room where her mother slept was a little rubbish-closet, scarcely large enough to stand in; this she cleared from its rubbish, and chose for her cell. The constant sickness and infirmities which she suffered after her illnesses at the convent prevented her from going out at night and contemplating the heavens, as had been her custom when a child. But she retained her old love for them, and contrived to make a little heaven of blue paper on the roof of her closet, and to cover it with gold stars; which, though but a poor substitute for an Italian sky—that sea of deep liquid sapphire, wherein float the bright stars, looking down like the eyes of the seraphim,—yet doubtless had its charm to the simple taste of its designer; and at any rate it reminded her, during the hours of her prayer, of the beautiful days of her childhood, when the heavens opened to her wondering eyes, and she became familiar with its inhabitants, and thought to get nearer to them and to her Lord by climbing on the roof of the house. Then at one end of the closet was a small altar, and on it a crib, and a representation of Mary, and the Divine Child lying on the straw,—much after the fashion of those still in common use among the peasants of Italy; for she always bore a special devotion to the mystery of the Infancy. A stool before the altar, a wooden bench, and two boxes, completed the furniture of her cell. There was no bed: she allowed herself but two hours' sleep; and this refreshment, such as it was, was taken on the floor, with her head leaning on the stool,—when she lay down in this way, the straightness of the closet preventing her from taking any position that was not painful or constrained.

Yet this strange prison, which she never left save to go to the neighbouring Church of the Bridgetines to hear Mass, was a paradise in Dominica's eyes; for here, at least, she was left at peace and with God. She kept a continual silence, and divided her time between prayer and work with her needle; and so perfect a mistress was she in all kinds of embroidery, that she obtained large sums of money by her labour. This she left in her mother's hands, who was thus well satisfied to leave her undisturbed in the possession of her little closet, whilst the profits of her daily labours kept the house. The austerity she practised extended to every kind of bodily denial. Her food was bread and water, taken so sparingly, that we are assured she sometimes spent a week without drinking at all: when she ate any thing, it was on her knees, as she bound herself ever to accompany the necessary refreshment of the body with interior meditation on the Passion. After some little time, she was moved to give the proceeds of her labour no longer to her mother, but to distribute them in alms to the poor; and feeling this inspiration to be the will of God, she immediately executed it, greatly to her mother's dissatisfaction and her own discomfort; for all the indulgence and toleration she had received at her hands so long as the profits of her work were at the disposal of the family, were now turned into sharp reproaches. Dominica, however, cared very little for the sufferings which her resolution brought on her; for God did not fail to evince His pleasure in many ways.

She was accustomed to wear the Bridgetine habit, with the consent of the nuns; not as belonging to their community, but because it was deemed advisable that she should have the protection and sanction of some outward religious habit in her present mode of life. As she returned one morning from church, a miserable beggar met her and asked an alms She had nothing to give him; yet, rather than send him away without any relief, she took the veil from her head, and giving it to him, continued her way. But presently she felt a great scruple at what she had done; the veil was part of her religious habit; and she accused herself of a great fault in appearing in the public roads without it, so as possibly to scandalise the passers by, and be taken for one who mocked the holy garb of religion. But as these thoughts passed in her mind, there met her a man, the surpassing beauty and nobleness of whose countenance revealed him to be her Lord. He carried in his hand the veil she had just given away; and throwing it over her head,—" Henceforth," He said, "My spouse, shalt thou have the poverty thou desirest, and shalt live for ever on alms, and as a pilgrim in the world, as I did." From this time she redoubled her labours in order to obtain large means for the purpose of charity, and besides this, spent much of her time in nursing and tending the sick, as well as relieving them by her alms; and whenever she did this, her own sicknesses and pains were for a time suspended, and she found herself endowed with strength sufficient for the most extraordinary fatigues and exertions.

It was during her residence at home, in her twenty-fourth year, that she received the sacred stigmata. These were not bloody, as in so many cases; but the exact form of the nails appeared in the flesh of the hands and feet; the head protruding on the upper part, and the point coming out in the palms and soles. The crown of thorns was not visible in like manner, though the pain of her head in the part which corresponded to its position was excessive; but very often, in after years, her spiritual children in the monastery of her foundation saw, as she prayed, how the crown appeared round her head in light, and bright rays came out from it and formed its points. Dominica strove to conceal the favour she had received, by wearing long sleeves to hide her hands; but the nails were so large and distinct, that it was impossible to prevent the fact from being known and observed by many. After a while, in answer to her earnest prayer, this extraordinary formation of the nails in the flesh disappeared, and the scars of the wounds alone remained, causing her excessive agony, which redoubled every Friday and during Passion-tide. At length, in her forty-fourth year, the wounds became invisible; but the pain of them continued during her whole life.

She remained at home for three years after the reception of the sacred stigmata. They were years of continual suffering and persecution. The violence and coarse selfishness of her mother's nature was vented on her in every way and on all occasions. She was made the object of the most bitter reviling, and had to listen to a torrent of abuse, and what was worse, of blasphemous cursing, whenever she appeared in her presence. Once her mother threw her so violently against the wall as to cause her to rupture a blood vessel; yet she bore all meekly and uncomplaining, until at length some friends who lived at Florence, having asked her to take up her abode with them, it was revealed to her that she should remove thither, which she accordingly did. The change of residence, however, brought her little or no relief from persecution; for after a few months, the women with whom she was staying, moved by some jealousy, or disgusted at the retired manner in which she lived, and refused to go about with them or join in their way of life, accused her of every crime they could imagine, and even attempted to poison her. Her mother, hearing of the sufferings to which she was exposed, was moved with a very natural contrition for her own cruelty to her, and set out for Florence to see her, and if possible remove her from the house.

Unable to obtain admission, she had recourse to one of the canons of the city, and implored him to take her daughter under his protection, and defend her against the cruel restraint and persecution to which she was exposed in her present residence. By his interference she was allowed to leave; and a charitable gentleman of Florence, named Giovanni, to whom the circumstances of the case were known, received her into his own home, where she—lived very peaceably for some time. In all these most painful and disturbing changes in her life, Dominica's tranquillity and resignation remained unmoved. She knew that the will of God had its own designs regarding her, and that these were not yet manifested; but until they were, she was content with whatever was assigned her, and received ill treatment, abandonment, and the desolate destiny of passing from one strange home to another, with an astonishing calmness and indifference. Her position in Giovanni's house was a very singular one. His wife was a weak and indolent woman, and with little religious character about her; she was the first of the family, however, over whom Dominica's influence was felt. In a short time her habits of vanity and self-indulgence were laid aside; and she began to pray night and morning, and to attend Mass, which till then she had neglected. Then one of the sons, who was to all outward seeming given up to the thoughtless dissipation of his age, and had always neglected his religious duties, was won over by her, and began a new life. Giovanni himself soon saw what sort of a person he had brought into his house, and that he was in fact entertaining an angel unawares. He therefore insisted on her taking the entire government of the family; and Dominica consented, with the characteristic simplicity which would have made her undertake the government of a kingdom, if her guardian-angel had assured her it was the wish of God. Whilst she ruled and directed them, however, in things spiritual, she herself did the servile work of the house, and waited on them in the humblest and most submissive manner. She never affected any other position than that of a simple peasant girl; but every one who came within her influence felt its power over them, and owned her as their mistress and mother.

It was whilst living in this way that God revealed to her that she was no longer to remain concealed and retired from the world; but that He was about to make her the spiritual mother of many daughters, and to do great things for His own glory through her means. Now Dominica was naturally of a very timid and bashful disposition; and when she heard of being brought before the eyes of the world, and called on to teach and guide others, she knew not what to think. Her diffidence, and what we should call shyness, was naturally so great, that she would turn pale if she had to speak to any one she did not know familiarly, and always at such times suffered from violent beatings of the heart. Therefore, when she considered the great things laid before her, she felt sad and a little frightened, and spoke to God with her usual simple frankness, saying, "O my Lord, how can this be? I am nothing but a vile peasant; the heart in my breast is a poor contemptible thing, that has no courage in it; my blood is peasant's blood; I am not fit for these great things unless you change it." Then God answered, saying, "And I will change it, and will give you a noble and magnanimous heart; wherefore prepare for keen and terrible sufferings; for it is by them that your heart and blood is to be purged and renovated, and fitted for My service in the eyes of men."

Scarcely had the vision ended, when Dominica felt the approach of the sufferings which had been promised; pain in every part of her body, a continual hemorrhage of blood, which seemed to drain every vein, and deadly faintings and weakness, reduced her almost to extremity. Then, after she had languished in this state for many weeks, a vision appeared to her of the same mysterious and significant kind as that related in the life of St. Catherine of Sienna. Our Lord took her heart from her breast, and supplied its place with one of burning fire. She rose from her sick-bed, and felt her whole nature renewed; every sense was quickened, and the powers of her mind enlarged and enno-bled;—nay, her very body seemed already to share in the glory of the resurrection. It gave out a wonderful odour, which communicated it-self to every thing which it touched. Her sight was so miraculously keen that she could see to embroider in the darkest night, and many *new* senses seemed given her; whilst those of smell and touch and hearing were also renewed in an equally extraordinary degree. But, at the same time, she lost the bodily vigour which had before enabled her to go through so many hard days' labour; and with her new heart she seemed also to have acquired a new and delicate bodily temperament which utterly incapacitated her for work, whilst she seemed to be wholly immersed in divine and interior contemplation. A strange elo-quence was now heard to flow from her lips, the infused wisdom and science of the saints was in her words; nay, she would often quote and explain sentences of the holy Fathers, or of the Scriptures, which it is certain she had never read or heard read. In short, God had bestowed on her the gift which He deemed necessary to fit her for the design He had regarding her; and still, with all the marvellous spiritual riches which she had acquired, she retained in her ways and thoughts and habits the old simplicity of the peasant child.

The first of the spiritual daughters given her by God was Gio-vanni's eldest child, who at her persuasion embraced the life of religion, and placed herself under her obedience. The second soon fol-lowed her example; and soon after a third. Another daughter, Catherine, still remained; like her mother, she was of a thoughtless and indolent character, much given to the vanities of her age, and the fool-ish pleasures of the world about her. She was accustomed to ridicule and mock at the conversion of her three sisters, and to hinder and dis-turb them in their religious practices; in short, she was about as hopeless a subject for Dominica to exercise her influence upon as might well be imagined. But one Christmas-day Dominica called her into her little oratory, and first turning to the crucifix, and spending a moment in silent prayer, she laid her hand on her breast, and said, "O hard and evil heart, be softened and yield to thy God; and bend to my will, which is, that thou be the heart of a saint!" Three days after this Catherine presented herself with her sisters, and implored Dominica to take her also under her teaching to convert the brothers; but by degrees she succeeded in persuading all to devote themselves to a holy and religious life; and the eldest, taking the habit of St. Dominic, lived and died in the order with the reputation of sanctity.

Her confessor about this time counselled her herself to take the habit of the third order; and the matter having been agreed upon, he provided a tunic and mantle of the usual kind for her clothing, and appointed a certain day for her to come to the Convent of St. Mark and receive it with the customary ceremonies. The circumstances which followed have a very marvellous character, yet there seems no reason to doubt the accuracy and reality of what is narrated. We are told that, on the morning of the day appointed, she being in prayer, was rapt in ecstasy; and in this state she saw St. Catherine and St. Dominic enter her room with the white tunic in their hands. St. Dominic himself gave it to her, pronouncing the words and prayer according to the rite of his order,—the responses being given by St. Catherine and the angels; and her guardian- angel gave the aspersion of holy water, first to the habit, and then to her; and St. Catherine received her as her daughter, and gave her the kiss of welcome. When she recovered from her ecstasy, she found herself really clothed in the sacred habit which had been thus wonderfully given her; and, full of joy, she appeared with it in public in the afternoon of the same day. This was a cause of great displeasure to the authorities of the order, who complained that she had assumed their habit without being regularly admitted into their society. The affair was brought before the Master-General, at that time Vio di Cajetan; and the complaint appearing just, he called on her either to lay it aside, or to explain the authority by which she wore it. The account she gave of the whole matter so satisfied the Archbishop of Florence of her sincerity and holiness, that he undertook to mediate in her behalf; and it was at length agreed that she should keep the habit, provided that she and her companions wore a red cross on the left shoulder, to denote that she had been clothed without the sanction of the ordinary authorities of the order, and was not subject to its jurisdiction; and, in fact, they did so wear it for six years, when, the Convent of the Holy Cross being established, they were afterwards fully admitted to the rights and privileges of the order.

After this point was settled, Dominica's next step was to retire with her little band of followers (which now included several others besides the daughters of Giovanni) to a small house, where they lived a regular life, supporting themselves by the labour of their hands. In time their gains increased to so wonderful a degree, that they found themselves enabled to purchase a more convenient residence, and then to enlarge it, and finally to rebuild it in the form of a cross. In short, in the course of a few years she saw herself at the head of a large community, possessed of a regular and extensive house, with a church attached to it, without any other means having been employed in its erection than the money which she and her sisters had earned by their own needlework. The Archbishop of Florence (the celebrated Julius de Medici, afterwards Pope) was so struck with the manifest expression of God's will in the whole matter, that he obtained permission from Leo X. for the regular foundation of the convent under the rule of St. Dominic. They were all solemnly clothed on the 18th of November, 1515, and proceeded to the election of their prioress. Their choice of course fell on Dominica, but she absolutely refused to accept the office; and used a power given her by the papal brief to nominate another sister in her place, whilst she determined to retain for herself the rank and duties of a lay-sister.

The ceremony of the clothing and election being therefore over, she made a solemn renunciation of the house and all it contained into the hands of the Archbishop-Vicar. Then she left the sisters, and went to the kitchen; and coming there, she sent all the other lay-sisters away, saying, it belonged to her to do what had to be done for the community for the first week of their settlement. She cooked the dinner, and sent it to the refectory; and whilst the sisters were sitting at table, she entered the room with a number of broken pieces of earthenware tied round her neck, and knelt humbly in the middle of them all, as one doing penance. The feelings of her children at this sight may be imagined; there was a universal stir; three or four rose from table, and would have placed themselves by her side. The prioress endeavoured to restore order; but the meal was broken by the sobs and sighs of the whole community. When dinner was over, she tried to return to her work in the kitchen; but the feelings of the sisters could no longer be restrained; they ran after her, and threw themselves at her feet. "Mother, mother," they cried, "it is a mother we want, not a saint; a guide, and not a servant,—this cannot be suffered." But Dominica tried to quell them, and to persuade them to let it be even as she desired; her entreaties, however, were in vain. They left her, and with the Prioress met together to consider what should be done; and it was determined that the Vicar should be called on to use his authority with Dominica, and bring her under obedience to take the office of Superior,—which, in short, she was compelled to do, with the title of *Vicaress*; for she persevered in refusing to be instituted Prioress.

When the time came for the profession of the new community, Dominica obtained permission from the Pope to defer her own profession; only to bind herself by a simple vow to wear the habit of the third order, and keep the rule of St. Dominic. Does the reader wish to know the motive she had for soliciting this singular privilege? He must go back some twenty years, and recall the time when the story of St. Mary Magdalen's retirement to the deserts of Marseilles had sent the little peasant child into the woods, to spend three happy days and nights in a hermit's cave too small to contain her, but which she considered as a Paradise; and where she would have been well content to have remained all her life, if such had been the wish of God. At thirty years of age, Dominica was still the same. Her simplicity had a touch of what one might call romance about it, and she had never forgotten her great project of a hermitage. She would not be bound to the Convent of the Holy Cross therefore, because she still hoped the time might come when she might find out the desert of Marseilles, and realise the life of penance and retirement, the account of which had made so deep an impression on her imagination. When she saw herself threatened with a perpetual appointment as Vicaress, she accordingly resolved to fly at once, and did actually escape by one of the windows, and set out towards Marseilles in the habit of a pilgrim. The community again had recourse to the Vicar, who sent a peremptory order for her return under pain of excommunication; and the messenger who carried it found her laid up in a little village with a swelling of both feet, which had put a speedy stop to her pilgrimage, and which she herself acknowledged to be the declaration that it was not God's will she should proceed in her design. She was therefore compelled to return and reassume the government of her convent, in which office she continued until she died in 1553.

With the circumstances which attended her death we must conclude. For months she had lain on a miserable pallet, unable to move or rise, and with the appearance of a living skeleton. But when Easter Day came, she felt it was the last she should spend with her Sisters, and determined to keep the festival with them all in community. She therefore caused herself to be carried to the chair, where she communicated with them. She took her dinner in the refectory, and afterwards held a chapter, where, after briefly and touchingly exhorting them to fidelity to their Spouse, she gave them her last blessing. Then, in order to assure them in the peaceable possession of their convent, she determined to make her solemn profession, which had never yet been done,—in conformity, we are assured, to the express revealed permission of God. She lingered on until the following August, and on the 5th of that month fell into her agony. When the last moment came, she raised herself on the pallet, and extended her arms in the form of the cross. Her face shone with a bright and ruddy colour, and her eyes were dazzling with a supernatural light; and so, without any other death-struggle than a gentle sigh, she expired, at the age of eighty years. Her life has been written at length by F. Ignatius Nente; but the principal facts were drawn up by the Abbess of Florence very shortly after her decease, at the instance of the Grand Duchess of Lorraine, and forwarded to Rome, to form the process for her beatification.

ANNE DE MONTMORENCY

THE SOLITARY OF THE PYRENEES.

ABOUT the year 1666, a young lady of the family of Montmorency, one of the most ancient and illustrious in France, disappeared at the age of fifteen from her father's house, because projects were being formed for her establishment, and she believed herself called to a different state of life. After having in vain endeavoured to alter the views of her family respecting her, she entreated permission one day to make a pilgrimage to Mount Valerian, near Paris, where were the stations of our Lord's Passion. When she reached that which represents our Lord on the cross, she implored Him whom she had chosen for her spouse, with many tears, to save her from the danger of being ever unfaithful to Him, and to teach her how to live from thenceforth as His own bride, unknown, and crucified with Him, with her body and soul given up entirely to His charge, and her whole being abandoned to the care of Providence.

With her mind full of these holy thoughts, she came down from the mountain, and without well knowing what she was going to do, she turned her steps towards the Bois de Boulogne; and when she reached the Abbey of Longchamp, feeling a strong impulse to enter the church, she dismissed for some hours the confidential attendants by whom she was accompanied, saying that she had still many prayers to recite; and accordingly they left her without suspicion to finish her devotions. No sooner were they out of sight than she left the church; and committing herself to our Blessed Lord and His Holy Mother, plunged into the recesses of the wood. She was following by mere chance an unfrequented path, when she met a poor woman, who asked alms of her. This encounter appeared to her an indication of the will of Heaven: she formed her plan in an instant, and began to put it into execution, by taking the clothes of the poor beggar, and giving her own in exchange; and to complete the disguise, she stained her hands and face with clay, and tried to disfigure herself as much as possible. She then turned in the direction contrary to that in which she thought pursuit would first be made; walked all the rest of the day, and found herself in the evening in a village situate on the Seine, some leagues from Paris. There she was met by some charitable ecclesiastics, who, touched by her youth, and the dangers to which it exposed her, took an interest in her situation, and found her first a temporary asylum, and afterwards a situation with a lady in the neighbourhood, who was very rich, and whose service was safe and respectable, as she was devout and regular in her conduct; but she was a difficult person to live with, being of a sharp and worrying temper, so that she had never been able to keep long either a man or maid-servant. Into this house, however, Jane Margaret, by which name only she was known, entered as lady's-maid; but as no servant but herself could remain, she found herself at the age of sixteen obliged to be cook and housemaid and porteress all at once. What consoled and even rejoiced her in this situation was the opportunity it afforded her of satisfying her thirst for crosses and humiliations, and also her freedom from all intrusion of idle curiosity, so that she felt her secret safe. She endured all the fatigues of so laborious a situation, and all the caprices of a harshness in temper, with unalterable patience and sweetness until her mistress's death; that is to say, for the space of ten years. And so faultless was her, conduct during all this time, that her mistress, on her death bed, publicly begged her pardon for all she had made her suffer, and insisted on leaving her the sum of four thousand francs in addition to her wages, of which she had as yet scarcely received any thing. Jane Margaret was with difficulty persuaded to accept this present, and when it was forced upon her, she distributed it among the poor, with the exception of a very small sum which she kept for her immediate wants. Feeling, however, that such extraordinary liberality on the part of a mere maid-servant would excite suspicion and endanger her secret, she resolved to escape the peril as soon as possible.

Accordingly, on her return from the funeral of her mistress, seeing the boat for Auxerre, she threw herself into it, without a moment's delay; and soon after her arrival in that town succeeded in finding another situation which she considered suitable. It was in the house of a master joiner, who was greatly esteemed both for skill in his profession and for general probity, and who was also clever in carving.

The early education of Jane Margaret made her very useful to her new master, who, in return, taught her how to handle the chisel, and she very soon became sufficiently expert to make wooden clocks. In this town, too, she was happy enough to find a director experienced in the ways of God, who confirmed her in the resolution she had taken. In about a year's time, however, she lost him; and despairing of finding another to whom she could give her entire confidence, she determined to return to Paris, in the hope of finding there a guide such as she required, believing herself sufficiently forgotten at this distance of time to run no risk of being recognised. She set forth, therefore, on the road to the capital on foot, and asking alms; for she had taken care before leaving Auxerre to give to the poor all that she had earned.

On her arrival in Paris she placed herself among the poor who ask the charity of the faithful at the church-doors; and begged every morning enough to maintain her for the day, for which purpose very little sufficed. All the rest of her time she passed in prayer in the churches, which she never left except at the approach of night. One day as she was asking alms, according to her custom, at the door of a church, it pleased Providence that she should address herself to a very pious and charitable lady, who kept a school at Château-Fort, and who was under the direction of a holy religious named the Father de Bray. At the first sight of the young and modest beggar, the virtuous schoolmistress felt moved, and discerning in her something which did not accord with her apparent state of life, ventured to ask her whether it was from sickness that she was reduced to that condition. Jane Margaret only replied that she believed herself to be fulfilling the will of God; which answer increased the interest she had already excited in the mind of the pious lady, who told her that in her state of weakness the air of the country would do her good, and offered to take her to Château-Fort. At the same time she spoke to her of Father de Bray, whose name and merit were well known in Paris. This last consideration was sufficient to determine Jane Margaret to follow a person whose sentiments were so congenial with her own.

As soon as Father de Bray became acquainted with her, he discovered in her one of those wonders which are wrought from time to time by grace for the confusion of the world, and set himself to second the designs of Heaven concerning this privileged soul. She too, on her side, convinced that she had at last found a guide such as she had been long seeking, bestowed on him her confidence without reserve, and continued to correspond with him as long as he lived.

In process of time, drawn more than ever by the Spirit of God, she left Château-Fort to go and seek a solitude hidden from all men; but it was almost two years before she could find what she desired. She traversed several provinces seeking for an asylum out of the reach of every human eye, until at last she arrived at the Pyrenees, where she established herself in a wild recess, which she names in her letters "the solitude of the rocks." It was a little space of a pentagonal shape, shut in by five rocks, which formed a kind of cross, and rendered the little spot of ground which they enclosed not quite inaccessible, but altogether invisible from without. From the foot of the highest of these rocks there gushed a spring of excellent water, and its summit was a kind of observatory, from whence she could espy any intruders who might venture to approach her abode. There were three grottoes at the base of the rocks, one of which was a deep and winding cavern; this she made her cell, and the two others her oratories. This solitude was at least half a league from any road, and surrounded by a thick forest, or rather by a brake, so tangled that, to get through it, the traveller must force his way among thistles and briers, by a path which seemed impracticable to any but wild beasts. Our solitary, however, met with none of these, except a bear, who was more afraid than she, and ran away. She found in her retreat shrubs which bore a fruit much like damsons; and the rocks were covered with medlar-trees, the fruit of which was excellent. The cold was not intense even in the heart of winter, while the heat of summer was tempered by the shade of the rocks, and of the woods which surrounded it. All these details are given in the letters of the solitary herself to her director, Father de Bray.

In this retirement she began to lead a life angelic rather than human; looking upon this earth as the blessed do from the heights of heaven, and consecrating every pulsation of her heart to God. For some time she used to go twice a week to the village to ask alms; but by degrees she weaned herself from the use of bread, and at last lived entirely on the vegetables and wild fruits which grew in the neighbourhood of her abode.

Her spiritual necessities were more difficult to supply. Not wishing to risk being recognised, she was obliged to use many precautions whenever she allowed herself the consolation of participating in the divine mysteries; but Providence had prepared for her a resource. At a little distance from the forest were two religious houses, one of men, the other of women. There she went to hear Mass and receive holy communion; and, in order to escape remark, she went sometimes to the church of the convent, sometimes to that of the monastery; and for her confessor she selected a good curate of the neighbourhood, who simply heard what she had to say, and asked her no questions. She had fixed for herself a rule of life, which she followed exactly: at five in the morning she rose, winter and summer; continued in prayer till six, when she recited prime, and either went to Mass or heard it in spirit; and then read some chapters of Holy Scripture. These exercises lasted till eight; after which she devoted two hours to manual labour, either mending her clothes, or practising sculpture, or cultivating a little garden which she had made round her habitation. At ten she recited tierce, sext, and none; and then, prostrate at the foot of her crucifix, she examined her conscience, and imposed on herself penances in proportion to the number and grievousness of her faults. All this lasted till about noon, when she took the only meal of the day, and after it her recreation, which consisted, in fine weather, of a walk to the summit of the rocks, where she contemplated the greatness of God in His works, and praised and blessed His infinite perfections in pious songs which she knew by heart, or with which Divine love inspired her at the moment.

On her return home she made her spiritual reading, usually from the Imitation, followed by an affectionate prayer, in which she poured out before God all the necessities of her soul; but asked of Him nothing but the accomplishment of His own good pleasure. Then she resumed her manual labour until four in the afternoon, after which she recited Vespers and the entire Rosary, accompanied or followed by pious considerations. This exercise brought her on to eight o'clock, when she went through the devotion of the Stations in a Calvary which she had built herself, and performed the penances and mortifications which she had imposed upon herself. At nine she retired to her cell, and, after a short examination of conscience, and some vocal prayers, slept till eleven, when she rose to recite matins, which she knew by heart, and to pray till two, when she retired again to rest till five. In order to regulate this distribution of her time, she had made herself a wooden clock. She made also several other pieces of workmanship, which were admired by connoisseurs, more especially a Crucifix made out of a single piece of corneil wood, which she presented to Father de Bray, and which afterwards fell into the hands of Madame de Maintenon, who valued it as a precious relic. She wrought also three other crucifixes, one very small, which she wore round her neck; another, three feet high, which, she placed in her cell; and a third, six feet high, which she carved out of the wood of a fir-tree, which had been struck down by lightning in the forest, and which she placed in the Calvary she had arranged on the summit of one of the highest of the rocks which enclosed her habitation.

For her communications with Father de Bray she made use of a wagoner, who, from time to time, journeyed to and from Paris, and who faithfully carried her letters, and brought back to her the answers to them, together with the small sums of money which her director sent her from time to time, and which she used to procure such things as were indispensably necessary to her, such as tools for her carving, needles, thread, worsted, and some pieces of calico and stuff to repair her garments, which were very simple, but always neat, especially when she appeared at church.

It may not be uninteresting to see an inventory of her few possessions which she sent to her spiritual director. A Roman Breviary, which she recited daily, and which she understood, having learnt Latin in her childhood; an Imitation; an abridgment of the Saints' Lives; a little book culled Horloge du Coeur, and another of Devotions to the Blessed Sacrament. Such was her library. Her workshop contained a supply of ordinary carpenters' tools, and a few more delicate implements for carving; while for her personal use she had a few hundreds of pins, some needles, some grey and white thread, a pair of scissors, and a copper thimble; two bowls and a cup, all in wood; a hair shirt, and a discipline. Her wardrobe, as may be supposed, was of the most simple description, but sufficient for decency and neatness.

Our solitary had but one fear in this peaceful retirement, that of being discovered; and it was long before her evident sanctity drew the attention of the people of the village, and excited the curiosity of so many people, that, in spite of all her precautions, they succeeded, by dint of constant watching, in finding out, if not absolutely her abode, at least the rocks which surrounded it. This was quite enough to force her to seek a more distant solitude.

Impelled, as she said in one of her letters, by an irresistible force, she transported herself to a distance of twenty leagues, still further among the Pyrenees, in the direction of Spain. She had dwelt for four years in the solitude of the rocks, and for three years more she abode in that which she called the Grot of the Rivulets. It was a place full of rocks and caverns, the retreat of wild beasts, enormous serpents, and monstrous lizards, which were the terror of the neighbourhood, so that none dared approach the spot. But when this barrier of rocks was once passed, which required good climbing, there was a little smiling valley enamelled with flowers, and intersected with rivulets from several springs of living water gushing out from the mountains; there, too, were several sorts of fruit of very good taste, and a quantity of wild honey, which the solitary pronounced to be excellent; so that altogether this abode would have been preferable to her former one of the rocks, if it had not been for the presence of the wild beasts. But of these Jane Margaret had no fear, depending on the help of the Lord, who has promised to give His servants the power of treading on serpents and scorpions, and of chaining the mouths of lions; and in truth these animals never disturbed her, though she passed their dens again and again; it seemed as though they respected her and all that belonged to her, for they never approached her dwelling, and even spared a little squirrel which she had found in this wilderness, and taken home with her for company.

Here, too, as in the neighbourhood of her first solitude, she found a convent of monks; but this was at a more considerable distance, for she had three leagues and a half to walk before she could reach it, and that through tangled thickets; but in this convent she sought a confessor; the Superior received her with great kindness, believing her to be a poor country girl, and asking her no questions but such as were suitable to the rural life he supposed her to be leading. For the holy sacrifice she went to the hermitage of St. Antony, a league and a half on the other side of the forest.

When once fixed in this new abode, our solitary peaceably resumed the course of her accustomed exercises. She arranged for herself two cells in the hollow of two rocks very near to each other, and in the space between the two she formed a little chapel, which she delighted in adorning with verdure and wild flowers. She divided her time, as before, between labour and prayer, and her trances and ecstasies became more frequent and more sublime than ever; but her great humility made her distrust these extraordinary favours of Heaven, and she required to be set at rest concerning them by her director, with whom she continued to correspond, and to whom she continued, even to the end, to pour forth all the secrets of her soul with the simplicity of a child. Her last letter is dated the 17th of Sept. 1699, and in it she expresses a great desire to go to Rome in the course of the following year, in order to gain the indulgence of the jubilee, but at the same time submits her own judgment entirely to that of him whom she regarded as the interpreter of the will of Heaven in her regard. Receiving no answer, she suspected that Father de Bray was no more; and in fact he had died that very year. She thought herself free to move, and set off for the Holy City, since which period it has been impossible to gather any trace of her. Whether she accomplished her pilgrimage, whether she died in Rome or in some solitude, has never been discovered; as though it pleased Providence to second, even after her death, the earnest desire of His servant to be hidden from the sight and knowledge of men; for the tomb, which often becomes the glory of the friends of God, only set the seal to her obscurity. At the last day, when the secrets of all hearts shall be made known, this treasure will stand revealed in the face of the universe.

Also from Benediction Books …
The Lives of the Fathers, Martyrs, and
Principal Saints
January, February, March
Alban Butler
Benediction Classics, 2011
892 pages
ISBN 978-1-84902-427-3

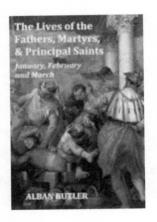

Available from www.amazon.com,
www.amazon.co.uk

Alban Butler (1710-1773) was an English
Roman Catholic Priest. He spent thirty
years studying the saints, culminating in him publishing his great
work, The Lives of the Fathers, Martyrs and Other Principal Saints.
The book has passed through many editions and translations and is
now available, once again, in four books.

This book (Book One - January to March) features a biography of Butler, a table of contents, an index of saints, a preface and some
introductory remarks. The copious numbers of footnotes have been
retained and it has been carefully reproduced.

Also available:
Book Two – April to June
Book Three – July to September
Book Four – October to December
They can be found by searching Amazon for
"Benediction The Lives of the Fathers, Martyrs, and Principal Saints"

Hurlbut's Story of the Bible
Unabridged and fully illustrated in BW
Jesse Lyman Hurlbut
Benediction Classics, 2011
976 pages
Size 11 x 8.5 inches
ISBN: 978-1849024556

Available from www.amazon.com,
www.amazon.co.uk

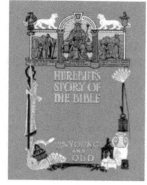

In the tradition of parents telling their children stories from the Bible, this new edition of a delightful book presents a continuous narrative of the Scriptures that brings the great heroes and events from the Bible to life. It is unabridged and features 168 stories from the Old and New Testaments, copious BW illustrations, a presentation page and a re-touched version of the 1904 cover. Since it was written in 1904 by an American Methodist Episcopal Clergyman, Jesse Lyman Hurlbut, over 4 million copies have been distributed.

From Ritual to Romance
Jessie L. Weston
Benediction Classics, 2011
188 pages
ISBN: 978-1-84902-415-0

Available from www.amazon.com,
www.amazon.co.uk

From Ritual to Romance was written in 1920 by Jessie L. Weston. The book was made famous by being mentioned by T. S. Eliot in the notes to his poem, The Waste Land. He says, "Not only the title, but the plan and a good deal of the incidental symbolism of the poem were suggested by Miss Jessie L. Weston's book". The book centres on an examination of the roots of the King Arthur legends and seeks to make connections between the early pagan elements and the later Christian influences. In particular, the book looks at the Holy Grail tradition and its influence.

Also from Benediction Books …
Wandering Between Two Worlds: Essays on Faith and Art
Anita Mathias
Benediction Books, 2007
152 pages
ISBN: 0955373700

Available from www.amazon.com, www.amazon.co.uk

In these wide-ranging lyrical essays, Anita Mathias writes, in lush, lovely prose, of her naughty Catholic childhood in Jamshedpur, India; her large, eccentric family in Mangalore, a sea-coast town converted by the Portuguese in the sixteenth century; her rebellion and atheism as a teenager in her Himalayan boarding school, run by German missionary nuns, St. Mary's Convent, Nainital; and her abrupt religious conversion after which she entered Mother Teresa's convent in Calcutta as a novice. Later rich, elegant essays explore the dualities of her life as a writer, mother, and Christian in the United States-- Domesticity and Art, Writing and Prayer, and the experience of being "an alien and stranger" as an immigrant in America, sensing the need for roots.

About the Author

Anita Mathias is the author of *Wandering Between Two Worlds: Essays on Faith and Art.* She has a B.A. and M.A. in English from Somerville College, Oxford University, and an M.A. in Creative Writing from the Ohio State University, USA. Anita won a National Endowment of the Arts fellowship in Creative Nonfiction in 1997. She lives in Oxford, England with her husband, Roy, and her daughters, Zoe and Irene.

Anita's website:
  http://www.anitamathias.com, and
Anita's blog Dreaming Beneath the Spires:
  http://dreamingbeneaththespires.blogspot.com

The Church That Had Too Much
Anita Mathias
Benediction Books, 2010
52 pages
ISBN: 9781849026567

Available from www.amazon.com, www.amazon.co.uk

The Church That Had Too Much was very well-intentioned. She
wanted to love God, she wanted to love people, but she was both ham-
pered by her muchness and the abundance of her possessions, and
beset by ambition, power struggles and snobbery. Read about the sur-
prising way The Church That Had Too Much began to resolve her
problems in this deceptively simple and enchanting fable.

About the Author

Anita Mathias is the author of *Wandering Between Two Worlds: Essays on Faith and Art*. She has a B.A. and M.A. in English from
Somerville College, Oxford University, and an M.A. in Creative Writing from the Ohio State University, USA. Anita won a National
Endowment of the Arts fellowship in Creative Nonfiction in 1997.
She lives in Oxford, England with her husband, Roy, and her daughters, Zoe and Irene.

Anita's website:
    http://www.anitamathias.com, and
Anita's blog Dreaming Beneath the Spires:
    http://dreamingbeneaththespires.blogspot.com